Ella Rose,
For your library... I hope you get
to see all these places...
Steve

5/18

# WEIRD KENTUCKY

STERLING
New York / London
www.sterlingpublishing.com

# WEIRD KENTUCKY

## Your Travel Guide to Kentucky's Local Legends and Best Kept Secrets

by JEFFREY SCOTT HOLLAND

Mark Sceurman and Mark Moran,
Executive Editors

# WEIRD KENTUCKY



Photography and illustration credits are found on page 253 and constitute an extension of this copyright page.

Library of Congress Cataloging-in-Publication Data Available

10 9 8 7 6 5 4 3 2 1

Published by Sterling Publishing Co., Inc.
387 Park Avenue South, New York, NY 10016



Distributed in Canada by Sterling Publishing
c/o Canadian Manda Group, 165 Dufferin Street
Toronto, Ontario, Canada M6K 3H6

Distributed in the United Kingdom by GMC Distribution Services
Castle Place, 166 High Street, Lewes, East Sussex, England BN7 1XU

Distributed in Australia by Capricorn Link (Australia) Pty. Ltd.
P.O. Box 704, Windsor, NSW 2756, Australia



**Sterling ISBN 13: 978-1-4027-5438-8**
**Sterling ISBN 10: 1-4027-5438-8**

For information about custom editions, special sales, premium and corporate purchases, please contact Sterling Special Sales Department at 800-805-5489 or specialsales@sterlingpublishing.com.

**Design: Richard J. Berenson**
**Berenson Design & Books, LLC, New York, NY**

*Weird Kentucky* is intended as entertainment to present a historical record of local legends, folklore, and sites throughout Kentucky. Many of these legends and stories cannot be independently confirmed or corroborated, and the authors and publisher make no representation as to their factual accuracy. The reader should be advised that many of the sites described in *Weird Kentucky* are located on private property and should not be visited, or you may face prosecution for trespassing.

# Contents

# A Note from the Marks

**O*ur weird journey*** began a long, long time ago in a far-off land called New Jersey. Once a year or so, we'd compile a homespun newsletter called *Weird N.J.,* then pass it on to our friends. The pamphlet was a collection of odd news clippings, bizarre facts, little-known historical anecdotes, and anomalous encounters from our home state. The newsletter also included the kinds of localized legends that were often whispered around a particular town but seldom heard outside the boundaries of the community where they originated.

We had started *Weird N.J.* on the simple theory that every town in the state had at least one good tale to tell. The publication soon became a full-fledged magazine, and we made the decision to actually do our own investigating to see if we could track down where all of these seemingly unbelievable stories were coming from. Was there, we wondered, any factual basis for the fantastical local legends people were telling us? Armed with not much more than a camera and a notepad, we set off on a mystical journey of discovery. Much to our surprise and amazement, a lot of what we had initially presumed to be nothing more than urban legend turned out to be real—or at least to contain a grain of truth that had sparked the lore to begin with.

After a dozen years of documenting the bizarre, we were asked to write a book about our adventures, and so *Weird N.J.: Your Travel Guide to New Jersey's Local Legends and Best Kept Secrets* was published in 2003. Soon people from all over the country began writing to us, telling us strange tales from their home states. As it turned out, what we had perceived to be something of very local interest was actually just a small part of a larger and more universal phenomenon.

When Barnes & Noble, the publisher of the book, asked us what we wanted to do next, the answer was simple. "We'd like to do a book called *Weird U.S.,* in which we could document the local legends and strangest stories from all over the country," we told them. So for the next twelve months, we set out in search of weirdness wherever it might be found in the fifty states. And indeed, we found plenty of it!

After *Weird U.S.* was published, we came to the conclusion that this country had more great tales than could be contained in just one book. Everywhere we looked, we found unwritten folklore, creepy cemeteries, cursed locations, and

all that was out of the ordinary about this state on his Web site Unusual Kentucky at www.unusualkentucky.com. This man, we thought, was a kindred spirit!

We contacted Jeffrey, and much to our delight he told us that he was not only familiar with our work, but that our *Weird N.J.* Web site was in part his inspiration for creating his Unusual Kentucky site. That was all we needed to hear: We knew we had found our *Weird Kentucky* author.

outlandish roadside oddities. With this in mind, we told our publisher that we wanted to document it ALL and to do it in a series of books, each focusing on the peculiarities of a particular state.

One state that we suspected would be fertile ground for weirdness was Kentucky. We can't really say why that is, but the mere mention of the name of the state was enough to conjure up mental images of dark and haunted hollers in the backwoods of Appalachia. Not only that, but as we discovered while writing *Weird U.S.*, Kentucky was also home to the country's most haunted abandoned sanatorium, a blood-drinking vampire cult, elusive colonies of little people and even blue people, cave ghosts, lake monsters, a sleeping psychic, and many more odd and unusual stories! Surely, we thought, there must be somebody out there documenting all these bizarre tales native to the Bluegrass State. Our research led us to a 2005 article in Louisville's *Courier-Journal* entitled, of all things, "Weird Kentucky." The piece told the tale of Jeffrey Scott Holland, a local artist who had been chronicling

There was no doubt that Jeff possessed what we refer to as the Weird Eye, which is what is needed to search out the sort of stories we were looking for. It requires one to see the world in a different way, with a renewed sense of wonder. And once you have it, there is no going back—you'll never see things the same way again. All of a sudden you begin to reexamine your own environs, noticing your everyday surroundings as if for the first time. And you begin to ask yourself questions like, "What the heck is that thing all about, anyway?" and "Doesn't anybody else think that's kind of weird?"

So come with us now, and let Jeffrey take you on a tour of his home state. If you are a native Kentuckian, we're sure that you will be familiar with some of the legends and folktales contained in this book. Even if you've lived in Kentucky all your life, though, we'll bet that many stories here will be completely new to you. It's all part of the unusual state of mind we like to call *Weird Kentucky*.

*–Mark Sceurman and Mark Moran*

# Introduction

There are two kinds of people on this planet—those who think "weird" is a good thing, and those who think it's a bad thing.

I'd like to believe that this book will help sway those in the latter category over to my way of thinking. After all, I take the widest, most all-inclusive definition of weird—meaning, basically, anything out of the ordinary and interesting. And Kentucky is a very interesting place. Weird doesn't all have to be lurid bloodletting tales of madness, murder, and monsters—sometimes it's as simple and as sweet as a restaurant's colorful psychedelic mural or a grave marker with a smiling piggy's face emblazoned on it.

Even as a child, I understood this on a visceral level: After going to places that were supposedly more interesting, like Walt Disney World and New York, I couldn't wait to get back home to the family farm and its ghosts. And in adulthood, no matter where I moved, I always ended up drawn right back to the hills of Kentucky. This is a real phenomenon that has been noted by many a Kentuckian, often jokingly referred to as the Kentucky Vortex, which holds in its sway all who were born here. When someone who's lived here their whole life announces they're moving to some distant locale, never to return to Kentucky again, my friends and I exchange a knowing glance or a wink. They'll be back.

So what is it that's so special about this place we now call the Commonwealth of Kentucky? It's a complicated thing, too diaphanous and wispy to capture in words, but I've tried. Sometimes it has to be sneaked up on. Hinted at. Talked around. Approached but not broached, lest it be frightened away like a distrustful feral cat. The nameless quality of Kentucky's magical weirdness can never be pinned down completely. After all, quantum physics tells us that the act of looking at something actually changes it. But this book contains all the pieces you need to put together why Kentucky is, without a doubt, one of the weirdest, wildest, and most wonderful states in the Union. If you're a Kentuckian, you might smile with recognition at some of these unspoken-till-now truths. And if you're from else-

where, let this tome be your tour guide to an assortment of puzzling and peculiar people, places, and things. You won't find most of them on "must see" lists of local tourist bureaus and historical societies. But you should. And maybe, just maybe, now you will.

The men behind the curtain in this book project—Management, I like to call them—are the Marks, Moran and Sceurman. The Marks know what I'm talking about when others may think I am either mad as a hatter or have downed one shot of Woodford Reserve too many. I'm thrilled and honored to be working with them and their *Weird U.S.* project, whose works I've been a fan of for years. It's very exciting to me that they've finally turned their attentions toward America's strangest region of all, and I can't wait to work with them again in the future. Keeping track of the kookiness of an entire nation is a thankless task, but someone's got to do it, and for that the Marks deserve all our undying gratitude.

*–Jeffrey Scott Holland*

# Ancient Mysteries

*Most of us were told in school* that the line of human occupation of North America goes from cavemen to Indians to Pilgrims, and that's that. And yet evidence to the contrary keeps piling up. In our state, there are signs that the region was visited in ancient times by the Chinese, Norse Vikings, Celts, Welsh, and ancient Egyptians (not to mention extraterrestrials). There once existed people in Kentucky whose description defies all known frames of reference, including a race of red-haired giants who inhabited this land before the people we now call Native Americans.

The amount of unexplainable artifacts that fly in the face of everything we think we know about history would be enough to fill a museum. At least it would be, had not so much of it been suppressed outright or destroyed by careless handling. There are accepted versions of science and history, sometimes created by people promoting their own agendas, sometimes just so embedded in mainstream thinking that it's almost impossible to dislodge them. But there remain those pesky things that won't fit into the official versions no matter how hard some people may try to force them. This chapter is about those things.

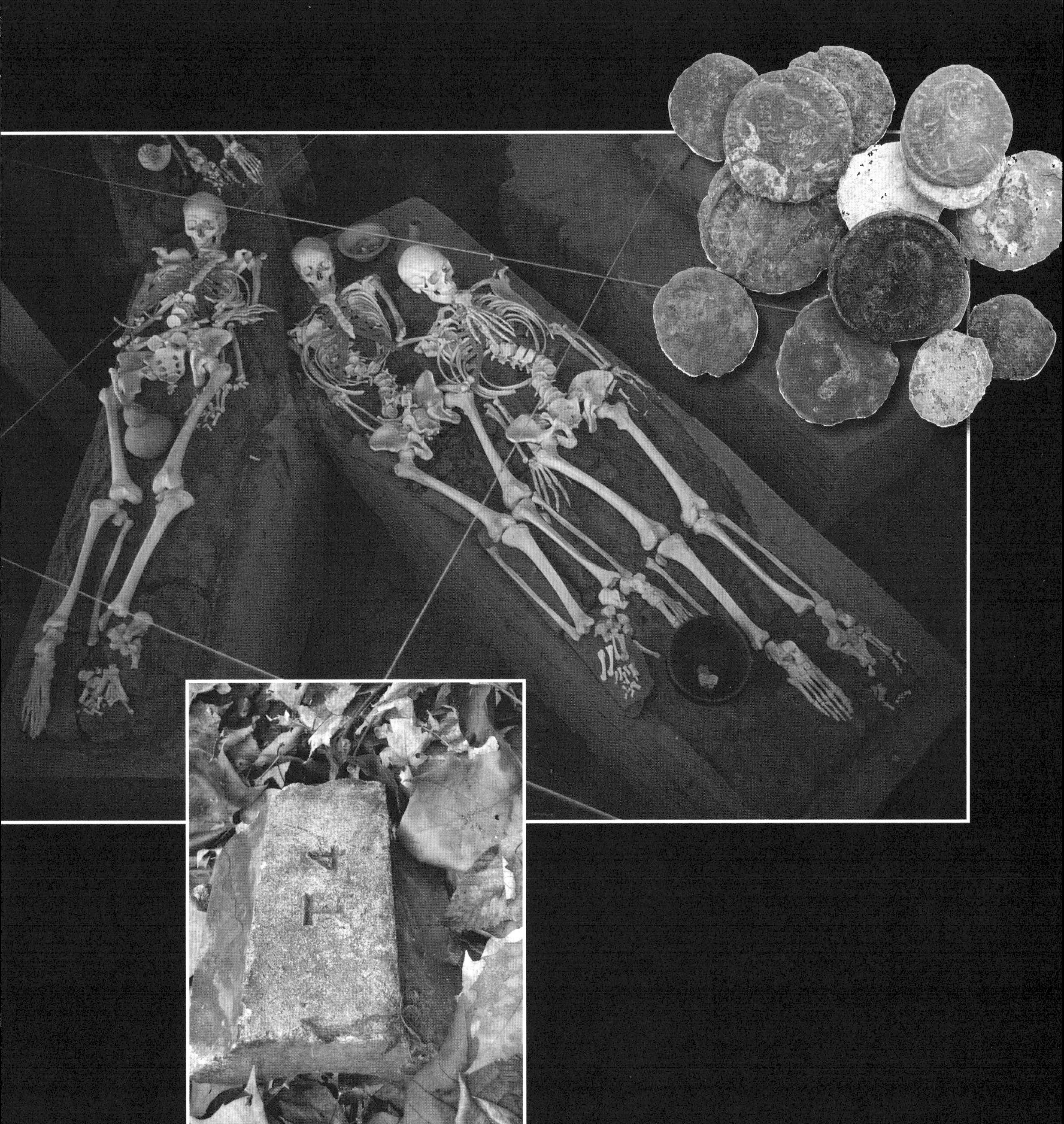

Over 150 such impacts on our planet have been documented, and there could be countless more hidden and yet unknown.

# Prehistoric Impact Craters

***There once was a time*** when people wondered why the earth isn't covered with meteor impact craters, since the moon is. It seemed like a darned good question at the time. Of course, we now know the earth IS covered with them—they're just harder to notice because of our planet's dense vegetation, erosion from weather, and incrustation of man-made structures.

Over 150 such impacts on our planet have been documented, and there could be countless more hidden and yet unknown. Here are the three most notable impact craters in Kentucky.

## The Middlesboro Basin

This is the most famous of the three, so huge that the entire town of Middlesboro was actually built inside it. The impact is believed to have occurred less than 310 million years ago. There have been numerous stories of poltergeist occurrences in the Cumberland Gap/Middlesboro/Gap Cave area. Although we don't know of anyone else making a connection between the crater's origin and such activity, we'll venture that whatever struck the earth in this spot could be related to paranormal phenomena in the area.

## Big Sink

You'll find this impact site on Big Sink Road in Versailles. It's a giant ring, one mile in diameter, consisting of many sinkholes and cracks, and is said to have occurred from an impact that took place no more than 445 million years ago. The site was well known to the Native Americans and was held in high regard. It's subtle when viewed at ground level, but is quite clearly a perfectly concentric ring pockmarked with sinkholes.

## Jeptha Knob

Located in Shelby County, almost equidistant between Lexington and Louisville, this crater was originally misidentified as a cryptovolcanic structure—one that mainstream science cannot explain. It's said by some to have been discovered in 1887 by a William M. Linney, although it had already long since been explored by Native Americans. According to some locals, it's also said to be haunted or to have a "spooky feeling" associated with it. "Jeptha," incidentally, is a Hebrew word meaning "set free."

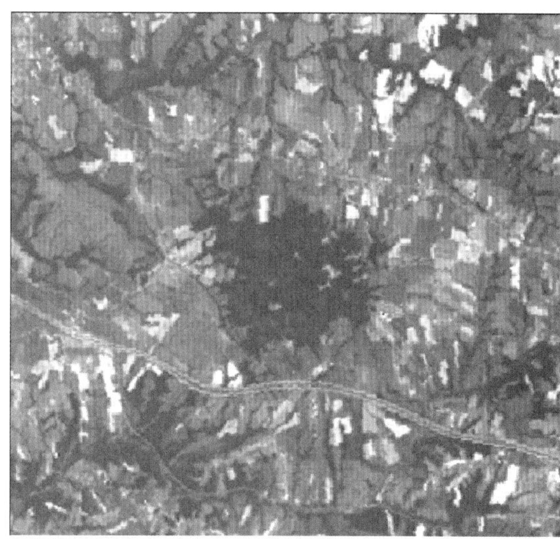

*A true color composite of Jeptha Knob. True color composite images most closely resemble the range of vision of the human eye.*

It should be noted that although it's generally assumed that these impacts were indeed created by meteors, we don't actually know that. Most meteors and meteorites explode on contact or just above the surface, but so might an alien-made craft.

# Footprints Left a Lasting Impression

***When you consider*** how conditions have to be just right for fossilization to occur, it's something of a miracle that we have as many fossils as we do. Somehow people have even been able to find dinosaur footprints that avoided being destroyed, smeared, or seriously altered long enough for the fossilization process to occur. The odds are against it, and yet there they are.

When fossilized human footprints are found, there's even more of a cause for amazement. Some of these prints are accepted by mainstream science, such as the 20,000-year-old human footprints discovered in New South Wales, Australia, in 2003. Others are questioned as being either just too perfect to be real or too vague to provide conclusive evidence.

Of all the alleged human fossil footprint stories, those concerning the prints from Rockcastle County are the most famous. In 1938, an announcement was made by Dr. Wilbur Burroughs of Berea College that a series of humanoid prints had been discovered on a nearby farm owned by Otto Finnell, and soon other scientists gave credence to his finds. By 1940, the story was being written up in *Scientific American* and presented not skeptically, but as a reasonable and potential anomaly.

Dr. Burroughs held an open mind to the possibility that these findings could turn upside down what we thought we knew about early man and be the cause for a rewrite of history. But he also proposed an alternate theory which suggested that more than one set of fossilization processes might have occurred, millions of years apart, with the end result having the appearance of one unified rock.

Creationists seized upon the story as vindication of their beliefs, noting that these humanoid prints were in Permian carboniferous rock (approximately 250 million years old) from a time when dinosaurs were not yet found on the earth. And everyone knows that man and dinosaurs did not cohabitate the planet. Ever.

In retrospect, it's surprising that the Kentucky prints were ever given as much benefit of the doubt as they were: The prints were comically distorted and did not look particularly humanoid at all. Some had five toes, but some also had four and even three. They resembled cartoon representations of feet more than anything else, though this may be partially because of the outline-chalking done to highlight the prints for *Scientific American*'s rather poor black-and-white photographs.

Unfortunately, the photographs are all we have today. As happens all too frequently with such finds, vandals destroyed the footprints in the 1960s, and only then did someone say, "Gee, maybe we should have done something to preserve or protect them." Modern analysis might have been able to tell us something conclusive about the footprints, but now we can only forever speculate. Because of the peculiar appearance of the prints, some have even said they'd believe these were some sort of bipedal alien footprints before they'd accept them as those of cavemen. A most intriguing idea.

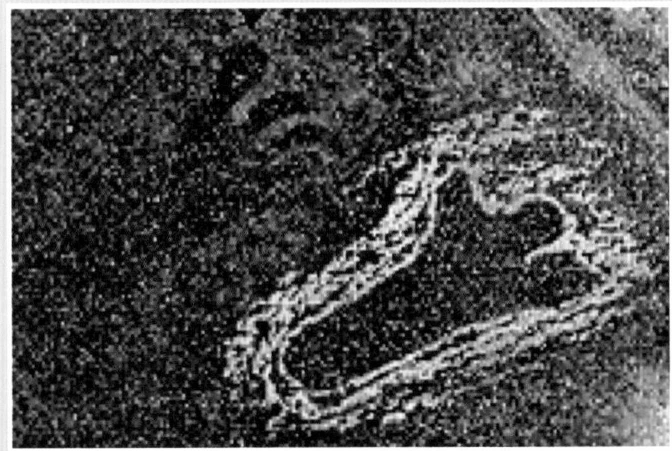

## Roman Riches in Kentucky

***Artifacts*** from ancient Rome tend to turn up in North America with alarming regularity. A Roman figurine head was found in a sixteenth-century Mexican burial site. A cave in Illinois was discovered to contain artifacts of Roman, Greek, and Egyptian origin, which were clearly left there in antiquity. Roman coins were unearthed in an Indian mound in Texas, and a Roman-style ship's remains were found at the bottom of Galveston Bay.

Kentucky is no exception. In 1963, as workers began construction on the Sherman Minton Bridge in Louisville, a large cache of Roman coins was dug up during excavation. According to one source, the coins were arranged in a way that suggested they had originally been buried in a bag or a pouch, which had long since rotted away. One of the coins bore the likeness of Emperor Claudius II, circa A.D. 268.

Two of the coins ended up on display in the Falls of the Ohio Museum in Clarksville, Indiana, but in 2004, were ordered removed by the state. Apparently, Indiana has a specific archaeological policy forbidding the suggestion that pre-Columbian contact with other cultures occurred, and so the coin exhibit was packed up and has presumably been filed away in some forgotten box in a dusty storage room.

Some years after the Louisville find, a man discovered Roman coins in a cave in Breathitt County. Interestingly, these coins were from the same general time period as the ones dug up in 1963—known as "antoniniani" coins, they're from somewhere between A.D. 238 and 305.

The Red River Gorge area in Powell County is rampant with unexplainable pictographic art and carvings, and some of them have been declared, at one time or another, to be seemingly of Roman origin. One such pictograph that purportedly depicted a Roman emperor with the "solar crown" motif was destroyed by vandals in the 1980s.

What, if anything, does it all mean? That the Roman Empire actually visited America? Possibly, but not necessarily. Anyone can purchase ancient Roman coins even today, and they were no doubt even more plentiful in centuries past. It's not unthinkable that some later travelers carried these coins here, although they would probably still have been pre-Columbian travelers and thus still fly in the face of historical decorum.

## Bar Kokhba Coins

***Since Roman coins*** keep turning up buried in Kentucky, perhaps it's only fitting that the state is also well known in some circles for its Bar Kokhba coins, from the Jewish revolt against Rome in A.D. 132.

Simon Bar Kokhba led the Jews in a split away from the Roman Empire and established a short-lived sovereign state, which was reconquered by the Romans in A.D. 135. His name is Aramaic for "Son of a Star" and was intended as a reference to Numbers 24:17, *There shall step forth a star out of Jacob.*

In 1952, a man in Clay City found a strange coin in his hog pen, located in a field alongside Route 15 that had recently been plowed for the first time. It was later determined to be a coin of the Bar Kokhba rebellion and was the subject of an article by Joe Creason in the *Louisville Courier-Journal* on July 12, 1953. However, in later years, several experts (including the curator of numismatics at the Israel Museum in Jerusalem) determined that the coin was a fake—but in a way, a real fake. The replica was indeed old; it has been postulated that it was made for tourists in the very early twentieth century as a souvenir of the Holy Land. How it ended up buried in a field in the middle of nowhere in an extremely remote part of Kentucky is still a fascinating question.

Other Bar Kokhba coins have been found, however. An article in the February 1980 issue of the journal *Current Anthropology* devotes extensive attention to the subject. Professor J. Huston McCulloch of Ohio State University has been researching the Kentucky Bar Kokhba phenomenon for some time and is aware of a Bar Kokhba coin that was dug up in Louisville in 1932, and yet another one found in Hopkinsville in 1967. Still others have turned up in other southern states. It's all part of the same confusing labyrinth of enigmas surrounding the civilizations that once inhabited this region before state lines were drawn.

# Cave Mummies

***What is it*** with Kentucky caves and mummies? Over the years, quite a few pre-Columbian mummies have been found in Kentucky caves, especially Mammoth Cave, Short Cave, and Salts Cave. Most of them are said to be of either unusually large or unusually small stature, and often have red hair.

Similar red-haired mummies have turned up elsewhere in the United States, as well as Russia, China, the Canary Islands, Egypt, Peru, New Zealand, and other locales. Their ethnic makeup remains a mystery, although some researchers, including Wisconsin's Mary Sutherland, have actually suggested the presence of extraterrestrial DNA. You can visit Sutherland on the Web at www.burlingtonnews.net.

The most famous of the mummies, known as Lost John, has been dated back to the fourth century B.C. while others, such as Little Alice, carbon-date to approximately 3,500 years ago.

Kentucky's mummies also include the following colorful characters.

## Fawn Hoof

Discovered in Short Cave in 1813, this elegant female mummy was wearing lipstick and was wrapped in deerskins when she was found. She was shuffled around from one group of incompetent scientists to another and fell into horrible disrepair in the process. According to some accounts, at some point after 1876 some geniuses at the Smithsonian Institution decided to dissect the mummy and subsequently discarded most of it.

## Little Alice

Discovered in 1875 in Salts Cave, she was sometimes displayed by carny promoters as the more popular Fawn Hoof. By the 1950s, the mummy had been so poorly cared for that she was deemed no longer suitable for museum display. Some researchers claim that despite her nomenclature and billing, Little Alice was actually a boy.

## Lost John

Legend has it that sometime in the very distant past this forty-five-year-old Native American entered Mammoth Cave on a gypsum-collecting expedition and inadvertently caused a cave-in as he hammered away at the crystals on the cave's ceiling. Two thousand years later tour guides discovered him in a perfectly mummified state, pressed under an immense slab of rock. Beside him were found his tools, his torch, and a lunch he'd packed but never got to eat.

## Scudder's Mummy

Discovered in 1814 in Short Cave, it was dragged off to New York City to be shown off in a venue called Scudder's American Museum, which was in turn purchased by carnival huckster P. T. Barnum. The whole place went up in flames in 1865, destroying the mummy and countless other treasures that were unfortunate enough to have ended up in Barnum's hands.

## More Giants of Kentucky

**The Bible says,** *There were giants . . . in those days,* and clearly, it was right. The archaeological record for ancient giant humanoids in North America (and especially Kentucky) is considerable.

In 1519, explorer Alonzo Alvarez de Pineda reported encountering giants on the Mississippi River. Panfilo de Narvaez and Cabeza de Vaca made a similar discovery in Tampa Bay in 1528. And in 1539, the explorer Hernando de Soto found giants in Florida, including the Native American cacique Tuscaloosa and his son.

Were these mere ancient anomalies? Maybe not. Martin Van Buren Bates of Whitesburg was over six feet tall at the age of sixteen and didn't stop growing until he was twenty-eight, at which time he had reached seven feet eight inches. He left a successful military career to join the circus, where he met and ultimately married Anna Haining Swan, who was even taller. They entered the record books as the tallest married couple ever. She died in 1888, he in 1919.

The highly controversial "UFO preacher," Sherry Shriner, claims that the gigantism that affected Bates, as well as Louisville's own Jim Porter, is caused by deliberate genetic interference by extraterrestrials. Some proof of that comes from Holly Creek, where in 1965, Kenneth White unearthed a humanoid skeleton that was almost nine feet tall. Interestingly, the eyes on the massive thirty-inch-circumference skull were slits, not round sockets, fitting the popular description of a typical extraterrestrial alien. The nasal passages on the skull were similarly slitlike, rather than normal open sockets. The late Kentucky folklorist Michael Paul Henson actually traveled to Wolfe County to examine the remains personally before White insisted on giving the body a decent reburial.

*Martin Van Buren Bates*

# Mysterious Mound Builders of Wickliffe

***Wickliffe,*** in Ballard County at the confluence of the Ohio and Mississippi rivers, is a hotbed of archaeo–logical research because it was once home to a mound-building community, about which we know very little.

What do we know about them? Well, they made beautiful pottery, especially of eerie-looking owls, symbolic of the underworld and the dead. They're generally regarded as having been part of the Mississippian culture, which is considered the probable ancestor of the later Native American tribes that populated the area by the time European settlers got here. It should be noted that the entire Mississippian geologic period was 360 to 320 million years ago, which is different from the Mississippian culture.

Probably. Possibly. Maybe. Archaeologists and ethnologists like to put things in boxes and assign things to categories as much as the next person, and so they separate the Mississippian culture into three extremely broad, extremely vague, and extremely arbitrary categories.

**1. Early.** Early Mississippian cultures are said to be those making a transition from a more primitive way of life to one of increasing sophistication. The Early Mississippian period is considered to be circa A.D. 1,000–1,200.

**2. Middle.** The middle period is considered the peak of the Mississippian people's development, because it was then that they instituted a form of government, being led by a chief in a chiefdom. The middle period of growth is considered to have taken place circa A.D. 1,200–1,400.

**3. Late.** This is where things get really interesting. The many tribes that we now retroactively classify as Mississippian were not necessarily connected or closely linked, and many lived out most of their existence isolated from one another. They didn't keep in touch with Web sites and e-mail, and they didn't have a newsletter. And yet, their civilizations all began to go

down the tubes at exactly the same time. A way of life that had sustained itself for centuries fell apart, and for no discernible reason. The tribes simply and completely vanished from Wickliffe.

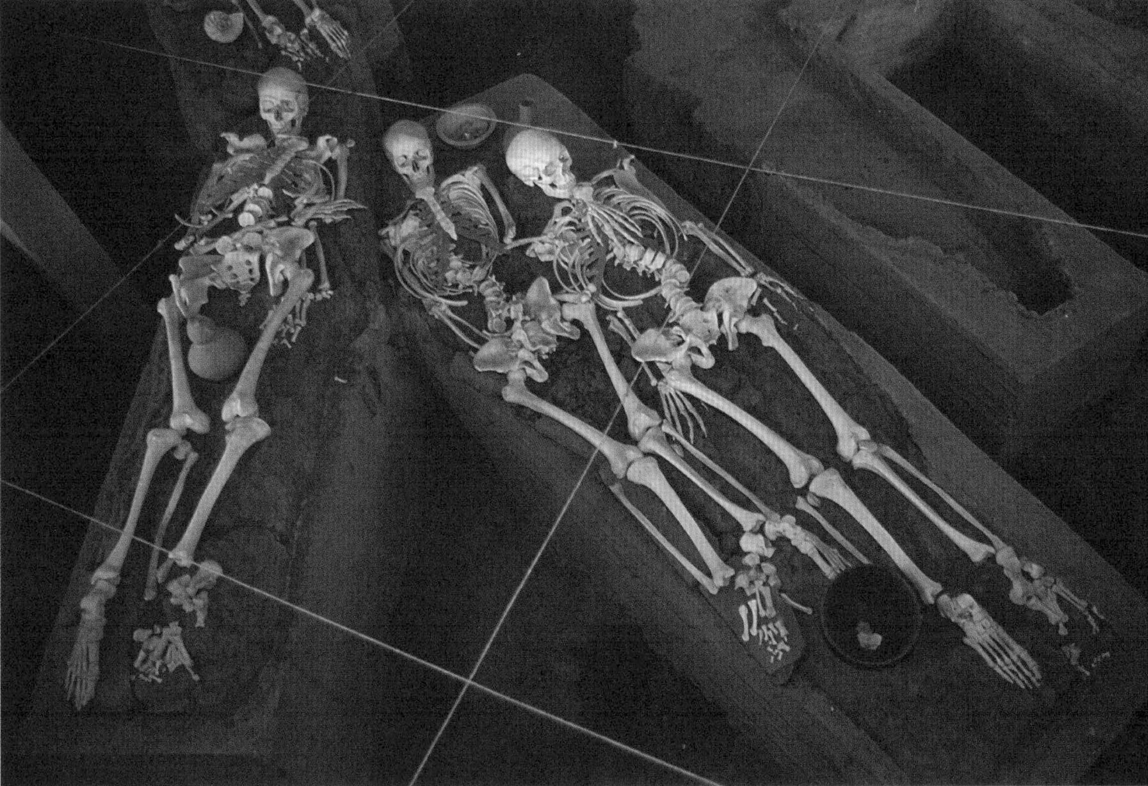

Why? We don't know. Is there any sign of war or disaster in the city's remains? No. Is there any sign of disease or epidemic? No.

Something made a centuries-old civilization pack everything up and move out. They left their burial mounds behind, which stayed intact for centuries—until 1930, when a man named Fain King looked upon the mighty works of those enigmatic denizens of the past and knew what must be done: He dug up the sacred mounds and turned the place into a tourist trap.

This sad state of affairs continued until 1983, well past the point when someone should have stood up and said, "Wait a minute, what the heck are we doing?" Thankfully, Murray State University finally reclaimed the site in the name of scientific research, and in 2004, the area became federally protected land as part of the state parks service.

Today you can visit the Wickliffe Mounds State Historic Site, its gift shop, and museum, which consists of three excavated mounds, demonstrations of Mississippian burial practices, and displays of artifacts from the site. These artifacts include peculiar figural pottery with haunting faces.

The most famous of all Wickliffe artifacts, however, was a creepy effigy of a great horned owl, which was unfortunately stolen by burglars in 1988 and never seen again. However, like priceless works of famous art heisted from museums, such items are nearly impossible to sell, even on the black market. The purloined owl totem probably currently occupies a display case or special perch in a secret room somewhere viewed by who knows who for who knows what purposes.

Let us take some minor comfort in knowing that whoever stole the owl and whoever currently holds it today will suffer a curse for their deeds and will pay sooner or later. Sure as there's feathers on a chicken.

## Buried Skulls

In 1792, an early settler, General John Payne, made a horrifying discovery while building his house in the Bracken County town of Augusta, just fifty-three miles southwest of the Great Serpent Mound, not far from the Ohio–Kentucky border. From *Historical Sketches of Kentucky by Lewis Collins,* Maysville, 1847, page 205:

> The bottom on which Augusta is situated is a large burying ground of the ancients. . . . They have been found in great numbers, and of all sizes, everywhere between the mouths of Bracken and Locust Creeks, a distance of about a mile and a half. From the cellar under my (Payne's) dwelling, 60 by 70 feet, over a hundred and ten skeletons were taken. I measured them by skulls, and there might have been more, whose skulls had crumbled into dust. . . . The skeletons were of all sizes, from seven feet to infant.
>
> David Kilgour (who was a tall and very large man) passed our village at the time I was excavating my cellar, and we took him down and applied a thigh bone to his. The man, if well-proportioned, must have been 10 to 12 inches taller than Kilgour, and the lower jaw bone would slip on over his, skin and all. Who were they? How came their bones here?
>
> When I was in the army, I inquired of old Crane, a Wyandot and of Anglerson, a Delaware, both intelligent old chiefs, and they could give me no information in reference to these remains of antiquity. Some of the largest trees of the forest were growing over the remains when the land was cleared in 1792.

After this, the skulls disappear from history, and another strange chapter in Kentucky's ancient past comes to an inconclusive close. To whom did the skulls belong? Why were some so large? We may never know.

## Ancient Civilization Under Lexington

***In his 1806 book*** *Travels in America,* Thomas Ashe writes of his experiences with an enormous underground chamber originally discovered in 1783 beneath Lexington. He describes it as three hundred feet long, one hundred feet wide, and nineteen feet high, containing exotic artifacts, a stone altar for sacrifices, human skulls and bones piled high, and mummified remains. The mummies were very strange looking and, like the Mammoth Cave specimens, had red hair. The local Native Americans claimed that these were not their people, but the remnants of an ancient civilization that died out long ago.

In 1872, respected historian George W. Ranck also discussed this "lost city" buried beneath Lexington. Again it is reported that local Native Americans identified the bodies as being from an ancient race that inhabited the area long before them. So strong was the evidence of giant caverns and the remains of ancient civilizations beneath Lexington that *Herald-Leader* columnist Don Edwards wrote that when one of the large hotels began construction downtown, they did far more core drillings than necessary, just to make absolutely certain they weren't building atop these caves.

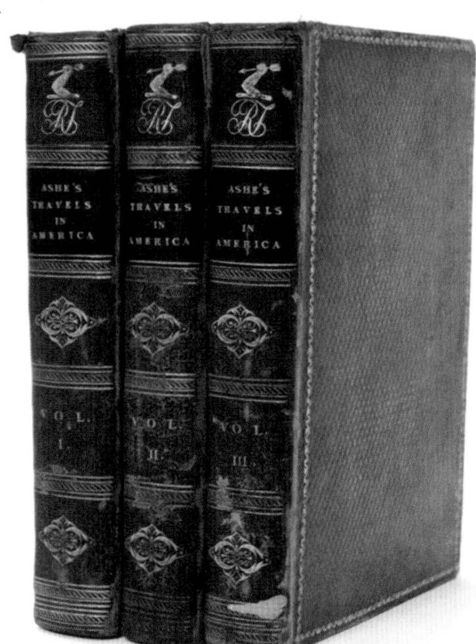

## The Brandenburg Stone

***In 1912,*** a farmer named Craig Crecelius found a large stone in a field on his farm in Brandenburg, about forty miles from the Falls of the Ohio. The stone clearly contained writing of an unknown language, going in a straight line across the rock's center. For fifty-three years, Mr. Crecelius exhibited the carved stone at fairs, during which at some point the rock accidentally was broken into three parts.

In 1973, so-called expert archaeologists examined the Brandenburg Stone and came up with the baffling assessment that the marks were simply natural scratches, nothing more. It remained in the possession of the Brandenburg Public Library for many years, and in 1998, a pair of professional Welsh historians from Cardiff recognized the script as being Coelbren, an ancient Welsh dialect from circa A.D. 500, and proceeded to translate the stone at long last: "Toward strength (unity), divide the land we are spread over, purely (or justly) between offspring in wisdom."

To many the revelation that the Brandenburg Stone is ancient Welsh serves as further evidence that the Welsh Prince Madoc arrived in North America centuries before Columbus and colonized Louisville's riverside area.

The stone is currently on display at the Charlestown Library in Charlestown, Indiana.

## Red River Gorge

***Forget the Grand Canyon, folks.*** The Red River Gorge in Kentucky provides the same grandeur and thrills for a fraction of the travel expense. The Grand Canyon is much bigger, to be sure, but it's mostly an empty hole in the ground, whereas the Red River Gorge is literally pulsing with life and energy, resonating with mystery and power.

So what exactly is the Red River Gorge? Well, when most people refer to it, what they're really talking about is a much larger general area known as the Pottsville Escarpment. This is a dense, mountainous area of forests and swamps combined with elaborate rock formations and outcroppings, the kind most people think of as being a feature of the western United States. The actual gorge is but one part of the escarpment. It's a huge canyon that includes natural bridges, waterfalls, and archaeological remains of ancient civilizations.

This area is well known for being a treasure trove of petroglyphs (rock art) etched by members of ancient civilizations. The petroglyph images include:

- **Footprints.** Drawing pictures of footprints was a popular pastime, it seems, for early man. Interestingly, those of birds seem to be the most popular, but footprints of humans, bears, and other animals were also rendered into rock walls in Kentucky.

- **Animals.** Images of bears, birds, lizards, cats, wolves, and fish have all been painted or chiseled into rock here.

- **Geometric and abstract designs,** including swastikas and swastika-like symbols. (The swastika, or gammadion, is a very ancient symbol popular for thousands of years before the Nazis adopted it as their own in the 1920s.)

- **Anthropomorphic figures.** Humans and humanlike figures have been portrayed in Kentucky rock art, including some that seem extraterrestrial in their countenance.

This area is very popular with rock climbers, campers, and outdoorsy types in general. There are spectacular rock promontories, a rock arch bridge with breathtaking views, other natural bridges sculpted by time and erosion, and a reputably haunted tunnel. You could spend your entire life here—and many have—and still not explore all that this region has to offer.

## Kentucky's Blue Hole

***I was reading*** the story about the blue hole in South New Jersey and was intrigued. I wanted to make it known that there is at least one other blue hole in the country and it is located in Bowling Green, at Lost River Cave. Lost River Cave is basically a park where tourists can tour the caves, ride boats through them, and purchase stuff from the gift shop. Some people even get married there.

There is a blue hole there as well that has a display sign in front of it like you see at many state and national parks describing the object, scene, etc. I cannot remember what they said the depth of the hole was, but it was extremely deep. They have it roped off so that no one can get close enough to fall in. It also is very blue. I'm not sure about the temperature of it though.

I just wanted to make you aware of this blue hole. Thank you for your time and keep up the interesting work.—*Travis*

# Middle Fork Ogam Rock Shelter

***Ogam***, the ancient Irish runic alphabet, has been found on numerous artifacts in North America, notably on objects and stone carvings in Kentucky and in West Virginia.

The Midwestern Epigraphic Society, a nonprofit organization that researches the ancient migrations of mankind to the Americas (especially pre-Columbian migrations to the Midwest), studied one of the most important and curious ancient sites in Kentucky, the Middle Fork Ogam Rock Shelter in Breathitt County. They posted their findings on their Web site at www.MidwesternEpigraphic.org.

> Having almost 600 ogam strokes, [the Middle Fork Ogam Rock Shelter] site is probably one of the largest in Kentucky and perhaps the United States. After discovery in the early 1990s by Mr Michael Griffith, Breathitt Co, Ky & Dr David Feldman of Lancaster, the leading amateur epigrapher in Kentucky, Dr John Payne of Berea became involved.
>
> Then D. Payne contacted the Midwestern Epigraphic Society in 2002 for the translator, Mr Michel-Gérald Boutet of Laval, Québec to translate. In Feb 2003 Mr. Boutet reported his initial analysis of this ogam site indicates the basic content concerns BOUNDARY MARKERS; and . . . the language appears to be Proto-Algonquian. In 2004 he announced that the site appears to be much older than he thought and considerably more work is needed before the message can be completely clear.
>
> The rock shelter is located on the middle fork of the Kentucky River and is the kind favored by old world Celtic people—one with a large boulder at the entrance just under the overhanging rock roof, and a nearby source of water, in this case a river. Both the boulder and the back wall of the shelter are covered with hundreds of ogam grooves.
>
> Its relative isolation and accessibility from only the river has protected the shelter from most modern graffiti. Periodic flooding has camouflaged the shelter entrance with debris and covered the lower levels of ogam grooves with protective layers of mud. All this made it hard to find once again in the Fall of 2002 for MES documentation and required washing the rock surface to reveal the ogam for tracing and photography. Every precaution was taken to preserve the site.
>
> Several "stars" appear in the ogam script, suggesting reference to those in the Kentucky night sky. If the translation does indicate astronomical references, site compass readings should be made to corroborate it. Natural circular depressions in the rock face seem to have been worked into the script and several possibly man-made "holes" may prove significance. . . .
>
> A Geologist who recently completed a scientific study of the Kensington Rune Stone will now study this rock shelter to verify its antiquity.

So how did Celtic runes end up in Kentucky hundreds of years before Columbus? Stay tuned.

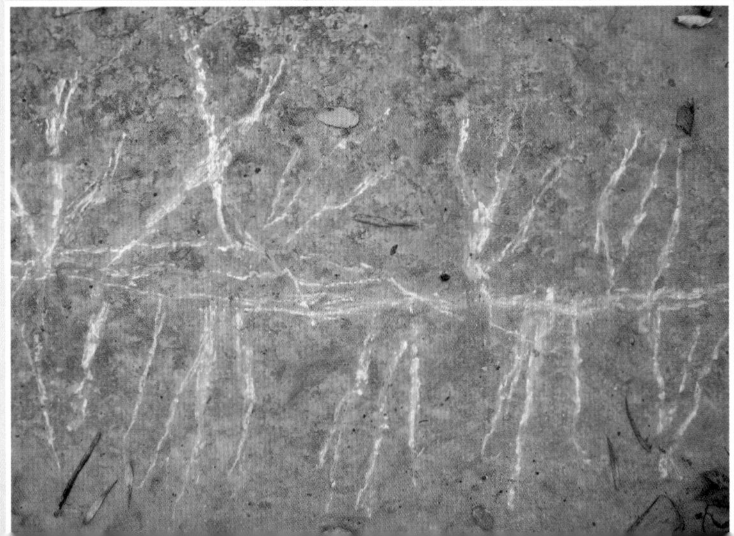

## Squire Boone Rock

***In the year 1770,*** brothers Squire and Daniel Boone were part of an expedition together in the general Kentucky area, but split up and went their separate ways in the spring.

Squire was traipsing across America in a north-south direction, heading down to North Carolina to load up on supplies, while Daniel progressed on a westerly route toward the Falls of the Ohio and the area that would soon become Louisville.

As legend has it, upon Squire's return to Kentucky, he carved his name and the year into a rock in the area that is presently between Berea and Big Hill, near Pilot Knob. This was allegedly intended to communicate to Daniel that he was back in the area.

Although its authenticity has been disputed by some, the prevailing consensus is that there's no reason to doubt the rock's validity. It's currently on display in the Madison County courthouse in Richmond. It remains one of the state's few prominent tributes to Squire, who in fact deserves every bit of the kudos and glory that have been bestowed upon Daniel, being just as courageous and trailblazing an American explorer as his more acclaimed brother.

## Digging for Ancient Mysteries

***Someone speaking about*** Louisville's great architectural details on rooftops once said that if you wanted to get a taste of the city's past, you had to look up as you walked. Quite true, and quite lovely stuff. But we tend to keep our eyes pointed down, not up. As Tom Waits says, *"There's a world going on underground."*

Consider the cobblestones. In some areas of Louisville, you can still find cobblestones that date far back in our city's history. Watch for dark brown ones, not the later salmon-colored replacements. Although there aren't as many of them as there used to be (in 2002, for example, a significant stretch of cobblestones was removed from Fourth Street), you can still enjoy their old-world charm in many places throughout the city.

And keep your eye out for bricks with words on them. They're everywhere. In the good old days, brick manufacturers stamped each brick with their imprint. These imprints are rarely seen—they were on the sides intended to be concealed in the mortar—but occasionally you can find them. Many older homes used imprinted bricks as makeshift cobblestones to pave a path or a driveway on their property.

And what's under these bricks and cobblestones? One of the great things about living in a truly old city is that there are so many opportunities to be an amateur urban archaeologist. If you live in the suburbs of a young town and start digging a hole in your yard, chances are you won't find much—maybe a Pepsi can and a plastic Pringles lid discarded by the construction workers who built your house. But in a place like Louisville, you can start digging anywhere, and you're likely to hit something interesting and old. After all, the ground of most old yards hasn't been messed with in almost a century.

Broken crockery shards from plates, teacups, and saucers circa 1920–1960 are the most common thing to turn

up in the dirt. Depression glass and milk glass fragments show up quite often, as do glittering pieces of so-called Carnival Glass and Fire-King's opaque green Jadite. Needless to say, don't dig on private property, don't dig on public property such as parks, and stay away from any grounds that are known to be sacred to any culture.

When we get to earlier strata of diggables, such as items from Native Americans, things get a little more complicated. Arrowheads are by far the most common item to show up in digs, especially on farmland that's been recently deep-tilled (deep-tilling is terrible for the environment, but good for archaeologists). Ask permission—I repeat, ask permission—before trespassing on someone's farm with a shovel. If you ignore this advice, don't come crying to me if someone blows your brains out with an SPR-94.

And another warning: If you're in it for money rather than the simple love of amateur archaeology, you're wasting your time. There are "price guide" books that list ridiculous prices for common arrowheads. They're total baloney, often made up out of whole cloth by collectors seeking to amplify the value of their own collections with the swoop of a pen.

If you find more advanced Indian relics than mere arrowheads, halt forthwith and notify someone like the Filson Club, the Kentucky Geological Survey, the Kentucky Paleontological Society, or a local professor. All Native American artifacts are protected by the Kentucky Antiquities Act, and it's best to check with an expert to make sure you aren't wrecking an important find.

Fossils are also another fun and fascinating thing to go digging and foraging for. Most of Kentucky's fossils are from very, very ancient times, almost always far older than the period when dinosaurs roamed the earth. Kentucky's sedimentary rocks that contain fossils are generally between 505 million and 1 million years old. This means that what you'll find here will likely be shells, mollusks, fish, plant life, coral, crinoids, and trilobites. As yet no dinosaur fossils have ever been found in Kentucky, but it's not entirely impossible.

It's beyond the scope of this book to tell you what to look for on any of these trips, but if your interest is aroused, a quick visit to a library will give you a start. Better yet, why not volunteer to take part in a professional and legitimate archaeological dig? There are plenty out there who could use your help.

If you do go digging on your own, document everything. Get a digital camera and take photographs of your dig sites, the moments of discovery, and so forth. Keep a diary or journal. Keep close track of what was found where. Treat even the most trivial discoveries of Mason-jar lids as if you were Louis Leakey unearthing *Australopithecus* skulls in the Olduvai Gorge. If you find something really important, tell an expert. Don't risk ruining an important discovery. And needless to say, if you find human bones, don't just call a professor, call the police!

Kentucky's opportunities for amateur archaeology, paleontology, and geology can be very rewarding. If you have soil, get thee to a shovel, and see what you can find.

# Fabled People and Legendary Places

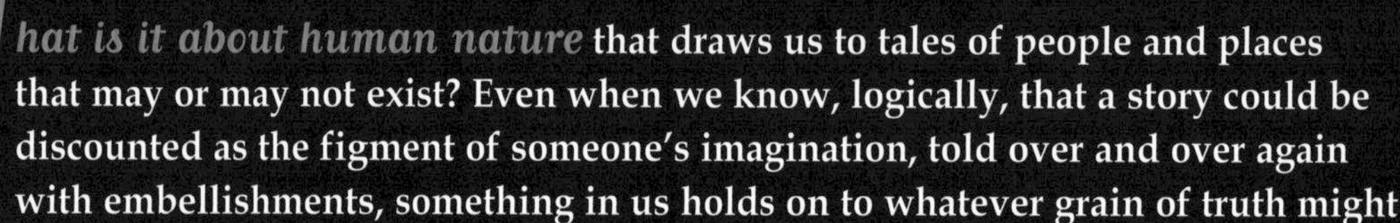

W*hat is it about human nature* that draws us to tales of people and places that may or may not exist? Even when we know, logically, that a story could be discounted as the figment of someone's imagination, told over and over again with embellishments, something in us holds on to whatever grain of truth might have engendered it in the first place. We grasp for that slim reed of possibility. Is it real? Could it be real? Is there such a place or person?

For instance, what about the Melungeons—that mysterious "race" of people with lumpy heads and shovel teeth? Were they roaming Kentucky long before the white folk landed? And after the Europeans "discovered" America, did some of them settle in the hills of our state and inbreed for so long that generations of their children were actually, well, blue? (This would, of course, give new meaning to the nickname Bluegrass State!)

As we comb the state in search of these mysteries and wonders, it's the grain of truth that keeps us going. Because as weird seekers are well aware, you just never know!

BLUE GRASS ARMY DEPOT
"PIONEER IN QUALITY"

*George Catlin painting from the 1800s of the Mandan tribe in their earthen forts. The cedar post they're dancing around represents the mysterious "Lone Man."*

## Wales Tale

***Did you know*** that an exploration team headed by a Welsh prince named Madoc ap Owain Gwynned (usually just "Madoc" for short) is believed by many to have settled in America in the year 1170? That's three centuries prior to when Cristoforo Colombo is generally said to have discovered America in 1498. (Yes, 1498. The children's rhyme says, *In 1492 Columbus sailed the ocean blue.* But he didn't actually arrive in the Americas until 1498.)

You won't find Madoc in the history books just yet, though. Scholars and historians aren't convinced of the veracity of the ancient legend or even of the existence of Madoc himself. While Owain Gwynned was a well-known Welsh ruler of the twelfth century, there is no record that he had a son named Madoc. Skeptics also point out that there is no known printed account of the Madoc legend prior to 1583, when it appeared in a book called, *A True Report of the Late Discoveries of the Newfound Landes.*

And yet, there are very good reasons why the Madoc legend persists.

In 1669, a clergyman named Morgan Jones was captured by a band of Tuscarora Indians known as the Doeg. Facing certain death, he began to pray out loud in Welsh. To his shock and amazement, the Indians understood Welsh and set him free. Jones found himself in the surreal position of suddenly being highly regarded and respected by this tribe of "savages" for his ability to speak Welsh, and he stayed with them for many months, teaching them about Christianity and preaching sermons to them in Welsh.

Many subsequent visitors to America encountered Welsh-speaking Native Americans, and one even claimed to find Indians in possession of a Welsh Bible.

So what, you may ask, does all this have to do with Kentucky? Well, it just so happens that the site where Louisville stands today is said to have once been a major settlement—possibly THE major settlement—of Madoc's exploration team and various Native Americans who learned to speak Welsh.

The Mandan tribe, who were originally located in the Ohio River Valley area near Louisville, had a legend about the "Lone Man" who came from an unknown land to rescue the tribe.

In his 1841 book *North American Indians,* George Catlin made a compelling argument for the Mandan tribe's being the descendants of Madoc; a definite Welsh influence was noted in the Mandan style of boatmaking, architecture, culture, and fair-haired appearance. Madoc's hand is also seen by some in the man-made fort mounds and a mysterious stone structure atop a natural rock formation called the Devil's Backbone, in Charlestown, IN. The Devil's Backbone protrudes into the Ohio River just across from Goshen, KY (just a few minutes north of Louisville).

# Melungeon Mystery

***According to some old legends,*** there is a strange race of people who call themselves the Melungeons. They are members of a secretive civilization that predates the European settlers in America and that had its own fortresslike cities deep in the wilderness. Supposedly, the Melungeons operated silver mines (and even minted their own coins) in the region where Kentucky, Tennessee, and West Virginia meet. It's a fascinating story that is told again and again.

Unfortunately, much of that story is baloney. There is a group of people called Melungeons, but they most likely did NOT predate European settlers. And the term Melungeon was not what they chose to call themselves; it was an insulting and pejorative general term given to any people of mixed ethnicity, used mainly by lazy government workers whose forms tended to classify humans only in terms of "white," "black," and "Indian." In fact, many so-called Melungeons openly stated that they were Portuguese.

Speaking on National Public Radio's *All Things Considered,* Dr. Virginia E. DeMarce of the National Genealogical Society said, "It's not that mysterious once you . . . do the nitty-gritty research one family at a time." DeMarce and other genealogists have traced Melungeon family trees back to Louisa County, Virginia, circa 1700.

That is, however, an inconvenient truth for many who prefer the mythologized and romantic versions of history. Many people have declared themselves to be Melungeons simply because they read about them on some Web site and suddenly decided they must be related because they have relatives with Melungeon-associated surnames in their family tree. Ava Gardner, Abraham Lincoln, and even Elvis Presley have all been rumored to be Melungeons. Recently reports circulated among treasure hunters that Melungeon silver coins (as well as statuettes of pigs and people) were unearthed in a cave near Elkhorn City.

I have to admit that even I briefly bought into the myth after being told years ago by a Melungeon "expert" that he was clearly descended from the original Melungeons because of physical characteristics such as "shovel teeth" and an "Anatolian bump" on the top of the skull. A little research, however, turned up the information that these features are extremely common in human physiology and that there's absolutely no scientific validity in pointing to them as indicative of Melungeon ancestry.

But what about those silver mines?

## Blue People in the Bluegrass State?

***Although the existence*** of the Blue People is a legitimate phenomenon that has been well documented and written about in all manner of publications from scientific journals to mass-market magazines, we really don't want to encourage readers to load their cameras and go on a gawking spree, bothering people. Still, it's too fascinating a story not to recount here.

Since 1800 or so, it was well known that multiple families of blue-skinned people lived along Troublesome Creek near Hazard. Because their offspring were always blue, it was often assumed that they were a distinct and separate race of people, even said by some to be aliens or descended from aliens, or even angels. The Fugates were the original blue-skinned family who came to the area in the late eighteenth or early nineteenth century. They descended from one Martin Fugate, who supposedly hailed from France.

But in the 1960s, a Lexington hematologist named Madison Cawein theorized that what was happening here was a rare disorder called methemoglobinemia, which creates an abnormally high level of methemoglobin in the blood, causing blue-tinted skin. While most people with methemoglobinemia acquire it through health-threatening circumstances such as heart and artery defects, nitrate poisoning ("blue baby syndrome"), or respiratory problems, the Fugates and the other blue families were in perfect health and lived long, robust lives.

Cawein's theory was correct, however. He administered a chemical substitute for a missing blood enzyme to some of the Fugates, and their skin turned pink within minutes. Once it was made known that the blueness could be cured easily, most of those afflicted came out of their rural seclusion to line up for the treatment. A very few, it is said, chose to remain blue, but the most recent reliable sightings of them occurred in the late 1970s.

It is unknown how many, if any, blue-skinned people still exist in the area. If there are any, they no doubt wish to be left alone. There's a story, apocryphal or not, about a Hollywood camera crew getting shot at and chased away by dogs when they trespassed on a blue person's land. The very few family photographs known to exist of the blue-skinned people were taken, alas, with black-and-white film.

A few years back we corresponded by e-mail with a distant descendant of one of those families. He was attending Eastern Kentucky University and reported that the only trace left of his blue heritage was a slight bluish tinge to his fingernails. And thus another marvelous bit of human uniqueness has been all but eradicated by modern technology.

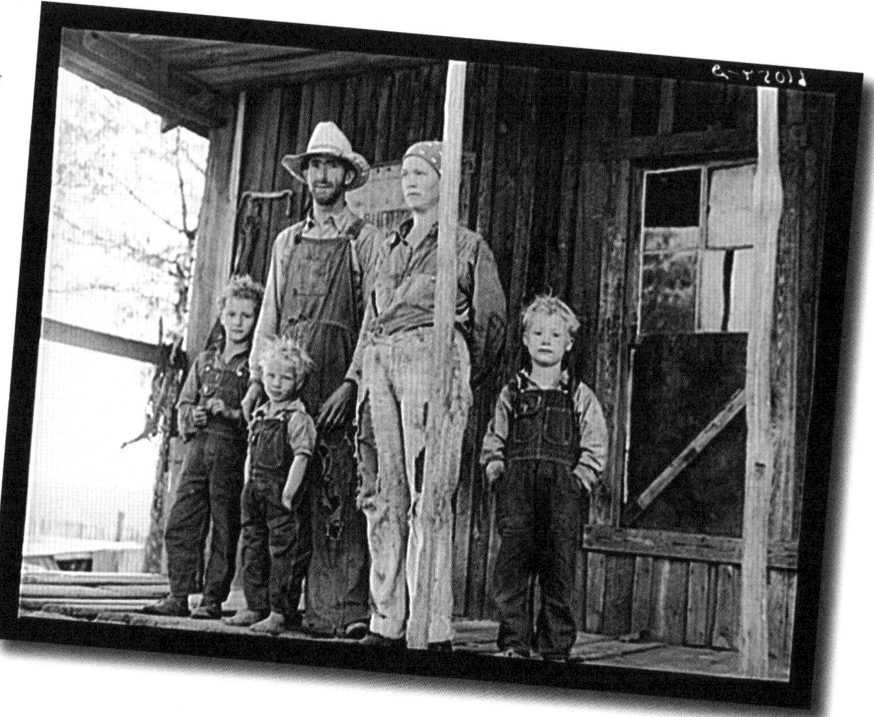

## Midget Communities

The idea of a so-called midget community is something that seems to have gained currency in the realm of myth and legend in recent years. More and more often around the country we find rumors about housing developments and gated communities populated entirely by little persons. While many of these stories are probably nothing more than urban legends, some of them are, in fact, real.

There once was a time when such remote communities were necessary so that their denizens could live in peace. Such communities were more than just housing developments; they were practically towns unto themselves, with a general store and a church. Nowadays we live in a more enlightened time (in theory anyway) and people with the medical condition known as dwarfism no longer need to isolate themselves from the rest of society—in fact, there is now a reality show featuring a dwarf family.

Be that as it may, we are still not going to divulge the location of the trailer park "midget community" in Kentucky, out of respect for the privacy of its occupants. But you can rest assured that it does exist. There's nothing to see there most of the time anyway, except that the mailboxes are closer to the ground and the door handles on the trailers are lower. Some of our correspondents, though, seem to have located their own Midgetvilles. We can't vouch for any of these, but here they are.

## Of Midgets, Squatters, and Cannibals

***There is a Midgetville*** in Kentucky, and I've been there on several occasions, both at night and during the day. It's in the sticks on U.S. 42, just south of Louisville on the road between Shepardsville and West Point. It's really an interesting little place. These cottages are arranged on a big square, high on a hill right off the main road. Most of them are built on the edge of a steep cliff. They are hanging off the edge of this cliff supported by long, narrow wooden stilts. In the center of the square is a rather large, funky looking church. My brother and I amuse ourselves by imagining it to be the secret headquarters of a super select cult of miniature Jim Jones enthusiasts. The cottages are tiny, and come complete with miniature doors, windows, porches and the smallest furniture I've ever seen this side of a Toys 'R' Us summer sale. There are about thirty or so little cottages.

There are also lots of squatters milling about during the daytime, though all of them appear to be of normal height, but that's about where the normalcy of their appearance ends, I'm afraid. One theory is that they are a wandering tribe of gypsy cannibals who assaulted and ate the previous residents before settling into the then vacant minuscule digs. I haven't been able to verify this theory, however, but one drive around the square is enough to convince the astute observer that this scenario is entirely feasible.

The squatters give you funny looks when you drive by staring at them, and they seem to sniff the wind a little more frequently when strangers wander through, but other than that, it seems friendly enough. Actually, that's not quite true; it seems pretty ominous to be honest, but in an unexplainable, Prozac-induced paranoia sort of way. There's also another weird little settlement in Louisville called Lake Dreamland that's worth a tale or two.–*Eric Crump*

## Tiny Houses 'Round a House of Worship

There really is a Midgetville, just outside Louisville. As a teenager back in the late '70s, my friends and I would drive out to Midgetville. There were a circle of tiny houses, and a small church in the center. More times than not, we ended up lost. I remember it being off Setonville Road.–*Poeticdebi*

## The Truth About Midgetville

The truth about this so-called Midgetville is that these houses were built around the church as a religious commune that is still in use today by a very strict sect of Jehovah's Witnesses, who are mostly of normal height. When you see these houses they may seem small, they only have a bedroom and bathroom in them. And if you approach them you would see that the doors are just big enough for a normal person. –*Chad Cummings*

## Mummy Unwrapping Parties

***In upper-crust*** Victorian-era society, it was once de rigueur to hold parties in which a genuine Egyptian mummy was imported by hook or by crook and turned into the subject of a parlor game.

The gimmick was this. Partygoers would take turns gingerly and slowly peeling away one of the ancient and crumbling bandages that encased the mummy. When the brittle and decaying material inevitably tore or crumbled, it was the next player's turn. These trendy socialites continued the ghoulish game until the body was naked. Unfortunately, we could find no historical memoir that states what happened next. Would there have been some dismay and loss of stomach contents once it was realized that, yes, a mummy really is a dead person, a shriveled human body, a corpse? Then again, maybe the partygoers all just shouted, "Hurrah!" opened another bottle of the good stuff, and put another Alma Gluck cylinder on the gramophone.

This was during the early days of archaeology, when nobody placed a high value on mummies and other Egyptian artifacts, which were surprisingly obtainable. Of course, exposing untreated mummy flesh to the open air often resulted in rapid decay. The bodies would literally turn to dust while the revelers' attention moved on to other parlor games. Hundreds of mummies were destroyed in this manner.

David Domine, author of such books as *Ghosts of Old Louisville,* reports that several of these bizarre mummy-unwrapping parties occurred in that city. This news is distressing enough if you believe (as we do) in the curses said to be associated with desecrating mummies and their tombs. It's even more troubling when you ask yourself, What did they do with the crumbling bodies and the dust and debris when they were done?

Apparently, in mummy-unwrapping events held in other cities, there were occasions when the mess they'd made was donated to science. However, given the questionable legal circumstances surrounding the whole thing, the more common practice was simply to get rid of the remains by any means necessary, including disposing of them in the trash or via backyard burials, some of which most likely occurred in Louisville.

## Be Still Our Hearts: The Story of Moonshine

***Moonshine***—the other legendary Kentucky drink besides bourbon—is a real Kentucky delicacy and not something Al Capp just made up for "Li'l Abner." It's amazing how many city folk still think moonshine is just a weird urban legend or simply a colorful euphemism for whiskey.

A Canadian chap approached *Weird Kentucky* after having read Lynda Barry's brilliant novel *Cruddy*. In it, the mentally unstable father of the main character hands her a jar of moonshine labeled CORPSE REVIVER and instructs her to drink some, saying, "It'll give you another eye." The person was inquiring whether such a beverage actually existed or if it was just a literary concoction. We were happy to tell him, and you, *Weird* readers, the answer is, Yes, there is a Corpse Reviver and the Kentucky area is its unofficial home. Can it really raise the dead? We're not sure. But we'll bet some folks have died trying.

Moonshine's confusion with whiskey comes from the fact that Kentucky bourbon is at least fifty-one percent corn-based rather than rye-based, and literary references to "corn liquor" might mean either bourbon or moonshine. Whiskey and bourbon have a different fermentation process, must be aged in special oak casks, and usually contain a blend of grains.

The most famous portrayal of moonshine in film was probably the 1958 film *Thunder Road*, in which Robert Mitchum played a bootlegger from Harlan County who drove a supercharged Ford with a secret compartment tank for transporting moonshine into Tennessee. The iconoclastic film, presenting Kentuckians flouting laws and eluding cops in high-speed car chases, was—for better or worse—the grandfather of all *Smokey and the Bandit*–type films that followed.

### Dead Drunk

The name Corpse Reviver was colloquially given to moonshine and other self-brewed moonshinelike concoctions made by hoboes during the nineteenth century. In the years since, many other drinks, mostly cocktails and brandies, have appropriated the name.

## Strange Doings at Seelbach Hotel

**Stepping into** the Seelbach Hotel in Louisville is like stepping into another era, one of mobsters and absinthe and Jazz Age records. It has so much mythic resonance, it should have been immortalized in great writing. Oh, wait, it was: F. Scott Fitzgerald wrote about the Seelbach in his novel *The Great Gatsby.* (The title character of Gatsby, in fact, was based in part on the life of George Remus, a wheeler-dealer local attorney and bootlegger.)

Although many of America's gangsters walked through the Seelbach's doors, Al Capone was the most famous and the most regular customer. His favorite alcove in the hotel's Oakroom lounge still exists, as does a giant mirror he had trucked in from Chicago so that he could always watch his back while having a card game.

Special spring-loaded doors were installed in the Seelbach that could be instantly closed and locked in seconds by one of Capone's watchful henchmen, in case of a police raid. And Capone also ordered that secret passageways be created for his surreptitious comings and goings; they led out to an alley behind the hotel and to another point around the side, on Fourth Street. The Seelbach management was apparently quite happy to comply with such arrangements, but then again, it may have been a request they couldn't refuse.

There's also a ghost on the premises: The "Lady in Blue" has haunted the hotel since 1936, when a young woman committed suicide by throwing herself down an empty ten-story-high elevator shaft. Because the sightings are said to have begun shortly after this incident, the ghost is generally regarded to be hers. As well as being seen, her ghost is often smelled, with a sickly sweet odor.

Most impressive of all the Seelbach's wonders is the catacomb-like bar in the basement, called the Rathskeller. Its dark, gothic,

Seelbach Hotel, Louisville, Ky.

subterranean chambers were another favorite partying place for Capone. The medieval-styled inlays are all Rookwood Pottery, which makes the room itself worth a small fortune. Strange designs and symbols pervade the ornate decor, a mixture of zodiacal, alchemical, Masonic, heraldic, and various other symbolism.

The classic Paul Newman film *The Hustler,* based on the novel by Kentuckian Walter Tevis, was partially filmed at the Seelbach. You can also glimpse the hotel in the Al Pacino film *The Insider*.

The Seelbach is located in downtown Louisville, at the corner of Fourth and Muhammad Ali Boulevard.

## Go for the Gold

***In the summer of 1960,*** a young boxer named Cassius Clay had a lot to brag about. Since 1955, he had fought and mostly won 108 boxing matches. He won six Kentucky Golden Gloves titles, two national Amateur Athletic Union championships, and two coveted National Golden Gloves crowns. To top that off, he won the gold medal in the light heavyweight boxing division at the 1960 Summer Olympic Games in Rome.

Clay's greatest glory days, when he would be known as Muhammed Ali, the heavyweight champion of the world, were still ahead. However, at this point, he was already renowned for the outsized ego and self-assuredness that would make him legendary. He surely now felt he was cock of the walk, baddest of the bad, king of the mountain. Imagine then, the shock he received in the diner of a downtown Louisville five-and-dime store. He expected to be hailed as his hometown's conquering hero, and the realities of racism probably hit him like a sucker punch when he sat down and tried to order a cheeseburger and a Dr. Pepper.

"Sorry," the anonymous, gum-chewing, know-nothing of a counterperson told him. "We don't serve coloreds."

Though the man in front of her had represented his country in the Olympics and brought home a gold medal, it did not register on her radar. Rules were rules, and standards were standards, and so Clay was refused service.

Clay's next stop is alleged to have been the George Rogers Clark Memorial Bridge, also known as the Second Street Bridge. It isn't known if he drove there or walked, but we can imagine that he clenched his teeth the entire way over as he fumed to himself and cursed the figurative river of racism that still ran deep and wide in Louisville. As he told the story for years, he went to the center of the bridge and hurled his gold medal into the Ohio River, flowing beneath it. He added, "That gold medal didn't mean a thing to me if my black brothers and sisters were treated wrong in a country I was supposed to represent."

Much later in life, Ali uncharacteristically backed away from his bridge story, possibly in the hopes of requesting a replacement medal. He changed the tale to say he "lost" the medal. Today, the newly opened Ali Center in Louisville maintains this version of events, though it's hard to see how something as coveted as an Olympic gold medal could simply be lost.

Regardless of the revised story, treasure hunters have scoured the river for the medal for decades. Louisville was in a dry spell in the summer of 1960, but rainstorms to the north might have made the river flow faster and higher than usual. Calculating this with the assumed weight of the medal (Olympic gold medals are not solid gold, but just gold-plated), it could have been carried away by currents to a distance greater than one might expect. Perhaps the strap attached to the medal snagged on debris or driftwood, which carried it even farther

**As he told the story for years, he went to the center of the bridge and hurled his gold medal into the Ohio River, flowing beneath it.**

away before it dislodged and sank.

The odds of finding Ali's 1960 gold medal are slim, but not impossible. Every year, a few people don scuba gear and take up metal detectors, entering the murky (and sewage-tainted) waters of the Ohio in pursuit of Ali's sunken treasure, hoping to win the gold for themselves. They might find it easier to take up boxing and qualify for the Olympics.

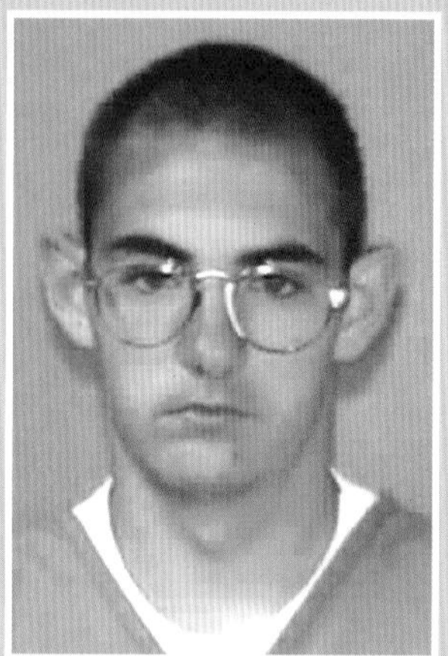
Howard Scott Anderson

## Murray's Vampire Clan

***Kids growing up*** in Madison County during the 1980s and '90s often told stories about a "vampire cult" that practiced ritual blood drinking. Most were no doubt just fantasizing, but who knows for sure how many of them tipped over the edge from fantasy to reality?

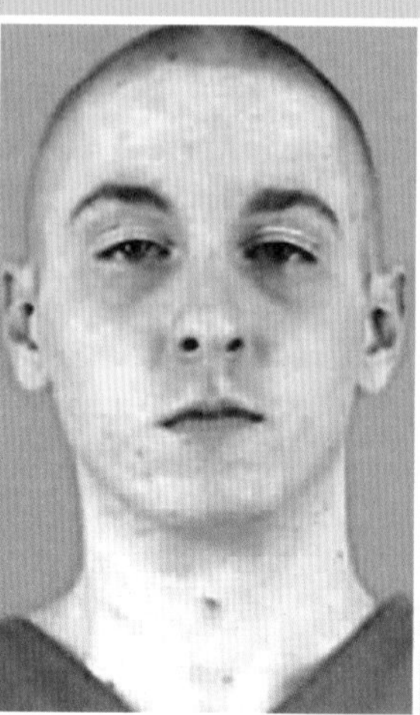
Rod Ferrell

A prime example would be the so-called Vampire Clan from Murray, headed by a teenager named Rod Ferrell. Rod and his Goth pals were obsessed with a vampire-themed role-playing game and ultimately completely lost touch with reality. Rod—or Vassago, as he liked to be called—and his cohorts quickly escalated their game to drinking each other's blood or, if if that wasn't available, the blood of some poor pet. Charming kids.

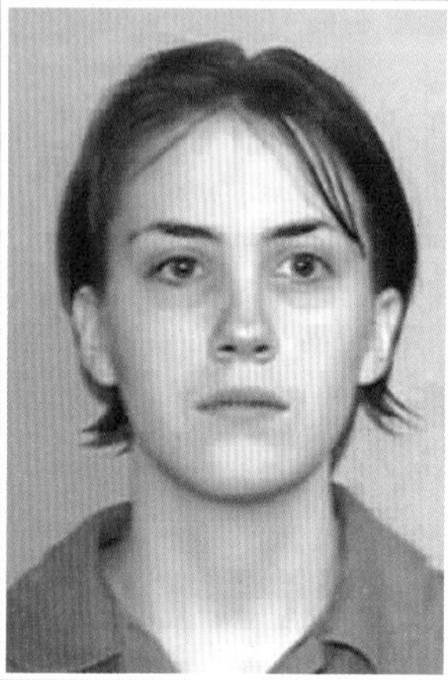
Charity Keesee

The kids' strange obsessions would eventually progress to humans. They loaded up the car for a vampire road trip for the purpose of murdering Ruth Queen and Richard Wendorf of Eustis, Florida. They were the parents of Heather Wendorf, an old friend of Ferrell's, and Ferrell had it in his mind that it was his unholy mission to "rescue" Heather from her parents.

Upon arriving at the Wendorf home, Ferrell and fellow cult mate Howard Scott Anderson—a native of Mayfield—broke in and found Richard asleep on the couch. Ferrell bludgeoned him to death with a crowbar and then did the same to Ruth Queen when she entered the room moments later. Ruth put up a good fight and managed to throw scalding coffee on Ferrell, but his youth and insanity gave him the edge.

The kids, along with Heather, then all piled into the car and hit the road, but it didn't take long for the cops to catch up with them. Rod Ferrell was sentenced to death and was at one point the youngest person ever to be on death row (an unfortunate first for Kentuckians), but in 2000, his sentence was overturned to life without parole. He is utterly unapologetic for his deeds and will bore anyone who cares to listen with his claims of being either a 60,000-year-old demon, a 500-year-old vampire, or Satan himself, depending on which way the gears in his troubled mind grind.

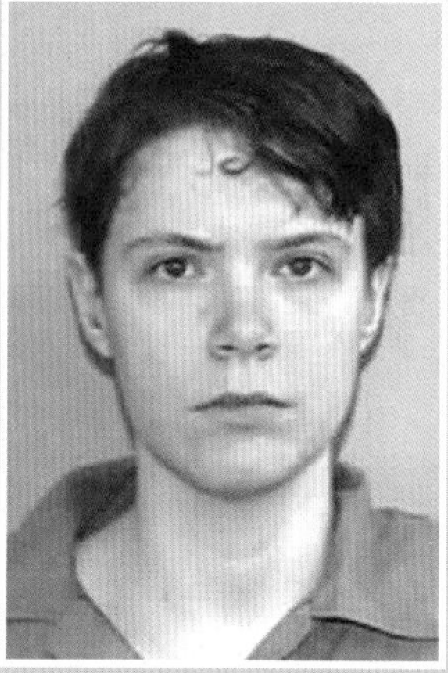
Dana Cooper

Today very few people in Murray are willing to talk about the cult. No one wants to dredge up unpleasant memories of such a monumentally stupid and horrible crime crew. The kids' favorite hangout—an old concrete building in the Land Between the Lakes area—nicknamed the Vampire Hotel, has been torn down and fenced off in hopes of eradicating all traces of the memory of the cult. People still make the pilgrimage to this site, leaving tacky gifts and quasi-occult graffiti. Exactly what they intend to commemorate with all this is anyone's guess.

VAMPIRE HOTEL
ACID

# Fast Food Strip Search

***You may have*** heard variations of the tale before: Someone calls a fast-food restaurant claiming to be a police officer and instructs the manager to strip-search a female employee. Eventually, the caller hangs up and everyone realizes they've been had. In fact, the story is no myth or urban legend. It actually happened, and it happened at a McDonald's restaurant in Mount Washington right here in Kentucky on April 9, 2004.

The prankster told the manager that she needed to bring an eighteen-year-old female employee into the office and order her to remove all her clothing except for an apron, ostensibly because she was accused of stealing someone's purse. Now, you may be noting that the logic here is already fuzzy, but wait, it gets even fuzzier.

The manager called home and asked her fiancé to come to the store and help out with the matter, an idea that was sanctioned by the "police officer" on the phone. While the manager tended to the store, she handed the phone over to her fiancé and he continued to follow orders given. The caller instructed him to remove the employee's apron, leaving her completely nude, and to have her do some strange exercises.

By now, alarm bells should have been going off in everyone's heads, right? Wrong. The fast-food interrogation went on for hours as the guy happily complied with the bogus cop's increasingly bizarre requests. There's no telling how far things would have gone if the manager had not called the main store manager on another line and found out that the police had not contacted him about this—even though the man on the phone had assured her that he had.

It was only at this point, they all claimed, that the long-overdue lightbulb went off over their heads. They suddenly remembered that in the real world, real cops don't ask managers to strip-search their employees.

Fortunately, someone had the good sense to dial *69 on the phone and found out that the imposter had been calling from a supermarket pay phone in Florida. Because the call was made with a calling card, police eventually were able to trace it to a correctional facility worker who was arrested and extradited to Kentucky to stand trial. The jury found him not guilty.

And what of the victim? After years of litigation, she finally emerged victorious against McDonald's in October 2007. A jury awarded her $6.1 million in punitive damages and court costs.

# A Glowing Report on Maxey Flats

***On your next*** family vacation, why not take the kids to Maxey Flats, Kentucky's catastrophic nuclear dump site? While not as famous as, say, Three Mile Island or Chernobyl, this fifty-five-acre tract of land near Hillsboro contains 4.7 million cubic feet of radioactive waste. It's sure to be great fun for any family on a Geiger-counter tour.

Kentucky first opened the Maxey Flats Nuclear Disposal Site in 1963. You'd think that two decades after having dropped the big one on Hiroshima and Nagasaki, they'd know a little more about the proper disposal of radioactive materials, but this was the original Maxey Flats method of nuclear waste disposal:

1. Dig some trenches.
2. Throw in nuclear waste, which was stored in metal drums and cardboard boxes.
3. Cover 'em up and walk away.

By the 1970s, environmentalists discovered that this primitive hazmat storage method created an ecological nightmare. It contaminated not only the soil but also the groundwater and the local water supply. Oops. Dumping stopped in 1977.

Those who come to the defense of such things point out that the stuff in the dump site is only "low-level" radioactive material. Others think this is a bit like saying that having one's head chopped off is a low-level amputation, or that Hillside Strangler Kenneth Bianchi was a low-level serial killer. A source claims Maxey Flats is filled with "transuranic" wastes such as plutonium, and tritium has been found in streams three miles away. Low level, indeed.

According to news reports, Maxey

Flats is now covered in some sort of protective black plastic, and underground filters and sensors have been installed to supposedly ensure that no radioactivity escapes. One report says that water from underground springs is routinely tested for unacceptable levels of contamination before being released into a local creek.

We've heard anecdotal legends of mutations and anomalies that have supposedly been brought on as a direct result of Maxey Flats. However, we haven't seen any of these firsthand, and no one can conclusively prove any connection between these legends and Maxey Flats's contamination.

Maxey Flats will probably never be on top of anyone's weirdest-places-to-see list. But list or not, you can't get in, anyway. It's a restricted area that's fenced in and patrolled—which is, no doubt, all for the best.

## Blue Grass Army Depot: Kentucky's Own Area 51

***For those*** who can't get to Nevada's famous Area 51—where among other clandestine operations the remains of a UFO crash are supposedly stored—there's always the Blue Grass Army Depot, located on the outskirts of Madison County. The depot likes to promote itself as a simple ammo dump for antiquated and abandoned conventional and chemical weapons from the '50s and '60s. But for a mere discarded-ammo dump, it sure sees a lot of action. Black helicopter and UFO sightings are so commonplace here that no one bothers to report them anymore.

In the early '90s, this author had a series of conversations about the depot with an eccentric person who shall remain unnamed. This person shared tall tales and unsubstantiated rumors involving what was going on in the site, though he declined to say how he could possibly know this information.

For example, he claimed that alien technology recovered from a crashed spacecraft was being used in experimental aircraft being tested at the depot. And no worries that the place didn't have a proper runway: He said runways were for airplanes. Flying saucers are VTOL (vertical takeoff and landing) craft and don't require an airport. He mentioned one such secret plane that was completely invisible because its hull acted as both a camera and a monitor, projecting what was on one side of the plane to the other side, no matter from what angle you were facing the plane.

He also had it on good authority that the alien spacecraft was stored, or at least had been stored at some point, underground at the depot. Kentucky was chosen because, as he said, "They wouldn't keep it where everyone expects it."

The depot, he went on to claim, was the military's main headquarters for chemical warfare, and the Gulf War was practically run from there.

Was this man to be taken seriously? It is true that all manner of cutting-edge secret aircraft have been tested at the depot, including the Stealth Bomber and many others that no one's ever heard of. But he certainly didn't look or act like the type of person who would have security clearance anyplace. He was pretty much drunk a large percentage of the time he told these stories.

But as it turns out, at least some of what the man said was true. During the first Gulf War, the Blue Grass Army Depot WAS the main source for the Department of Defense's chemical weapons program. This information can be found right on their own Web sites. And while the invisible plane story seems outlandish (didn't Wonder Woman fly such a plane?), such an experimental aircraft DOES exist, with a technology called electrochromatic panels, according to well-respected researcher Norio Hayakawa.

Tightened security in the post–9/11 world resulted in dramatic changes to, or the complete disappearance of, most of the Web sites by, for, and about the depot. Even its own Web site closed up shop entirely. Some sites had stated in no uncertain terms that the Blue Grass Army Depot was the Department of Defense's primary center for chemical weapons. Not A primary center, but THE primary center. The Blue Grass Chemical Activity houses U.S. government chemicals in containers on 250 acres within the Army Depot. Others went on in great detail about special operations projects and work being done on-site by depot "tenants" such as Raytheon and their related entities like E-Systems and Serv-Air. All are major suppliers to the Department of Defense and NASA in matters related not to ammo, but to aircraft—both conventional and unconventional.

And so we come out of the woods just about where

we went in. It remains to be seen whether the future will provide us more details regarding the UFO and black helicopter activity around the depot, and whether the planned multimillion-dollar hazardous materials incinerator scheduled to be constructed there will change matters any. One thing is for certain. Blue Grass is not just a simple army ammo dump, as indicated on their press releases and on the calendars they give away to the community each year.

*Blue Grass Chemical Activity has a restricted area where 1.7 percent of the nation's original stockpile of chemical weapons, is being stored. There are multiple security measures to protect the weapons. The stockpile is kept in a secure restricted area that covers one square kilometer. The entire area is surrounded by two fences that are topped with coiled concertina wire.*

*Blue Grass Chemical Activity stores 523 tons of chemical weapons in earth-covered igloos.*

*Visitors to Blue Grass Chemical Activity must go through this security gate. All visitors must provide identification to enter the installation.*

*Blue Grass Chemical Activity uses 45 igloos like these above and below to store chemical weapons. The projectiles and rockets contain nerve agents GB and VX, as well as mustard agent.*

# Unexplained Phenomena

Kentucky has always been, and continues to be, a very puzzling state. Just as the early Native Americans knew there was something not quite right about this territory, visitors today often pick up on a certain feeling—the knowledge that something odd is in the air here, but they're unable to articulate precisely what.

There are phenomena in Kentucky that are deeper and older than humanity itself, like the bottomless pits that can be found in caves such as Mammoth. And then there are more recent phenomena: Ghost lights shine in the nighttime hills and hollers, mysterious meat falls from the sky, the image of a dead girl is seared into a window pane. Kentucky has its own history of leaping weirdos, strange coincidences, and black helicopters. Much of the state's weirdness is connected to UFOs and alien abductions, which may or may not be traced to the large presence of the military and its covert intelligence entities here.

Whatever the source for our commonwealth's inexplicably weird vibes, embrace and rejoice in them, because it certainly makes life interesting in Kentucky. Who would want to live somewhere dull?

# Mysteries in the Barnyard

***Paranormal barnyard mutilations*** are alive and well in Kentucky, even if the mutilated critters aren't. Never heard of such a thing? A quick tutorial, then.

Starting in Colorado in 1967, with the strange death of a horse the media dubbed Snippy, observers of the paranormal began to see a pattern of unexplained mutilations of animals—particularly cattle—in the United States, often allegedly carried out with surgical precision and often involving the animals' private parts. Some reports even described the animals as being completely drained of blood. Various explanations have been proposed, such as voracious coyotes, satanic cult activity, UFOs, and government agents in black helicopters, all of which the Bluegrass State has.

Why would aliens or government operatives want to stealthily snip away at farm animals in the middle of the night? And even if we knew the reason, would it make any sense? Not likely. Nevertheless, it happens, and all too often.

In the summer of 2001, the *Cincinnati Enquirer* ran a story about a spate of livestock mutilations in Kentucky's Grayson County. The article reported local phenomena dating back for at least twenty-five years. Among the incidents on record were:

- An Appaloosa colt found dead near Nolin Lake with its reproductive organs removed and a small hole in its abdomen. There was no exit wound or bullet found.
- A heifer calf found dead in the woods, also near Nolin Lake, missing several of its vital organs. There was no blood in the vicinity.
- A Hereford bull in Sadler (about ten miles south of Leitchfield) found dead in a creek sans private parts and hoofs. Long hairs from his tail were found to be hanging up in a nearby tree. The hoofs were later found lined up perfectly on a nearby rock. Perhaps the work of coyotes with a sense of feng shui?

After the 2001 incidents, detectives from the Grayson County sheriff's office sought to place some logic to the illogical events, with little success. Meaningful clues are few and far between. The cause of these animal mutilations remains unknown.

## Decomposition Composition

When some friends and I went into the forest behind the house of one of us, we found a cow bone (possibly a leg bone). We found it in a mud puddle, and there were basically—well—"bubbles" coming out of the mud. We told my friend's mom and she was gonna call the cops and tell them about this. Before the police came, I went home because I didn't want to get questioned about any of it.
*—Michael Schelling*

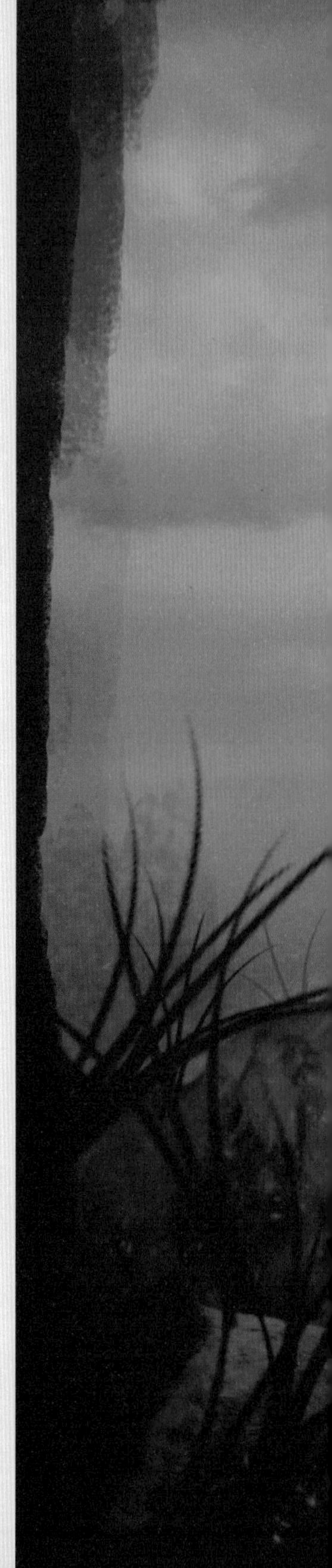

## Death Waits in the Dark

***There was a time*** when the notion of black helicopters scuttling around on nefarious covert military missions was considered the stuff of tinfoil-hatted kooks writing manifestos in their mothers' basements after watching one episode too many of *The X-Files.*

But as with so many other things, Agent Mulder turned out to be right in the end: We now know there really are black helicopters in the military. And does it come as any surprise that they're based in, of all places, Kentucky?

More black helicopters than you need to develop any conspiracy theory are at the 160th Special Operations Aviation Regiment (SOAR) at Fort Campbell. The craft, known as Little Birds, use a specially formulated paint that protects them from chemical attacks and is also non-radar reflective to help them do whatever it is they're doing out there. The helicopters are used for all manner of covert Special Operations purposes, which can cover quite a lot, most of which we're not supposed to know about. After all, the motto of the 160th is "Death waits in the dark," and its insignia is the grim reaper riding a horse.

You can see some interesting video footage of these Little Birds at the Don F. Pratt Memorial Museum, located at Fort Campbell. There's even a real black helicopter—a McDonnell-Douglas AH-6 Cayuse, to be exact—on display, hanging from the ceiling.

Even if you couldn't care less about seeing the unmarked helicopters, there's plenty else to see at the Pratt Museum, and visiting it is highly recommended. Enter the fort through gate 4 and have your ID ready. They're closed on Sundays.

Meanwhile, black helicopters can also be seen buzzing across the state, especially in and out of the Blue Grass Army Depot in Madison County, often to a helipad very close to the road.

## Bottomless Pits

***While Kentucky can't boast*** the deepest bottomless cave pit in the world (that honor goes to a Croatian cave called Velebita), it does have more than its share of cavernous pits, of which Mammoth Cave's 104-foot-deep pit is the most famous. It is rumored that Mammoth Cave, in the hills of the south-central part of the state, contains other such pits. The vast majority of Mammoth Cave's labyrinthine tunnels have yet to be explored.

Even deeper than Mammoth Cave's deepest pit, however, is the one in Frenchman's Knob Cave, in Hart County, which is 180 feet deep.

Many years ago, before the depth of these pits was known, they were thought to be bottomless. All manner of objects, including lit lanterns, were hurled down them, only to vanish without a trace, with no sound of their impact below. Scientists still haven't worked out the exact mechanics behind the formation of these enormous vertical underground shafts, and we can only guess at what secrets they hold.

## Red Meat in the Sky

***In March 1876,*** in full view of many witnesses, large hunks of fresh red meat fell all over Allen Crouch's property in Bath County. Although the meat was generally thought to be beef, some people tasted it and declared that it had a gamier flavor, more like venison.

In subsequent articles in medical journals, doctors and scientists reported their findings after analyzing the flesh. The samples they received, they said, consisted mostly of lung tissue from a large mammal, with human infants or horses being the most likely source.

The only attempt at a scientific explanation put forth was the theory that a very large flock of buzzards must have, en masse, flown over the farm and regurgitated the meat on the wing. This, of course, ignores the fact that no buzzards or birds were reported overhead during the meat rain, and that the chunks were far larger than any that could be chewed off, swallowed, and disgorged by any buzzard we've ever seen.

## Foal Play?

***In the spring of 2001,*** disaster struck Kentucky's billion-dollar horse industry when hundreds of pregnant mares across the state began miscarrying simultaneously. Roughly one out of twenty foals died, which added up to well over $225 million in lost sales and stud fees.

Kentuckians followed the story in the media and waited for the investigators to come up with an explanation. And waited. The days turned into weeks and the weeks into months, but no solid leads were found. The best official explanation anyone could come up with was quite an exercise in Rube Goldberg science. Most people couldn't even take it seriously at first, but in the absence of any other explanation, it gradually became the accepted cause:

- The weather had been highly erratic during the previous winter.
- Extra-long winters can sometimes increase the cyanide content of cherry leaves.
- Horses might have eaten some.

Then it was pointed out that there weren't cherry trees on most of these horse farms. So the official explanation was amended:

- The weather had been highly erratic during the previous winter.
- Extra-long winters can sometimes increase the cyanide content of cherry leaves.
- Tent caterpillars might have eaten the cherry leaves.
- Then these cyanide-laden tent caterpillars could have traveled to horse farms, where they would leave waste behind.
- The horses must have eaten the caterpillar waste.

It sounds like an absurd scenario out of *South Park,* but most of the general public responded to this explanation with, "Oh, of course! That makes sense! Well, that settles that!" Only a few would regard the poisonous caterpillar-waste theory somewhat incredulously.

As it turned out, over seventy percent of the affected horses were Thoroughbreds. Would cyanide-eating tent caterpillars be more likely to hang out around a Thoroughbred than say, some common workhorse? And come to think of it, would cyanide be more likely to induce miscarriage in a horse than in any other type of animal? And why only in this area? There are tent caterpillars and cherry trees in other parts of the continent, are there not? But, hey, what do we nonofficials know?

## Spring-heeled Jack

*In 1837,* a frightening humanoid, bedecked in a black, leathery cape and equipped with batlike wings and pointy horns, allegedly began assaulting women in England. This strange rogue's myth grew into an enduring legend, with reports of sightings being quite common throughout the nineteenth century. Some people say the creature was ultimately the inspiration for Jack the Ripper and comic book characters such as Batman. Still others have noted the resemblance to the legendary Mothman, a frequent bogeyman in Victorian times.

This creature was dubbed Spring-heeled Jack for his ability to leap great distances in a single bound, a feat testified to by many sworn eyewitnesses of the day. Even the British army became convinced that Jack was no mere urban legend when he was spotted leaping onto the rooftop of one of their sentry buildings in 1870. They tried to trap him, but to no avail.

Could Spring-heeled Jack, whoever or whatever he was, have sprung his way across the big pond to Kentucky? Researcher Jim Brandon tells of reports from 1880 describing a "tall and thin weirdo" that appeared out of nowhere and began a terror campaign in Old Louisville, frightening the locals and ripping the clothing from females in the streets. Eyewitnesses describe his superhuman ability to escape by jumping impossible distances and springing over objects as tall as a horse-drawn carriage, leaping and climbing away to safety on rooftops. This creature was described as wearing a cape and helmet, and having an eerie glowing light emanating from his chest. The descriptions of his outfit seem to oddly match the British entities. We can also deduce that the creature appeared in outlying farms as well as downtown, because one sighting has him jumping over haystacks and completely disappearing on the other side of one.

Even stranger, the *Louisville Courier-Journal* reported that on July 28, 1880—the very same day that the Jack-like person began his attacks—many citizens downtown spotted a tiny open-platform craft of some sort flying through the air. It flew low enough so that they could see that it was being piloted by a seated man surrounded by machinery, which he operated with his hands and feet. It sounds quite like an autogiro—a tiny, helicopter-like modern craft often not much bigger than the pilot's seat. But this was years before the invention of said craft, and even more years before they became that compact. Perhaps this Jack also had wings to go along with his springed-heels?

## By George!

***There's a very famous story*** that is often told by "Weird But True"-type columnists, and is also popular with statisticians and lecturers on probability and chance. It concerns one George D. Bryson, a businessman who, on a whim, stopped overnight in Louisville on his way to New York. He chose the Brown Hotel on Broadway, and after having registered and being given his keys to room 307, he passed the mail desk and jokingly inquired if there was any mail for him. To his astonishment, the desk clerk produced a letter addressed to "George D. Bryson, Room 307."

As it turned out, the previous occupant of room 307, who had checked out that morning, was also named George D. Bryson!

The odds against such a thing happening are mind-boggling, and many have used the Bryson anecdote as a way of illustrating their contention that reality is indeed wild, wiggly, shifting, and thermoplastic. Researchers such as the late, great Robert Anton Wilson have expounded and theorized at length about the true nature of what we call coincidences. They posit that those moments of serendipity act as a sort of signal of quantum significance—though the meaning of the signal isn't always comprehensible to those who experience it, and may not make sense until years, decades, or centuries later. As of this writing, the quantum significance of room 307 at the Brown, and its separated-yet-conjoined twin, George D. Bryson, is unknown.

## The Girl in the Window

***Russellville*** is located in the far southwest corner of the state, but the fate of the "Russellville Girl" has been told in every corner of Kentucky. The story goes that a young girl was waiting for her lover to pick her up one night for a dance. It was a stormy and dangerous night, as lightning illuminated the sky and rain fell in sheets. She was very anxious about her boyfriend's driving in such weather and stood near the front window of the house, anxiously watching the dark road outside and hoping for some sign of his oncoming headlights. Just then a bolt of lightning struck the house and somehow passed through the front window, instantly killing the girl.

These days no one seems able to remember just what this girl's name may have been, but they don't have any trouble remembering what she looked like. By some freak of nature, the lightning created a photographic imprint of the girl on the pane of glass in the front window.

For many years, on every occasion when it rained, the girl's image would appear on the glass. The story became famous, and people came from miles around to see the image. No matter how hard the owners cleaned the window, they could not erase the imprint. As years passed, the window was boarded over to keep away the curiosity seekers. More recently, it has been painted over.

The house where the girl's image was imprinted on the window is a private home on Clarksville Road. It now serves as the residence for the caretaker of Maple Grove Cemetery.
*–Troy Taylor*

# Mystery Lights in Estill County

***The first time*** I'd ever heard anything about "mountain ghost lights" in Kentucky was in the early 1980s, when I dated a girl who told me the story of large floating lights that appear and disappear on several different mountains in Estill County.

I have a lot of kinfolk in the deep-rural area and spent a good chunk of my childhood in this peculiar and spooky place. I thought I'd experienced all there was to experience there but had never heard of this phenomenon. Intrigued by the concept, I fired up the video camera and set about arranging some camping trips in the area so my girlfriend could show me these mystery lights.

The problem—or the charm, if you enjoy tall tales—with mystery lights is that when you do see a weird light on a mountain in front of you, you have no way of immediately verifying anything. I learned this the hard way when I spotted a suspicious light for the first time and started trudging up the hill like Teddy Roosevelt. Of course, I lost sight of the light when I started climbing, and when I finally got to the top, I found nothing. When I slogged my way back to camp, my lady friend reported the light had gone out just as I'd started going up. After that unnecessary exercise, I chose to simply watch and wonder from our vantage point instead of going after the answers.

After a summer of trying, we never did conceive proof of a genuine "ghost light" sighting. I chalked it up to a rural legend and filed the case in that very small section in my mind reserved for things I considered debunked. But the story of this ghost light wouldn't go out. A decade later, while I discussed paranormal matters with a retired gentleman at a flea market in Ravenna, he brought up the mystery lights with no prompting from me. His story placed the lights in Cobb Hill, a totally different area than the one to which my friend had led me. According to him, these lights weren't just stationary or floating, they were darting all around the surface of the mountain like, in his own words, "a hundred pound lightnin' bug."

This leads me to suspect some sort of electromagnetic phenomenon, rather than ghosts or UFOs, but that ain't bad.

I have long suspected that some sort of ley line type of strange energy runs through Estill County, and this could be the first step toward demonstrating that in some palpable way.

I recently spent several nights trying once again to document this phenomenon, to no avail. Because it's such a remote area, there aren't a whole lot of locals with doors to knock on and ask, but I have spoken to others who have indeed heard the rumors of ghost lights, none of whom would go on record as having actually seen them in person. I am determined to not only photograph it, but figure it out. *Weird Kentucky* will keep you posted.

## *Sand Mountain's Ghost Lights*

Sand Mountain is a towering section of knobbed hills that joins the national forestlands of the state. It lies about twelve miles south of Mount Sterling, and is located between the towns of Jeffersonville and Means.

In the early1900s, before the wide use of automobiles, people in the region near Sand Mountain reported seeing mysterious lights on the steep slopes. Firsthand accounts often claim the lights appeared along the roads and paths of the mountain. They sometimes seemed to follow passing travelers, as if they had an intelligence of their own. One man claimed a ghost light often appeared along a certain stretch of road, hovered in the air, and then vanished.

As the area near Sand Mountain has grown more populated, sightings of the ghost lights decreased. Some have suggested that natural-gas wells may have caused the phenomena but no one really knows for sure.—*Troy Taylor*

## The Chemtrail Conspiracy

***You might not be aware*** of the conspiracy theory regarding chemtrails: the white jet trails we see crisscrossing the sky. Since the early '90s there has been an increasingly vocal group of people who claim these are actually sprayed chemicals and part of an elaborate and sinister scheme to . . . well, no one's really sure what the scheme is, but they're sure it exists and it ain't good.

So what's the basis for all of this? It does seem that there are more jet trails in the sky than there used to be, which is normal given increasing airline travel. But it also seems that the trails used to vanish without a trace shortly after being left behind; now they seem to linger longer in the air as they gradually dissipate into a hazy cloud cover.

Some researchers have noted the unusual activity of these alleged "sprayer" planes, or have reported strange white fibers falling from the sky directly beneath the trails. The most famous of all chemtrail researchers, Clifford Carnicom, claims to have conducted extensive chemical analysis of residues from these trails and found all manner of mysterious substances, including red blood cells.

We don't know what it all means, but we do know that many people, ranging from ordinary citizens to devoted conspiracy researchers, are convinced that something screwy is going on with these jet trails and that Kentucky plays a significant part in the screwiness.

But few people want to go on the record about chemtrails, especially if they believe there's something to the story. Those in a position to know anything about the phenomenon have jobs that could be jeopardized by "coming out" about the notion of substances in some of our nation's jet exhaust that aren't supposed to be there, especially in this post–9/11 era.

The closest thing to an official acknowledgment from anyone in any position of authority comes from an anonymous source connected with Louisville International Airport. The source brought up the fact that in 2001, Ohio Congressman Dennis Kucinich mentioned chemtrails as a "space-based weapon" in his H.R. 2977 bill that called for enforcement of peaceful uses of outer space. The reference was subsequently deleted from future versions of the bill.

## UFO Files

Kentucky may be best known for its grass, its derby, and its bourbon, but a lesser known thing we've got in abundance is UFO sightings. They have been reported all over the state, by everyone from pilots to rural farmers. And the experiences are as wide-ranging as the hats you'll see on Derby Day. Among them are lost time, crop circles, tragic plane crashes, and potshots at aliens from farmhouse porches. The government might even be encouraging alien visitations on our very own Lynch Mountain. While the existence of UFOs is still up for debate to some, *Weird Kentucky* thinks there's little moonshine behind the following Blue Grass alien encounters.

## Stanford UFO Abduction

***It was around eleven fifteen p.m.*** on January 6, 1976. Three middle-aged women—Mona Stafford, Louise Smith, and Elaine Thomas—were driving along Hustonville Road in Stanford, headed for the home of Mrs. Smith.

Things started to get strange when the car began driving as if it had a mind of its own, reaching 85 mph even though Mona was hitting the brakes. They then saw a glowing red UFO descend from above. It emitted a bright light that had a gaseous, hazy quality. The UFO stayed close, and the women described it as enormous, metallic, and disk-shaped with a dome on top, a ring of red lights around its midsection, and a yellow, blinking light on the bottom.

After that, things get a little vague. All that the women could report was that at some point, they found themselves in the car, still driving down the road at a normal speed. But the three were now covered with burns. Upon reaching Mrs. Smith's home, they realized it was one twenty a.m. on January 7. They had lost two hours.

They contacted the police, and soon their story hit nationwide headlines. UFO investigators studied their case eagerly and found a few strange, verifiable phenomena connected to the women. Mechanical and electrical devices often stopped working after they handled them. Mrs. Smith's pet bird went wild with fear in her presence and would no longer allow her near it.

All three took and passed polygraph tests administered by the Lexington Police Department. Under a series of hypnotic sessions, the women all recalled being abducted by alien beings on a spaceship and probed in many uncomfortable ways. Their descriptions of their experience have provided the basis for the classic alien abduction scenarios seen repeatedly in movies, television, and books. There were also several sightings of the UFO independent of Stafford, Thomas, and Smith, including by two teenagers who followed the red light all the way to Danville.

No one has been able to dispute the evidence that something did abduct these women. They sought no fame or fortune from their experience and, in fact, tried hard to be left alone. They had no reason to mutually fabricate an elaborate alien hoax. The polygraph sessions proved that these respectable ladies, two of whom were grandmothers, were not lying.

The Stanford incident is Kentucky's best proof of alien entities on earth, even over the Thomas Mantell case, which occurred on the same date years earlier. Read on.

## Death of Thomas Mantell

***What may be*** the first documented death resulting from someone chasing after a UFO occurred in Kentucky on January 7, 1948. The story begins at one fifteen p.m. when the Kentucky State Police contacted officials at Godman Air Force Base, just outside Louisville, with reports of UFO sightings in Maysville. Twenty minutes later the state police would call again: UFOs had also been sighted in Owensboro and Irvington.

In ten minutes, the control tower at Godman got its first glimpse of the UFO as it approached the base. At that time, they ascertained that the object was not a weather balloon or a plane. They described it as gray, metallic, conical, and rotating.

At two thirty, a team of four F-51 fighter planes happened to approach the base. The control tower called the flight leader, Captain Thomas Mantell, briefed him of the situation, and asked him to investigate. One F-51 in the fleet was running low on fuel and continued on its course, but Mantell took his other two planes and went after the UFO.

Mantell sighted the UFO above him and followed it to 20,000 feet while his men dropped back at 15,000 feet. He had maintained active radio contact with the control tower, but suddenly stopped responding. His plane could no longer be seen. There are reports that he flew to perhaps 30,000 feet and may have passed out from lack of oxygen. Whether because of this or something related to the UFO he was pursuing, Mantell's plane crashed in a farm field 130 miles away from Godman. His watch allegedly stopped at three sixteen p.m.

The control tower at Godman lost sight of the UFO in the next half hour, but reports of a UFO occurred throughout the Midwest about four hours later.

Early in the morning on January 8, Captain James F. Duesler arrived to investigate Mantell's crash site. He saw that the plane appeared to have belly flopped straight down, which was totally inconsistent for a crash of this type. There should have been damage to surrounding woods from an angular trajectory, and the nose-heavy weight of the plane should have brought it down nose first. He also saw that although the wings and tail had broken off, the fuselage sustained little damage.

Duesler found no blood in the plane's cockpit. Mantell's body had already been taken away, but others at the scene allegedly informed Duesler that "nowhere on the body had the skin been punctured or penetrated, yet all the bones had been crushed and pulverized."

The air force maintained that Mantell must have been chasing Venus and run out of oxygen. After it was pointed out that Venus was nowhere near that position in the sky at the time, they changed their story and insisted it was a balloon that Mantell was chasing, even though the control tower had earlier verified that what they saw had not been a weather balloon.

Regardless of what he had actually been chasing, Mantell's quest to get to the bottom of the unknown took him a little further into it than he planned on going. His body was laid to rest in Louisville's Zachary Taylor National Cemetery.

## Kelly Creatures

***Another famous alien*** encounter in Kentucky occurred on August 21, 1955, in the small rural community of Kelly, just outside Hopkinsville. Elmer "Lucky" Sutton and his family, as well as their houseguest, Billy Ray Taylor, claimed to have been invaded by large alien creatures.

It began when Taylor saw strange lights in the sky around seven p.m. He tried to tell the Suttons about what he'd seen, but no one paid much attention to his story.

About an hour later Taylor and Sutton went outside to investigate why the family dog was barking. As they tell it, what they then encountered was an enormous humanoid figure with elephantine but pointed ears, luminous eyes, and unthinkably horrible hands with long, pendulous webbed fingers and sharp talons. The creature was metallic silver, but they could not determine whether this was its skin or some sort of protective clothing.

Taylor and Sutton's response was, of course, to do the logical thing one does when finding an intruder (metallic or otherwise) on one's rural Kentucky property in the 1950s. They grabbed their guns and started shooting at it. As they opened fire, the creature did somersaults in the air and cartwheeled itself off into the wilderness.

While the two men were discussing whether or not they had wounded the intruder, and debated about whether to go in search of it, another taloned hand from another creature reached down from the porch roof above them. They shot this one too, only to spot a third beast in a nearby tree. Gradually, more of the creatures trudged toward their home, clawing at the doors and peeking in the windows, in what sounds like a scene from *Night of the Living Dead,* if the dead were aliens. For several hours that evening, the family held the creatures at bay, firing round after round of bullets at them with seemingly no permanent effect.

Running out of ammunition by eleven p.m., the besieged group made a break for their cars and sped to the Hopkinsville Police Department. After they had convinced the sheriff that something bizarre was going on, a posse composed of local and state police, press, and citizens descended on the Sutton farm. The creatures were nowhere to be found, and the only evidence left to prove they had been there was a luminous spot on the ground where one of them had been shot.

After the search was called off at two fifteen in the morning, the family reportedly attempted to calm down and tried to get some sleep. But later that morning cops, detectives, reporters, and curious citizens converged on the scene. Again, no tangible evidence of the alien invasion was found, and the luminous spot had vanished. Bullet holes from the men's gunfire abounded in and around the house, and researchers would note later that even for the sake of a hoax, a poor family could ill afford to have shot out their own windows and caused so much damage to their own property.

The ensuing media circus embarrassed the family, who sought no profit from their story and quickly clammed up about the whole matter to the press or to anyone else. If it was a hoax, it was an extremely elaborate one between seven people (including children and a church-going grandmother) that seemed to serve no purpose but to make its accessories miserable for years.

As is often the case in such matters, skeptics' attempts to explain the Kelly incident are usually as outlandish-sounding as the event itself and often require an extreme degree of mental gymnastics to convince oneself of the explanation. One such theory claimed that the entire family mistook owls for aliens!

In the years since, the legend of the Kelly creatures has snowballed into an iconic myth that the local people no longer shun, but celebrate: They hold a Little Green Men Festival every year to commemorate the incident and draw worldwide attention to the area as a key location in any UFO buff's vacation travel itinerary.

# Strange Sounds from Lynch Mountain

***Secluded*** in the Kentucky jungles, deep in the heart of darkest America, you'll find the small mining town of Lynch and nearby, what is locally known as Lynch Mountain. (The government lists it as Black Mountain, but what do they know?)

Lynch Mountain gained notoriety with Internet conspiracy theorists around 1998, when reports of UFO sightings became a regular occurrence here, as well as in the general area. These UFOs are often described as being oval or egg-shaped and, in one case, consisted of a smaller oval connected to a larger one. Triangles and cylinders are also seen occasionally. Sometimes the objects are clearly craft of some sort, but the ovals more often seem to be blobs of energy.

More distressing than the UFOs, however, are the reports of black helicopters and white military jeeps, trucks, and Humvees generating traffic up and down the mountain to a government-protected radar tower at the top. According to many locals, there is an active, though secret, government installation at the mountain's peak, with Area 51–like security. Many who have attempted to enter this area have been immediately intercepted, ordered to leave, and followed all the way back down to the bottom of the mountain.

And that's not all: Extremely loud and peculiar noises have been heard coming from the area – sometimes booming explosions, sometimes eerie, maddening hums not unlike the famous Taos Hum in New Mexico. Often the sounds seem to come not from the mountain's peak, but directly from underground.

Some suspicious souls have taken this to mean the government has been hollowing out the mountain since the 1950s and making it into an underground black-op CIA-NSA base for whatever nefarious purposes those spyboys might have. But, being more paranoid than the average, we here at *Weird Kentucky* can go you one better. Whatever's going on may not be human at all. The historical record shows that the weird sounds coming from the mountain actually predate the government outpost there. In fact, all the way back to the eighteenth century, the adjacent area was called Sounding Gap, because even then the very first settlers heard those unexplained ground sounds.

## Crop Circle in the Rye

***One common aspect*** of the paranormal that Kentucky doesn't have a wealth of is crop circles. A notable exception is one that appeared in a field of rye in Flemingsburg in 2003. It was not as ornate or picturesque as some of the better-known crop circles, but is notable for its proximity to other paranormal events. Another crop circle had recently appeared not far away in southern Ohio near the Great Serpent Mound, and a few months later a low-flying UFO was seen in Morehead, which is just a few minutes south of Flemingsburg. The Morehead sighting was accompanied by the sounds of a female voice, which could clearly be heard screaming for help.

If these incidents are indeed related, those who favor the "friendly new age aliens with crop circles" point of view are going to have to work overtime to square their worldview with the opposing "scary aliens who probe into sensitive places" archetype!

# Train Collides with UFO!

***On January 14, 2002,*** twenty miles north of Paintsville, a train carrying coal had a close encounter with a large hovering object that was flying along the railroad tracks in front of it.

Seeing lights coming from around the bend, the crew assumed another train was approaching on another track and thought nothing of it. But as the train rounded the curve, the computer and other onboard instruments began going berserk, and the engines spontaneously shut themselves off. One crewman's watch stopped at two forty-seven a.m.

The crew saw three UFOs with searchlight beams scanning the nearby river, as if looking for something. The train was still rolling on inertia at about thirty miles per hour, and struck the first object, clipping the tops of the first three cars and leaving severe gouges in the train's steel hull. All the objects immediately vanished.

After getting emergency power systems going, the crew notified their dispatcher and apprised him of the situation. They were advised to continue on to a milepost near the abandoned Paintsville yard and assess the damage there. Two hours later the damaged train hobbled into Paintsville.

What happened next sounds like something out of the movies, but it's the crew's story and they're stickin' to it. They were greeted by a huge entourage of government officials who immediately took charge of the train and everyone aboard. Teams were already in place ready to disconnect the damaged cars from the rest of the train and roll them into a large tent they'd erected to conceal them. The crew were allegedly held for hours and interrogated, given medical tests, and told to keep quiet about the entire incident due to "national security." They were then taken to Martin, where they were questioned all over again by railroad officials, given drug tests, and released.

They were sent back to work just eight hours later after a short nap, and they noticed as they passed through Paintsville again that the tent, the cars, everything connected to the incident was packed up and gone. There was still noticeable coal spillage twenty miles back where the collision had taken place, however.

The story, if true, would seem to indicate that these UFOs were experimental aircraft of our own creation, given the fast response time and containment set in place by these shadowy government agents. The disk that collided with the train was described as being silver with multicolored lights, approximately eighteen to twenty feet long and ten feet high. That sounds like the current trend in our own cutting-edge craft, which tend toward a triangular shape, but who can say for sure?

RAIL ROAD
CROSSING
9993
CSX

## Kentucky Contactees

***It's difficult to assess*** the impact of the alien abduction phenomena in any given area, because people are so reticent to talk about their experiences. Some people are absolutely convinced they have been abducted by aliens, but are unwilling to tell their whole story, much less submit to hypnosis or testing. They seek no fame, glory, or attention, and are in fact often too embarrassed by their experiences to go into much detail. Therefore, they don't turn up in the case files of most online armchair UFO enthusiasts. But they are indeed out there.

Abduction counselor Donald Worley writes of his encounters with abductees from Kentucky and Indiana who display a demonstrable ability to disrupt "electron flows" in any nearby electronic devices, similar to what the women in the Stanford UFO case experienced. If they drive or walk under streetlights, the lights may go on or off. Radios, computers, and all other manner of electronic equipment can be affected by whatever is happening to these people. The energy coming from these abductees, Worley says, is undetectable yet obviously causing an effect, and seems to be intermittent.

An organization called Southern Ohio Alien Abduction Research (SOAAR) also deals with cases from nearby Kentucky, which they publish on their Web site. In one such case, "Mark" (not his real name) tells of alien encounters throughout his life, from a childhood UFO encounter in Nicholasville to visitations in his dorm room in Morehead and a visitation with missing time somewhere between Lexington and Mount Sterling.

Another SOAAR case file, Louisville subject "Danny," underwent regressive hypnosis to recall his abduction experiences in which he and his mother were captured by aliens in a triangular craft, stripped naked, and held prisoner together in a strange room aboard the vessel.

A Freudian fantasy or the real thing? Draw your own conclusions.

## Squares in the Sky

***Square objects*** don't often turn up in UFO lore, so it makes sense that Kentucky appears to be a hotbed for them.

In 1985, glowing cubes were seen silently hovering over Berea, not far from the Blue Grass Army Depot. Those who saw them gave wildly varying guesstimates as to the objects' size, but all witnesses agree that what they saw hovering in the sky was square, not oval.

In July 1986, a square UFO was spotted in Oneida by multiple witnesses, including a local restaurant owner and a forest ranger who described it as square and having a pair of red lights on two of its sides. It was also said to travel at both very high speeds and very slow hovering speeds, neither of which is possible for any known conventional craft.

And in the spring of 1999 there was a rash of square UFO sightings in Richmond, not far from the site of the 1985 Berea sightings. Some of these reports described the object as not necessarily cubelike, however, but more like a flat platform or at least something with a base that appears as a square when viewed from below.

One eyewitness said, "I've seen them flying low. You can see them up close. I could even see a place on the bottom where I guarantee you landing gear ejects from. I don't think they're meant to go far, 'cause square planes aren't aerodynamic, you know? I think they're small and probably only have one man inside. I don't think they're UFOs, I think they're man-made."

# Bizarre Beasts

Kentucky's rolling wilderness happens to be located in an especially insular part of the United States. Far less populated and less bulldozed than its neighbors Tennessee and Virginia, Kentucky provides a convenient pocket for animal life to range and roam. Some of the nation's wildest wildlife still dwell here, like packs of enormous wild boar and feral hogs, coyotes, mink, foxes, bears, and bobcats.

With all the wildlife creeping around, it's not too much of a stretch to surmise that these woods might also hold critters that mainstream science doesn't even recognize yet. This is the subject of cryptozoology—the investigation of unknown animals. Factor in Kentucky's extensive labyrinth of underground caverns that are almost completely unexplored, and you have the potential for discoveries that could turn the scientific community on its ear. For example, a strange new bacterium discovered recently in Mammoth Cave has the creepy ability to halt formation of new blood vessels in human tissue and therefore is being investigated as a tumor-fighting tool.

Without question, it is a good time to be a cryptozoologist in the Commonwealth!

# Herry the Lake Monster

***Kentucky's most famous*** aquatic monster is said to dwell in Herrington Lake, although the creature—if he exists—has been quiet in recent years. He did enjoy a spurt of interest in the 1970s, coinciding with the newfound mass popularity of eerie-themed television shows like *In Search Of,* but interest in Herry, as he is sometimes called, had mostly ebbed by the 1980s.

In February 1990, however, a Junction City resident reported sighting a large alligator in the lake. At the time, some doubted this claim, but in fact, alligator populations have been stealthily making their way north since the 1960s. In 2001, an alligator was captured in the Kentucky River at Clays Ferry, near Winchester. In the summer of 2006, a gator showed up on a Lexington woman's porch.

With its three hundred and fifty miles of shoreline and sprawling shape, there's plenty of room for something to be lurking out of sight beneath Herrington Lake's surface. A professor named Lawrence Thompson described encounters with a creature with a piglike snout protruding above the water and moving along at about trolling speed. Some are convinced it was an alligator, while others point to a fish called an alligator gar as a candidate. It has a snout that extends above the water like a shark's fin, can grow to enormous size (over twelve feet long and more than three hundred pounds), and even experienced fishermen don't always recognize one.

Pollution has been a recurring problem in these waters. "If you go fishing in Herrington Lake, or in Lake Cumberland, be careful about who eats your catch," says Andy Mead in an article in the *Lexington Herald-Leader*. "Fish in those and other Kentucky waters have accumulations of mercury in their tissue at levels high enough that more than one meal a week can cause nerve and brain damage in children under 6, and can be passed from mothers to unborn children." It's entirely possible that a lake creature did exist at one time but has since died off from the toxins—or morphed into something you wouldn't want to meet on a moonlight cruise.

**Alligator populations have been stealthily making their way north since the 1960s.**

# The Lake Barkley and Kentucky Lake Monster

***What sets this tale apart*** from most lake monster stories—Kentucky's or otherwise—is that whereas most are strictly visual phenomena, this one is experienced. The monster, or monsters, in these lakes is never seen but always FELT. Overturned boats, drownings, unusual malfunctions with equipment, or just a general feeling of anxiety—such occurrences are blamed by some fishermen on the "curse" of the lake monster. It's one thing to see a log floating in water and mistake it for a prehistoric plesiosaur; it's quite another to actually have your boat overturned by an unseen creature!

One fisherman put it this way: "I don't think of him as a Loch Ness monster kind of thing. He's more like a ghost. But I think he's just, you know, mischievous." Others, who have blamed deaths and drownings on the entity, might disagree.

Lake Barkley and Kentucky Lake are enormous twin lakes located side by side, with the territory between them known as Land Between the Lakes. It's not clear why they're given separate names when they're really one huge lake connected by a canal, but there it is. They were created as part of a controversial 1966 TVA plan that evacuated entire towns and flooded the area. People were driven from their homes and their property seized under eminent domain. To this day, you can still don scuba gear, go underwater, and see the remains of buildings, railroad tracks, streets, and so on.

The Army Corps of Engineers was supposed to dig up all the graves in all the cemeteries—and that's a LOT of graves—and reinter the bodies elsewhere. There's been quite a bit of speculation about whether or not things were done by the book. Cemeteries were not always transferred intact, and families that had originally been buried together in one cemetery were often needlessly split up across four others when moved. Some headstones didn't even make it to their new locations. Many graves in those old cemeteries had no stone at all, especially those of babies, slaves, and paupers. There's no telling how many of the dearly departed were left behind to be submerged forever under hundreds of feet of water.

Perhaps it is this and not the presence of an unknown beast lurking beneath the water that gives people the sense that there is an invisible entity—or entities—in and around the lake. It's not hard to imagine the involvement of ghosts who are extremely displeased about what happened to their homes, their relatives, their headstones, and their graves.

## Bigfoot and the Spottsville Monster

***Where there's dense wilderness*** in America, you'll usually find Bigfoot sightings. Kentucky is no exception to this rule. There's actually more logic to the idea of a primitive humanoid surviving in Kentucky than in a lot of other states, because the terrain here is so pockmarked with caves that lead to thousands of miles of underground caverns that are still mostly unexplored to this day. If Bigfoot exists, he might well be a Kentucky cave dweller.

The area surrounding Uniontown has long been a hot spot for Bigfoot sightings. Folkloric legends of tall bipedal cavemen, ape-men, or gorillas roaming these woods have been common among locals for years and actually predate the Bigfoot concept, which began in 1958.

In 1988, two deer hunters from Indiana were chased away by a classic Bigfoot-type creature at the Higgins & Henry Wildlife Area outside Morganfield. In November 1996, a woman had a close brush with a ten-foot-tall Bigfoot and watched it walk away slowly and meanderingly, directly in front of her, heading toward the Ohio River.

In 1996, two fishermen sitting in a parked car alongside Lake Barkley at night startled a Bigfoot when they turned on the headlights, unaware that the beast had wandered close to them. It ran into the woods, made loud howling sounds, then apparently doubled back toward the car and hurled an enormous log at them. Both men attested that the log was so large and so heavy that the two of them together couldn't lift it.

In 2004, two campers were four-wheeling on trails in the Land Between the Lakes area and encountered a seven-foot-tall creature with glowing red eyes and a peculiar snout. Although the beast quickly disappeared and there was no confrontation, one of the campers was gripped with an "overwhelming feeling of dread" after returning to camp and decided to pack up and get out.

In September 2006, a Trigg County woman was surprised to find a Bigfoot-type ape-man on her rooftop in broad daylight. Not being a believer in Bigfoot, she assumed it had to be some crazy person in an ape suit and attempted to talk to it by yelling things like "Okay, you're funny, joke's over, now who the hell are you?" which elicited no response. "It was like something out of a bad old movie," she said. "It didn't look real at all. It totally looked like a man in a really fake gorilla suit, and I didn't think he was doing a very good job of acting like a gorilla either." But as she was rummaging through her purse looking for her cell phone so she could call a neighbor for help, the ape-man rolled backward, did a sort of a somersault, leaped an incredible distance off the corner of the roof to a utility pole—something no human could have done—and deftly swung from the pole to the tops of nearby trees with great speed. It was out of sight in seconds. Good work for a guy who likes to put on an ape suit and scare people.

Henderson County is another extremely active area. Kentucky cryptozoology expert Bart Nunnelly tells of a Bigfoot sighting at a specific spot on Collins Road in Reed in 1968, and again in the same place in 1971. Nunnelly's family had many close encounters of their own in 1975 at their farm in Spottsville. In fact, Bigfoot sightings on their property became such a regular occurrence that the local police stopped answering calls regarding them, even though people in Hebbardsville and other adjoining areas along the Ohio River were also seeing the creatures. The *Henderson Gleaner* dubbed it the Spottsville Monster, and this term is sometimes still applied to local Bigfoot sightings.

In 1999, a pair of Bigfoots were seen in a field close

**In 1999, a pair of Bigfoots were seen in a field close to Highway 60 in Baskett.**

to Highway 60 in Baskett. This incident illustrates well the "hidden in plain sight" axiom that applies to all paranormal phenomena. The person who reported the creatures noted that traffic was heavy that day, with lots of cars in front of him and behind him, and yet no one else bothered reporting the sighting. In 2004, two witnesses in Hebbardsville saw a similar pair of creatures eating cornstalks near a church, and in 2006 a Hebbardsville man found an anomalous tooth that he believes to be from a Bigfoot. It has characteristics resembling a human tooth more than one from any other animal and yet is far too large for any human mouth.

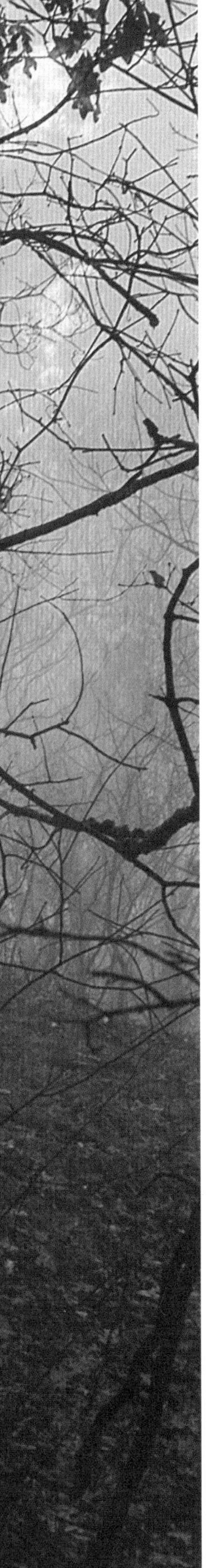

# Feral Humans

***The subject*** of feral humans brings another, rather fascinating element to any discussion about Bigfoot. Some people feel that a certain percentage of Bigfoot sightings might actually have been of humans who have, for one reason or another, entered a wild, animalistic state. Here are three cases of note.

**Date: December 24, 1983**
**Location: Union County**
Jan Thompson reported seeing a very tall (over six foot) naked man with unhealthy-looking pale skin and a head of long, flowing hair, walking at night on Christmas Eve. The person seemed to be in a completely feral state and had blood in its hair and on its hands and face. Because of its animalistic facial features and behavior, not to mention solid red glowing eyes, Thompson was inclined to think of it more as a Bigfoot-type creature than a human being, especially since Bigfoot reports are common in Union County.

**Date: Summer 1985**
**Location: Estill County**
After local residents began reporting a manlike figure prowling in the woods near their houses, Bigfoot rumors began circulating like wildfire in the area. Police combed the wilderness and apprehended a man, a native of Irvine, who had been on the missing persons list for quite some time. According to reports, he was naked but covered with mud and foliage to the extent that vines and moss and lichen were actually growing in his hair and on his body. He was in a completely animal-like state of mind, could not or would not speak English, and had to be forcibly subdued. He was taken to Pattie A. Clay Hospital in Richmond. There were no further reports on his recovery in local media.

**Date: Spring 1990**
**Location: Red River Gorge, near Slade, in Powell County**
The author encountered, face-to-face in the wilderness near Cloudsplitter Rock, an adult (in his thirties) Caucasian male, walking in the woods, naked but covered with mud, leaves, and vines, which were matted into his hair and beard as well, giving him an almost absurd "ZZ Top turned Swamp Thing" appearance. He walked with a hunched, apelike gait. He spotted me moments after I spotted him, and we stared at each other for what at the time felt like an eternity. Finally he turned and fled. His eyes seemed to show some intelligence, but he was still extremely animal-like and seemingly unable to speak. I made no effort to follow him. I have heard similar stories over the years from locals in Slade about old "Mountain Men" who have lost their minds and are now living deep in the wilderness, reverted to an animal-like state.

# Albino Ape-Man of Mason County

***If Bigfoot is an apelike creature,*** he doesn't always come in apelike colors. In October 1980, Charles Fulton and his family were watching television in their Mason County home when they heard a loud thumping on the front porch, along with the sound of a chicken in distress. Fulton peeked out the front door and found himself staring face-to-face with a white, hairy, pink-eyed creature, approximately four hundred pounds and seven feet tall, clutching a rooster in a massive hand. The creature had long, white, flowing hair like a horse's mane. Fulton described it as more manlike than animal, although its eyes lacked human intelligence behind them.

Fulton chased the intruder away, firing directly on it with a .22 pistol as it ran out of sight.

A month later an Alabama truck driver named Noble Clay was hauling a load of steel through Mason County. He slowed down as he saw what he thought was a person standing in the road in the opposite lane. As he got closer, he realized the figure was an enormous apelike creature with white fur, similar to the critter Fulton had encountered in the area weeks earlier.

Clay first contacted locals on the CB to inquire if there was a zoo or a circus nearby that had lost a large albino ape, then reported the incident to police. This was his first time driving this particular route, and he knew nothing of the prior albino ape-man–Bigfoot sighting.

## Anorexic Werewolves Just Passing Through

***After reading*** [Linda Godfrey's story about Wisconsin's] Beast of Bray Road in *Weird U.S.*, I literally have goosebumps. It's an interesting thing to know that you're not completely crazy after seeing something that no one will believe.

I was working as a night shift security guard for a construction site in Bowling Green. One foggy night I was doing my patrols down the small country road that flanked the site, when I saw something moving in the mist. At first I thought it was some sort of large breed dog or one of the coyotes that had been around the last few nights, but as I drove closer, I started realizing that it was much bigger. Thinking it was a deer, I shined my spotlight at it, only to see it stand up on its hind legs, and jump nimbly over the perimeter fence along with a second creature I hadn't noticed.

They stood a good 7-8' tall, and were covered in brown fur. They were very gaunt looking, which was surprising for their size. I'll never forget those eyes reflecting in the light and how effortlessly they jumped a 4' fence. The closest thing I've ever had to describe them as is "Anorexic werewolves" but they didn't quite look like anything from the classic horror movies.

Now the automotive plant they were building is finished, so I can only imagine they've been driven from the area, but I've always had the feeling they were just passing through anyway.—*Chris Cooper*

## The Pope Lick Monster

***One of Kentucky's*** most famous and enduring legendary creatures, the Pope Lick Monster, is said to be a half-man, half-goat animal that once made frequent appearances in the vicinity of a railroad trestle in Fisherville. According to one version of events, the beast was actually from the Canadian wilderness and was caught in the late nineteenth century by a traveling circus. As legend has it, it escaped while on board a train passing through Fisherville and then remained in the general area. Other versions of the tale portray it as more of a supernatural being, with abilities to vanish, teleport, and control minds. One of its favorite tricks, it's said, is to control the minds of youth through hypnosis and make them walk up on the railroad tracks high in the air on the trestles.

Many kids and teens have indeed met an untimely end on those dangerous tracks, and some of them were there specifically because of their interest in the Pope Lick Monster, making the whole thing sort of a self-fulfilling prophecy. Not to mention ensuring that the site is indeed haunted, if not by a monster, then by the ghosts of all these kids who died horrible deaths here.

Ever read the Stephen King book, *Stand by Me,* with the kids daring each other to go out on the trestles? It's exactly the same situation here. Once you're halfway across the tracks, there is no time to turn and run back if a train suddenly appears coming around the bend, and there is absolutely no chance for survival if you jump off the trestle.

The earliest reports of the monster seem to be from the turn of the last century, and peaked again in the '50s and '60s, during which time an entire Boy Scout troop, including the scoutmaster, were allegedly attacked by the creature, which wailed in a loud shrieking howl and threw rocks at them.

There are no credible reports in recent years that we've heard of, but that doesn't stop anyone from making regular pilgrimages to the legendary stomping grounds of this monster.

## Pope Lick's Goat Man

Taking the Taylorsville Road exit from the Gene Snyder freeway may take you into some uncharted territory. About a mile from the exit there stands the infamous, yet abandoned, train trestle where there is a myth about a devastating creature, The Goat Man (also dubbed the Pope Lick Monster), half goat half man, that will make you wish you had never stopped anywhere near him.

According to some legends, many teenagers who are just looking for a thrill will get more than they bargained for. One case is that a young man decided to walk across the trestle and then fell to his death. The reason he jumped is that the Pope Lick Monster can create the sound of a train and cause an illusion for the trespassers. I have been to the area just once, but thinking about it is something that still makes me shiver every time I tell this story.

Some friends of mine decided to take me and another friend to introduce us to the myth. As I got out of the car it was the worst feeling in the world. It was really overwhelming and I immediately wanted to get back in the car, but for some reason I didn't. As we are walking along this road we come to a fence that has a small sign that says NO TRESPASSING. We did follow the rules and decided to turn back since there was nothing there for us to see. So we were getting back in the car and I got in first cause I was sitting in the back and my friend who was riding shotgun got in next. He then proceeded to put his drink in the cup holder and all of the sudden our passenger door closed, not violently, but a typical shut. Not sure what just happened we both pointed fingers at each other but neither of us could have done it because I was in the back and couldn't reach the handle and he was leaning toward the cup holder. We immediately left and never looked back. I've never been back again and probably won't go back anytime in the near future.—*Christopher Stivers*

## Close Encounter of the Goat Man Kind

As a kid growing up I heard of the Goat Man. He was half human and half goat with a human torso and a goat head. The stories my grandfather told were of this screaming devil jumping a fence, grabbing two full-grown pigs and jumping off with them. There are stories of him that are over sixty years old.

On highway 69 outside of Dundee, I was heading home and I saw something leap across the road. I hit the ditch to keep from hitting it. It was so unreal, almost deformed. It had a monkey-like face, small horns, strange arms like a kangaroo, thick legs and a long tail. It was far from human. I think this was the Goat Man.—*Doug Oller, Paducah*

## Goat Man, the Orc-like Monstrosity

Has anyone ever heard of a set of abandoned train tracks that run across a broken bridge on the outskirts of Kentucky? It's one of the creepiest places I've ever seen, as well as one of the most frightening experiences this former Louisvillian has ever known. Supposedly, underneath the bridge lives "the goatman"—a weird orc-like monstrosity that kills and buries folks that snoop around the area too much (especially high schoolers). Sure, this all sounds like a familiar fairy tale, BUT, I led a caravan of about 3-4 cars to the tracks. This was circa 1991. No goatman appeared, but the place was the most scary place I'd ever been to. AND, the dilapidated bridge actually shadows the entrance to a hidden roadway.

On a dare, we flew through the road, which was one of darkest, winding roads with no shoulder and odd houses every mile or so. The legend also mentioned that at the end of the road was "four winds," a satanic headquarters in Louisville located on a hidden farm. I didn't believe it, until we shot down that road. On every side were either drop-offs, wrecked and abandoned cars and houses with candles LIT IN THEIR YARDS, until we suddenly hit a straightaway, where on the left was a farm with NO TRESPASSING signs surrounding it, and a sign reading FOUR WINDS. The fence encasing it was painted entirely in red and black.

Anybody ever heard of this? I'd ask the members of my caravan, but they're all dead or insane (true story).—*B. Manley*

C. Wilkins

## Lizard-Men of Kentucky

***Elsewhere*** in *Weird Kentucky*, you'll learn of the preacher William Branham, who maintained that the biblical serpent in the Garden of Eden wasn't actually a snake but a humanoid lizard-man sent to earth to plague mankind. And maybe, just maybe, Branham was onto something.

In the October 28, 1878, issue of the *Courier-Journal*, we find a story of a "Wild Man of the Woods" being captured and placed on public display in Louisville. The humanoid creature was said to be over six feet tall, possessing eyes twice as large as a human's, and with scales for skin. Whatever became of this reptilian wild man is not known.

In 1966, there was a sighting of a bipedal lizard-man in Stephensport, near where Sinking Creek meets the Ohio River. Described as "very amphibious looking" and covered in brownish green scales, the creature appeared outside a home late at night and ran off into the darkness on its hind legs when confronted.

In October 1975, in Trimble County, alongside the Ohio River, there were sightings of a "giant lizard" that, according to eyewitnesses, ran on its hind legs. According to Peter Guttilla, the creature was "about fifteen feet long, had a foot-long forked tongue, and big eyes that bulged something like a frog's. It was dull-white with black-and-white stripes across its body with quarter-size speckles over it."

In the 1990s, Mary Burlington, a paranormal researcher from Wisconsin, became convinced that three-toed reptilian humanoids walk the earth and are more common than people realize. She's gradually been collecting evidence from her own archaeological digs and cave investigations in Kentucky. Her research has taken her on a wide-ranging ride through ancient Egyptian serpent cults who occupied Kentucky in prehistory, John Swift's lost silver mines, the Great Serpent Mound in nearby southern Ohio, and so on. Burlington has compiled numerous reports of evidence (mostly footprints) of the lizard-men in Kentucky, ranging from Red River Gorge to the Prestonsburg area.

### Slimy Creature in the Deep

There's a report that dates back to August 1955, in which a Mrs. Darwin Johnson was attacked by an unknown creature in the Ohio River near Henderson. In full view of a friend she was swimming with, Mrs. Johnson was pulled underwater by something with a large clawed hand that grabbed her by the leg. She wriggled and managed to free herself, only to be grabbed by it again. Finally the two women were able to scare it—whatever it was—away.

Inspection of Mrs. Johnson's leg showed visible claw marks where the slimy hand had seized her, and there was a green stain that reportedly could not be washed off for days.

One of the lizard-men? Or something else?

## Cyclopean Ape

***According to Greek mythology,*** a cyclops was a member of a primitive race of giants, each with one big eye in the middle of its head. But maybe the mono-eyed big guys weren't such a myth after all.

In 1831, a one-eyed ape was reported in Jessamine County by an outdoorsman named Patrick C. Flournoy. According to an article in *Saga,* Flournoy stated, "Whilst descending the cliff on the north side of the Kentucky River I encountered a being whose visage was most horrible. He was lying upon the ground, his tail tied to the limb of a tree. The tramping of my horse frightened him and he bounded up a tree, climbing by his tail. Nearing the tree I surveyed his appearance. His hair was long and flowing, and he had but one eye, in the center of his forehead, which was white and near the size of a silver dollar."

The exact height of this ape wasn't made clear, but we can assume that it was of considerable size, since even a one-eyed chimp wouldn't exactly be a "visage . . . most horrible." A one-eyed gorilla isn't terribly likely either, and, besides, they don't have tails.

## Devil Deer

***You know,*** it's funny, in the 1970s and '80s, we went through a period during which wild animal populations were dwindling and seldom seen, and now we're in a peculiar moment in history when they're dwindling more than ever, but we're far more likely to encounter them now because their natural habitat is so encroached upon by civilization. Case in point: Just a few years ago I was walking through a small semi-wooded area being cleared for a forthcoming subdivision. There were a lot of bulldozers around and hammering going on, making it the last place I'd expect to see deer.

As I walked down a recently paved road, an impossibly enormous elk jumped out of the shrubbery and charged straight for me. All my life, it's always been deer running from me, not straight at me! Its antlers were crazy—multi-tined and asymmetrical—and its eyes were like evil, black, soulless marbles. I moved out of the creature's way, and fortunately, it kept on charging along its prescribed path, crashing through the shrubbery on the other side of the road. And then it was gone.

I recounted the incident to an old-timer hunter, and his eyes widened. "You know whatchoo saw!" he exclaimed. "Son, you saw the DEVIL DEER! Do you know how many hunters would give their left [arm] to see the Devil Deer?" Prodded to elaborate further, he told me, "All serious big-time hunters know about Devil Deer, and that they're the most dangerous thing in all the wilderness. They're bigger, meaner and crazier than regular deer, and they cain't be killed!"

What I don't know about the world of hunting, you can almost fit into the Hollywood Bowl. So I remain unsure if this guy was either crazy or just pulling my leg with some sort of "Great Pumpkin" story for drunken outdoorsmen.—*JSH*

966G
CAT
As I walked down a recently paved road, an impossibly enormous elk jumped out of the shrubbery and charged straight for me.

## Legend of the Wampus Cat

***The mountains of Kentucky,*** Tennessee, and western Virginia are dotted with country folks whose occupations range from farming to coal mining. Many of these people have often told tales of the paranormal: coal miner ghosts, Indian legends, strange creatures who live in the hills and hollows. One of the oldest of these is the tale of the Wampus Cat. There are at least two versions of the story of how this bizarre feline came to be.

The first version is an old Native American legend. It was said that a young Indian woman did not trust her husband. It was the custom for the men of the tribe to hunt while the women did things around the encampments, as the women were forbidden to hunt. One night, the distrusting wife placed the hide of a mountain cat on her body. Then she sneaked out to spy on her husband to see what he did on his hunting trips.

As the hunters gathered around their campfires, the woman watched them. She became fascinated with the stories and the magic that the medicine men of the tribe presented to the men before their hunt. But she was not meant to see these things. The poor woman was caught, and for her crime she was transformed into what is known as the Wampus Cat, half woman and half mountain cat. The Wampus Cat is said to still walk the hills of Kentucky, Virginia, and Tennessee: On full moons, you can see it slinking in the woods and hear it howling. Just remember this when you are out camping sometime. If you hear her wail, she is near and may come to visit you.

As the second version of the story goes, there was an old woman who lived by herself in the hills. Townsfolk swore she was a witch. People complained that their cattle were being hexed and other farm animals were coming up missing. They all blamed the old woman. Supposedly, she would turn herself into a cat, sneak up to a house, and hide until someone would open the door. Then she would dart in and wait for her victims to fall asleep. She would cast a deep sleeping spell on the family and then would slip out of the window to steal a farm animal. The witch was so good at what she was doing, she was never caught.

After a while, the townsfolk decided they were tired of their livestock going missing or turning up dead. They devised a plan to catch the witch in the act. One night they watched her as she turned herself into a cat and then sneaked into an unsuspecting house and placed the whole family under her spell. When they were deep in sleep, she jumped out the window as she had always done and went straight for the barn. Once she got there, she began chanting spells to change herself back into human form so she could carry off one of the animals.

In the middle of the spell, however, several people jumped out and surprised her before she had the chance to complete her transformation. Time is important for a witch, and the spell she had cast upon herself could never be reversed or fixed. She was left half woman and half cat—a ghastly sight. The creature howled with fright and ran off into the night, doomed to be the Wampus Cat for all eternity.

On nights when the moon is high and the wind is blowing hard, you can see this creature. It howls and walks upright like a human but has the body of a large cat. Supposedly the Wampus Cat still stalks the hills of Kentucky; it is said to go after farm animals but likes young children best.

## *Is the Wampus Really a Black Panther?*

I live in Estill County and all of my life I have heard stories of people seeing or hearing large black panthers or some kind of large cat that they claim is much bigger than a German Shepherd. This is not to be confused with bobcats or wildcats. I mean basically this is considered common knowledge by some folks. Most people have only heard them and they claim they sound like a woman screaming, only higher pitched. One friend who coon hunts with his dogs, claimed first that his dogs were mean and usually afraid of nothing, and second that on occasion his coon dogs have cried like babies because the alleged black panthers were near. Also, a friend of mine from Breathitt County told me he has heard many tales like this in that county also.—*Robert*

## *Taking Potshots at "Caleb"*

I'm in Madison County. A friend of mine's dad saw [a] creature on Dogwood Drive in Berea. He fired a shot at it and missed. He said it stood to its hind legs, had green eyes, screamed like a woman, and took off. Its local nickname is "Caleb."—*Letter via e-mail*

## *Don't Believe What the Game Wardens Tell You!*

I live in Lawrence County and for about three years straight, we had a "large cat" of some kind killing our animals. One night around 1 a.m., I heard one of my little puppies yelping as it ran towards my house. When I got to it, its side had been completely ripped open, with three large claw marks, as clean as a razor. The puppy's mother was never seen again; we assume she was killed while trying to protect her babies. A few nights later I heard this cat, and as I shined a light near the tree line, I saw two big bright yellow eyes and then it ran away. Similar things followed the next few years, and there were lots of reports of people's dogs, goats, horses, and other animals being attacked. One of our neighbors claimed to have seen this black cat during the day. However, any game warden will happily tell you, those kind of animals do not exist in this area.—*Letter via e-mail*

# Local Heroes and Villains

*Every state* has its local heroes and its local villains. What's interesting about Kentucky's is that you can't always tell which are which. Take those infamous feuding families, the Hatfields and the McCoys. Are they heroes or villains? Both sides committed a lot of atrocities, but they did it for what they perceived as protecting the interests of their own flesh and blood, their family, their kin. Would you not go to any extreme to protect your own children? At what point does protection go from noble to nutty?

And how about Kentucky's own Bill Monroe, the undisputed king of Bluegrass music? Let's face it: We don't love Bill Monroe for the kind, gentle friend of humanity he became as he mellowed out with the passing of time. We love Bill Monroe because he was, aside from Jerry Lee Lewis, country music's last great crank. We admire him for the mean-spirited, stubborn gumption to not speak to Lester Flatt and Earl Scruggs for twenty-three years! *Weird Kentucky* would like to tip our hats to anyone with such self-determination and principle.

There are many people in small Kentucky towns right now doing heroic and villainous deeds. Few, if any, are likely to have books written about them, but maybe they should. As filmmaker John Waters once noted, there are all manner of humans playing out incredible scenes of mythic proportions in our own hometowns, if we'd all just slow down and pay attention. Here are a few worth more than a passing glance.

## Belle Brezing: Gone with the Wind

***The greatest madam*** the Commonwealth has ever known, Belle Brezing, was born Mary Bell Cox on June 16, 1860, to an unwed dressmaker who was known to turn a trick or two herself. Belle acquired her surname when George Brezing, a Lexington saloon operator, grocer, and alcoholic, married her mother, thus turning her into an honest woman. Or a reasonable facsimile for the times.

Belle was pregnant by the age of fifteen, but since she was fooling around with at least three older gentlemen at the time, the father of her child is unknown. By 1879, she was working at Jenny Hill's bawdy house on Main Street, which today is known as the famous Mary Todd Lincoln House. Wonder if the tour guides there mention this fact?

Like the cream in milk, Brezing quickly rose to the top of her chosen field. She was amazingly successful as a prostitute. She also turned out to have a good head for business and a knack for making friends in high places. Though arrested more times than any other citizen in Lexington of the day, when serious prison time loomed, she received a pardon from Governor Luke P. Blackburn.

By necessity, Brezing kept moving around town and plied her trade in a number of locations. For a time, she did business in a row house on Upper Street that now contains Transylvania University's sports offices. Later, she moved her bordello down the street to 194 North Upper Street, where Jonathan's, the Gratz Park Inn restaurant, now stands. Later still, she relocated to a mansion at 59 Megowan Street, and it was here that her career hit the high mark.

Belle's mansion was decorated in over-the-top Victorian splendor. Loaded with cash, she hosted lavish parties for men who came from all over the United States, lured by the thrill of Belle's fast girls and Lexington's beautiful horses. Soldiers spread the good news when they were stationed in the city during the Spanish-American War. During this high point in her career, Belle met William Mabon, brother-in-law of Confederate colonel Richard C. Morgan. They were together until he died in 1917.

The red lights dimmed forever on August 11, 1940. Brezing died at four thirty a.m., addicted to morphine and suffering from uterine cancer. She was buried in Calvary Cemetery (with a marker that unfortunately misspells her name as Breezing, a common error). To this day, her grave is rarely without flowers and visitors. For reasons of their own, many people make pilgrimages to her tombstone and leave elaborate reverential offerings.

Oh, and by the way: Belle Watling, the elegant madam in the film *Gone with the Wind,* was based on Brezing, from stories the author, Margaret Mitchell, said she heard from her husband, who had lived in Lexington for a time.

## Edgar Cayce, Sleeping Psychic

***World-famous*** at one time and with an almost cultlike following, Edgar Cayce, born and raised in the small town of Hopkinsville, had a surprising success as a psychic diagnostician and healer. Cayce claimed the ability to enter a deep trance and, during his slumber, come in touch with an invisible library of information (the "Akashic Records") that exists outside our realm of reality.

Cayce's psychic abilities are said to have begun when a blow to the head by an errant baseball in 1892 knocked him into a stupor, during which he mumbled that a specific type of poultice should be applied for treatment. He emerged back into consciousness with new and amazing abilities. In the years that followed, Cayce gave thousands of "readings" in a trance state. Subjects he expounded on during these readings were usually of a medical nature, but also veered off into philosophical, religious, and paranormal matters.

Skeptics like to point out that Cayce's readings weren't always correct, and that some of his "cures" were rather far-out. (For breast cancer, Cayce prescribed "the raw side of a freshly skinned rabbit, still warm with blood, fur side out, be placed on the breast for cancer of that area.") On the other hand, many of them were correct and seemingly without explanation as to how Cayce could have come up with such information.

A devout Christian, Cayce was startled to find that he was giving rather New Ageish revelations in his trances. Most of his strange remedies were generally accepted at face value by his followers, but even the faithful started scratching their heads when he began getting into superhuman civilizations, endorsement of ancient Egyptian religious precepts, Hindu meditations, chakras, kundalini, and the exploits of an ancient, evil secret conspiracy called the Sons of Belial.

Cayce's endorsement of the notion that we have had past lives was an especially hard pill to swallow for his Christian admirers, and many broke ranks with him over the subject. Ironically, not long after his death the subject of reincarnation blossomed in the 1950s with a mass audience for books like Morey Bernstein's *The Quest for Bridey Murphy* and L. Ron Hubbard's *Have You Lived Before This Life?*

Cayce's A.R.E. (Association for Research and Enlightenment) organization still exists and is headquartered in Virginia Beach, Virginia. It conducts expeditions searching for the lost continent of Atlantis, following information from Cayce's trance readings. We'll keep you posted.

## Colonel Sanders

***Kids today*** generally don't realize that Colonel Harland Sanders was a real person. But the goateed man in the KFC commercials, bedecked in an old southern-gentleman white suit, really did exist and once roamed the countryside, touring from one Kentucky Fried Chicken restaurant to the next, promoting the brand.

One might say that Sanders lived a more action-packed life than any average man. During his early years, he was a firefighter, a chef, a soldier stationed in Cuba, a traveling salesman, a steamboat operator, and the head of several small businesses, including a gas station in Corbin.

It was at this humble station that Sanders's life turned a corner. He was cooking his own fried chicken and selling it to his customers as they filled up their gas tanks, and finding that the sales of his chicken were quickly surpassing the few cents per fill-up he was making. Soon his living quarters in the back were turned into a makeshift dining area, which grew to such proportions that, by 1932, he had to create a full-fledged restaurant, and then a motel to boot. The popularity of Sanders Cafe Chicken was by then a huge phenomenon; in 1952, it was renamed Kentucky Fried Chicken.

In 1956 came Interstate 75, which ran parallel to U.S. 25, but at that time had no exit in Corbin. Fearing this would be devastating to his business, Sanders sold the property and moved his headquarters to Shelbyville. In 1964, he sold the entire Kentucky Fried Chicken empire to John Y. Brown Jr. (who would later go on to become governor) and became the chain's mascot, staying on the road almost perpetually, making appearances as a company spokesman.

Sanders wasn't always thrilled with the way things ended up. In 1975, he was even sued (unsuccessfully) for libel by Kentucky Fried Chicken for complaining in interviews that they'd turned his famous gravy recipe to "sludge." He died of leukemia in 1980, at the age of ninety.

## Grillo the Clown

***This well-known*** roving street character has spent a good deal of his life on the sidewalks of Lexington, Richmond, Berea, and other central Kentucky cities. Wearing an elaborate costume constructed from cardboard, wires, car floor mats, and other trash, Grillo is a self-styled performance artist whose stage is the street. He usually wears some combination of hockey masks, crude homemade space helmets, saucepans, and colanders on his head. Somewhere along the way, he started calling himself Grillo the Clown, even though he doesn't look much like a clown (except very occasionally, when he has a red clown nose duct-taped to his mask).

The stories of Grillo's misadventures and malfeasance are legendary and worthy of compilation in a tome of their own. Here's just one.

### A Grillo Gag

Yes, everyone around downtown Lexington has seen Grillo at least once in their lives. He asks for money and asks you your name and makes up stupid songs on the spot, using your name. A long time ago he used to have little Casio keyboards duct-taped to each of his arms, haven't seen him with those lately, he probably hocked them for something.

My favorite Grillo story happened to my friend Cody, who said Grillo handed him a huge package and said, "Will you hold this for me for a moment while I go in the bank? I'll give you a dollar." Cody said sure, and Grillo handed him a dollar and went in the bank. The dollar stunk to high heaven! After like 20 minutes he hadn't come out yet, and Cody went in to say "Hey dude, I don't have all day," but Grillo was gone. He had walked right out the back door as soon as he entered. Cody never opened the package, he trashed it because he thought maybe it was a bomb or some kind of trick. What a wuss, I'm dying to know what might have been in it!
*—mimefield*

## Patrick Moore

***Flipping channels*** recently in Jefferson County, we caught this fellow's highly idiosyncratic public-access television program. Our first impulse was to laugh out loud at the strangeness that unfolds on the screen: A middle-aged Arlo Guthrie–like man in a loud flowered shirt was driving around what appeared to be Hawaii, warbling along with his own CD in the car as a video camera was perched on his dashboard, giving the viewer an unsettling nostril-cam view of the driver as he sang along with himself. The songs were dizzyingly psychedelic folk-rock that often veered into avant-garde Syd Barrett territory, whether intentional or not. Combined with the vertiginous visuals, it was a train wreck. We couldn't stop watching.

But you know what? For days thereafter, those earnest little songs rattled around in our heads. Soon we were actually tuning in to the public access channel specifically to catch his program again and again. A check of his Web site (mooresongs.com) delivered the news that he's doing quite well, thank you very much: He's traveled and performed around the world, released many DVDs of it all, and is still going strong, daring to promote a "peace and love" message in this nanotech-ridden, RFID-tag-laden new millennium of security cameras and untested artificial sweeteners. What really makes Moore so "weird" in today's modern world is his honesty, and that's something we really can't get enough of.

## Real Inventor of the Radio

***Some Kentuckians*** just don't get no respect. Take Nathan Stubblefield, for example. Born in 1860, Stubblefield was an eccentric melon farmer from Murray. He was a voracious reader and styled himself as a self-taught scientist and inventor.

As early as 1885, Nathan had invented several different wireless telephone devices. And wireless telephony is, of course, the whole point of radio. This was years before Marconi got official credit for inventing radio. (Even without Stubblefield, Marconi still wouldn't be the true inventor of radio. Nikola Tesla invented it well before Marconi, who, in fact, used Tesla's patents as research materials.)

In 1892, Stubblefield performed the world's first wireless broadcast in Murray, transmitting speech and music. Later he gave a very successful demonstration on the Potomac in Washington, D.C. Yet, without proper marketing credit for his invention eluded him. He entered into a business partnership with a company that promised to promote his wireless telephone but instead let it languish, suppressed his patent, and paid him only $800 and a trunkful of worthless stock certificates.

Stubblefield eventually died of starvation, a crazed hermit in his shack in the wilderness of Almo, but not before destroying all his prototypes, fearful his inventions would be stolen again by big-city slickers. He was buried in Stubblefield Cemetery (also known as Bowman Cemetery) on Route 2075 in Calloway County. A road near his place of death has been renamed Radio Road. But for poor old Nathan Stubblefield, that's too little and way too late.

## Sweet Evening Breeze

***Suppose we told you*** that an openly gay cross-dressing man lived much of his life publicly in drag between the 1930s and the 1970s? And not only that, but that he was African American and in the South, no less! One might think, how could that even be possible in such a repressive time?

Believe it. Not only did Sweet Evening Breeze survive safely, she lived for a century.

Lexington is known for its unique characters, but none can surpass the notoriety and fame of Miss Sweets, as she was often affectionately known. At a time in history when the idea of being "out" was nearly unthinkable and when most who chose cross-dressing not just as a hobby but as a lifestyle had to keep it on the q.t., Sweet Evening Breeze would have none of that. Instead of sneaking and slinking around, she walked brazenly down the city streets of Lexington in broad daylight.

And somehow it worked. Sweets, thanks to her powerful charisma and charm, gained a huge and curious following of friends, fans, and admirers. She had friends from all walks of life, from well-to-do fellow members of the Pleasant Green Baptist Church to pals and acquaintances met in restrooms of the Phoenix Hotel. Sweets even obtained a good job as a nurse at Good Samaritan Hospital, remaining employed there for decades, and she participated in staff basketball games on weekends—as the cheerleader!

As was the case in many cities in those days, Lexington had a law on the books forbidding cross-dressing. There's a story that when Sweets and another young black drag queen were thrown in jail, they entertained the sympathetic guards with the same routines they performed in cabaret clubs, and ultimately swayed the judge with Sweets's persuasive argument that the cross-dressing law was unconstitutional.

Sweets lived for years in a nice house by the railroad tracks on Prall Street, which was a very old African American community near the University of Kentucky. The house still stands today.

Sweet Evening Breeze died on December 16, 1983, and was buried in Lexington with a gravestone bearing her real name (James Herndon), by which few people knew her.

## Walter Tevis

***A good ol'*** Madison County boy who served in World War II at a young age, Walter Tevis had two big passions: playing pool and writing fiction. He went to college at the University of Kentucky and somehow managed to juggle those passions well enough to earn a master's degree. Even after becoming a schoolteacher in small towns like Science Hill, Irvine, and Carlisle, he spent a great deal of time in the smoky, dirty pool rooms of Richmond. Later he went on to become a professor at U.K. and then at Ohio University. His pool shark's life of drinking and smoking caught up with him in the end, however, and in his final years he battled alcoholism and lung cancer. He died in New York in 1984.

*Jackie Gleason (left) as Minnesota Fats and Paul Newman in the film version of "The Hustler."*

Oh, and he also just happened to be the author of three best-selling novels: *The Hustler, The Color of Money,* and the science fiction classic *The Man Who Fell to Earth*, all three of which were also made into blockbuster Hollywood films.

The nationwide pool craze created by Tevis with his book *The Hustler* and the subsequent movie version single-handedly revolutionized the billiards industry, giving it enormous new popularity and the respectability it still enjoys.

For what it's worth, Tevis also inadvertently gave the world Minnesota Fats, a.k.a. Rudolph Wanderone Jr., the world-famous pool player who achieved fame by appropriating the name of a character in *The Hustler* and claiming that Tevis (whom he had never met) had based the book on him. Tevis denied this and called Wanderone a fraud, stating, "I made up Minnesota Fats just as Walt Disney made up Donald Duck."

Tevis is buried in the Richmond Cemetery in Madison County, not far from the last of the great old Richmond pool halls, Taylor's Billiards, which still exists.

# Charles Manson, Native Kentuckian

***The name Charles Manson*** is invoked second only to Hitler's as a generic expression of evil, often by people who don't really know what that whole "Helter Skelter" thing was about. They just know it had something to do with the Beatles, right?

Contrary to popular belief, Manson was not an Ohioan, but a Kentuckian. His family lived in Ashland and simply chose a hospital in nearby Cincinnati for the birth in 1934. Charlie's mother, Kathleen Maddox, was only sixteen and unwed when Manson was born. He was later determined to be the son of a mysterious Colonel Scott, who was ordered to pay Maddox the princely sum of $5 per month for his support. Reportedly, the colonel didn't come through on even that meager payment.

In his youth, Manson spent a lot of time in and out of boys' reformatories, special homes, and jails, which kept him shuffled around the country from West Virginia to Indiana to Washington, D.C. to California. Along the way, there was a little armed robbery, a lot of other crimes, and a lot of guitar playing. Manson idolized the Beatles and the Beach Boys and even auditioned to be a member of the Monkees.

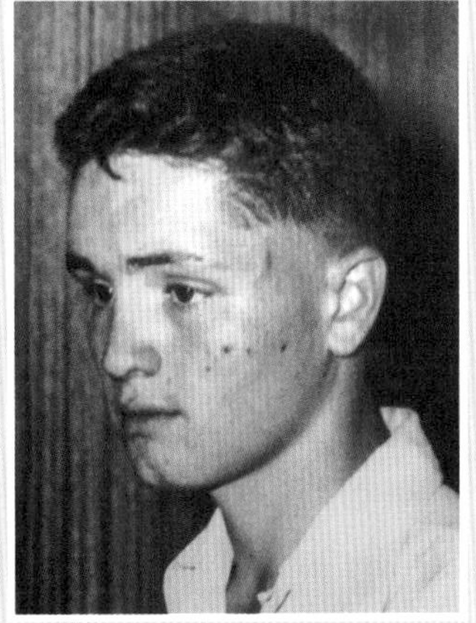

*Charles Manson at age 14*

Hanging out in California during the 1960s, he set up the apocalyptic Manson Family cult in the desert, surrounding himself with drug-addled hippie chicks and other drifters. Soon murders were being carried out allegedly in Charlie's name and on his instructions. One of the most gruesome slayings was that of pregnant Sharon Tate, a Hollywood actress best remembered today for her appearances in *Valley of the Dolls*. After a chaotic trial, Manson was sentenced to life in prison.

The Manson Family violence may have even come back to Kentucky's dark and bloody ground. James Willett, another Manson Family victim, was born in Kentucky in 1946. In November 1972, three Manson women—Nancy Pitman, Priscilla Cooper, and Lynette "Squeaky" Fromme—were charged with Willett's murder, allegedly to keep the twenty-six-year-old from blabbing about their robberies.

Manson frequently makes people's top ten lists of serial killers, although as far as we know he never actually killed anybody. He even denies that he ever told his minions to kill anybody. Currently he resides in California's Corcoran State Prison, inmate number B-33920.

## Donald "Angel of Death" Harvey

***Forget Charles Manson***—Kentucky produced a REAL serial killer, boasting one of the highest body counts of all time. Donald Harvey spent his formative years in Appalachia in Booneville. He now claims to have killed eighty-seven people, but the official toll is somewhat lower—between thirty-six and fifty-seven. He calls himself the Angel of Death, but his mother told a reporter, "My son has always been a good boy."

Harvey earned good grades in high school but dropped out because he found education boring. Drifting along aimlessly, he became a factory worker in Cincinnati for a while, but returned to Kentucky and the town of London in 1970 when his grandfather was ill. Harvey spent a lot of time at Marymount Hospital visiting his grandfather. The nuns took a shine to him, and one of them offered him a job as a hospital orderly. He jumped at the opportunity and started work the next day.

After just a few months of changing bedpans and inserting catheters, something snapped in him. No one really knows what exactly happened, but Harvey started to kill patients. Was he alleviating suffering, as he avers; was he angry with them; or did he just like to watch people die? In any event, one evening Harvey was checking on a stroke victim, when the patient became unruly and angry, lashing out at him. Bad move. "The next thing I knew, I'd smothered him," Harvey said. "It was like it was the last straw. I just lost it."

Amazingly, no one suspected foul play. Three weeks later Harvey disconnected an elderly woman's oxygen tank. Again, no one thought anything of it. Unlike most serial killers, who use one favorite technique, Harvey tried many different murder methods— plastic bags, drugs, you name it. Being exceptionally bright, he wanted to experiment, no doubt. One of his most sadistic murders involved a patient who suspected Harvey was trying to kill him. The patient hit Harvey with a bedpan. Harvey regained his composure, bided his time, and shoved a coat hanger in the man's catheter. The patient developed sepsis and died slowly and painfully.

One night, under arrest for burglary, Harvey, who was drunk, started blabbing about all the people he'd killed over the past year. The cops couldn't substantiate his claims, so he wasn't charged with murder. He pleaded guilty to theft and hightailed it out of town. Whew, that was a close one! Then he joined the air force. However, he had problems in the military and was discharged after less than a year.

In 1975, he took a job at the Cincinnati V.A. hospital, where, with little supervision on the night shift, he was able to dive back into his killing sprees, studying medical journals to learn how to disguise the murders. He killed patients with rat poison in their dessert (it's some kind of testament to the tastiness of hospital food that the patients couldn't tell any difference!), put arsenic and cyanide in their juice, suffocated them with plastic bags and wet towels, and injected cyanide into IVs. In the 1980s, he branched out from helpless hospital patients. He slipped arsenic into his lover Carl Hoeweler's food to make him too sick to leave the apartment they shared. (Harvey suspected Hoeweler was being unfaithful.) He put hepatitis serum in a neighbor's drink and put arsenic in another's pie. When Hoeweler's father had a stroke, Harvey visited him in the hospital and put arsenic in his pudding. He died that night.

Eventually, Harvey landed at Drake Memorial in Cincinnati, where he killed twenty-three patients over thirteen months. Not until 1987 did it all begin to unravel. At the autopsy of patient John Powell, the coroner smelled burnt almonds, a sign of cyanide. Powell's friends and family were cleared, so hospital

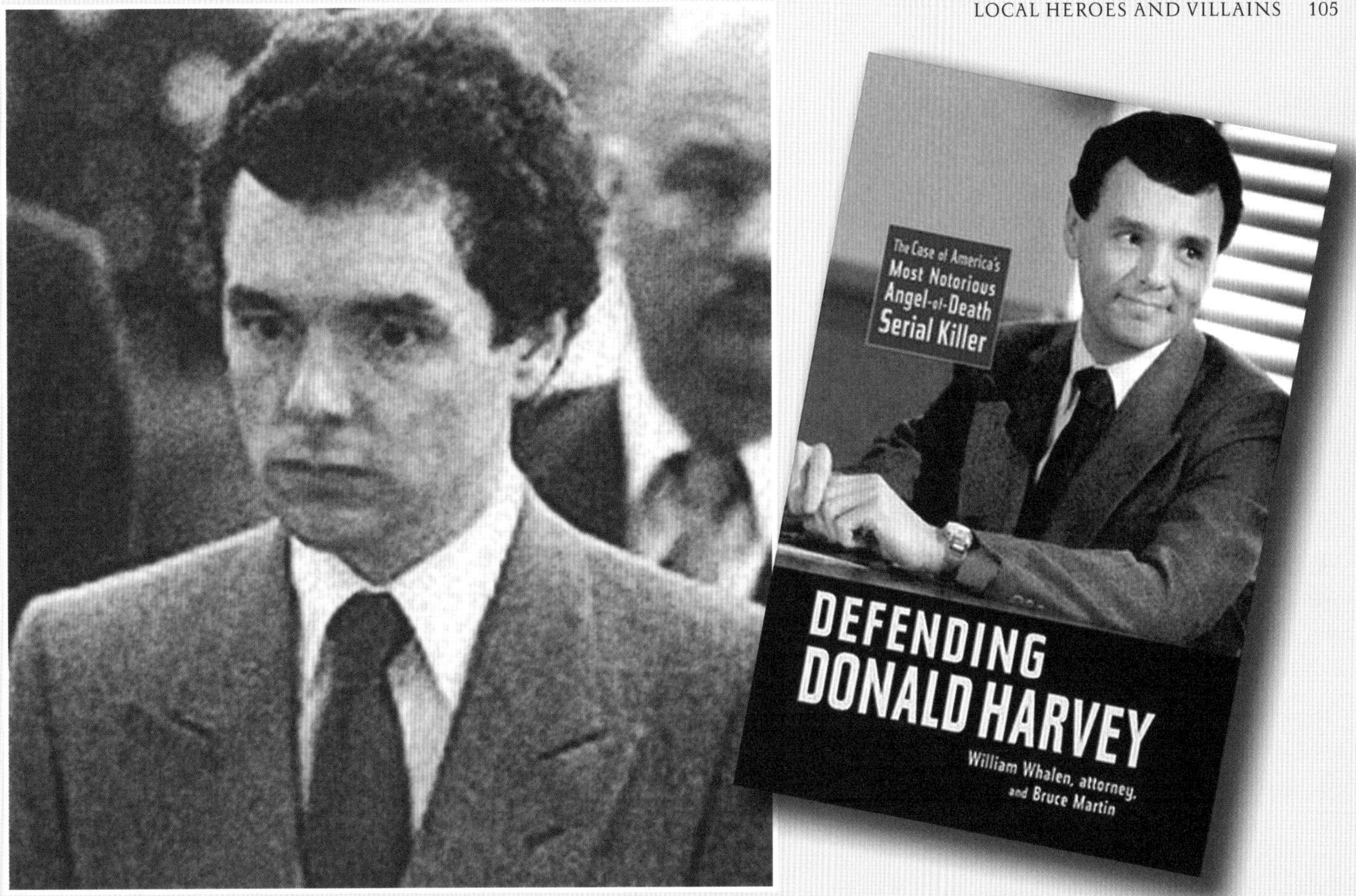


employees were suspected. When investigators found out that Harvey was called the Angel of Death, because he always seemed to be nearby when a patient died, their radar finally went off.

A search warrant for Harvey's apartment paid off big-time. Police found jars of cyanide and arsenic, occult books, "how to" books on poison, and a diary! Why do serial killers keep diaries?

When first caught, he confessed to his public defender, William Whalen, that he had committed thirty-three murders over seventeen years. But the number kept growing until it reached seventy. Investigators were skeptical that anyone could kill so many people without arousing suspicions, and Harvey's mental state was tested. He was found, in their assessment, to be mentally sound.

Harvey is now serving multiple life sentences for the murders in Ohio and Kentucky. When a *Columbus Dispatch* reporter asked why he killed, Harvey said, "Well, people controlled me for 18 years, and then I controlled my own destiny. I controlled other people's lives, whether they lived or died. . . . After I didn't get caught for the first 15, I thought it was my right. I appointed myself judge, prosecutor, and jury. So I played God."

Harvey is eligible for parole in 2047, when he'll be ninety-five. Still not too old to slip a pinch of arsenic into some little drink somewhere.

# Hunter S. Thompson

***The great antiestablishment icon*** of the 1970s and 1980s, Kentuckian Hunter S. Thompson, allegedly took his own life with a handgun in his Aspen, Colorado, home on February 20, 2005. He left the single word "counselor" typed haphazardly in the center of a sheet of paper in his typewriter.

Thompson was a Louisville native who grew up in the Highlands and attended Male High School. He escaped robbery charges as a teenager in Louisville in 1956 by joining the U.S. Air Force but was soon discharged because his superiors feared his haughty, rebellious attitude would rub off on the other men. Thompson moved to New York and studied creative writing at Columbia University. He devised his own method of learning to write: He retyped *The Great Gatsby* and *A Farewell to Arms* to learn the authors' styles.

While running for political office on the Freak Power ticket, Thompson dropped in on *Rolling Stone* editor Jann Wenner and proposed an article about the race. He narrowly lost the election, but gained a foothold at the magazine as a political correspondent. *Rolling Stone* was not the first to publish Thompson's gonzo style of writing (in which the subject and author are blurred manically). That honor belongs to the now defunct *Scanlan's Monthly,* in an article called "The Kentucky Derby is Decadent and Depraved." Hunter didn't consciously create his signature style—he was simply under a tight deadline and sent his editor whatever was in his notebook. Bill Cardoso coined the term "gonzo" to describe the style, and the description stuck.

Best known for his book *Fear and Loathing in Las Vegas,* Thompson was named a Kentucky Colonel by Governor Paul S. Patton and received keys to the city of Louisville.

## "King" Solomon

***One of the most*** amazing things about human beings is that there's just no telling how they will react in a crisis. In the early 1800s, William "King" Solomon was well known as Lexington's town drunk and is specifically described as such in historical texts. He supported himself and his alcoholism with occasional odd jobs such as digging ditches. But one day the police decided that they'd had enough of this man's lowering the class of their fair city, and they busted him for vagrancy. His sentence was to be auctioned off as a servant to the highest bidder. If anyone at the time felt this was an extreme penalty for the "crime" of standing on a street corner without money, history did not record their sentiments.

Ironically, Solomon was sold (for eighteen cents) to a free African American woman, who put him to work hawking her baked goods at roadside stands.

Then came the summer of 1833. It was the year of a horrible cholera epidemic that swept across the land. Half the population of Lexington evacuated the city, leaving the streets literally filled with over five hundred corpses of those not so fortunate. There was an "every man for himself" sense of anarchy and panic in the air, as law enforcement broke down and city officials refused to go near the bloated bodies for fear of contracting the plague themselves.

Solomon volunteered to deal with the bodies. Completely without help, he transported the corpses all the way out to the cemetery and gave each of them a proper burial. It took over two months of around-the-clock work. He paused only to sleep (and presumably, for an occasional swig from his hip flask), and even then, he slept on the ground right there in the cemetery and immediately resumed his task upon waking.

By autumn, the epidemic had passed; the good citizens of Lexington returned to their homes, and life settled back to normal. Solomon was made a free man once more. It is written that on the first day of court session that fall, the judge noticed that Solomon was one of the spectators in the back of the courtroom and came down from the bench to shake his hand. All the other citizens gathered round to shake Solomon's hand as well.

King Solomon died in 1854 and was originally buried in an unmarked grave, until years later when someone finally decided maybe he deserved a little better than that.

Why didn't Solomon contract cholera himself while handling all those corpses? Because, unbeknownst to people in 1833, cholera is not spread person to person, but primarily through contaminated drinking water, and, well, Solomon didn't drink water!

## Ray Chapman and Carl Mays

***The unusual distinction*** of being the only pro baseball player ever killed during a game goes to Kentuckian Ray Chapman. Ironically, the person who killed him was also a Kentuckian. Chapman, a shortstop for the Cleveland Indians, was killed on August 16, 1920, by a spitball thrown by one of baseball's most disliked bad guys of the day: New York Yankees pitcher Carl Mays, a native of Liberty.

Chapman, born in McHenry, was an extremely charismatic and well-loved player, which made fans all the more outraged when Mays killed him. Mays was already a *persona non grata* before the Chapman incident, after he injured two fans in Philadelphia by angrily throwing a baseball into the stands.

Many of those at the game insist that Mays clearly and deliberately threw the spitball directly at Chapman's face. Contrary to popular belief, spitballs were often treated not with spit, but with all manner of gooey substances such as grease, oil, lard, or peanut butter. This treatment made it harder for a bat to glance a proper blow off the slippery ball, but it also had the effect of making the ball travel in an erratic pattern that was difficult for the batter's eye to follow. The spitball was outlawed after Chapman's death.

Mays would later be investigated for accusations of throwing the 1921 World Series. His image wasn't helped any by his apparent lack of remorse over the Chapman event. He would later be traded to the Cincinnati Reds, then briefly to the Brooklyn Dodgers, where he would eventually give up and go into early retirement.

*Carl Mays (inset) and Ray Chapman (above)*

Though both men were born in Kentucky, neither was buried here. Mays's grave is located in Oregon; Chapman's can be found at Lake View Cemetery, Cleveland, Ohio.

## Beulah Annan, the Real Roxie

***A sensational murder trial*** riveted the public in the 1920s, when Kentuckian Beulah Annan went on trial for murdering her lover, a charge for which she was eventually acquitted. Many felt strongly that she was guilty and that justice had not been served. Others saw her—and still see her—in a more romanticized "Bonnie and Clyde" way.

In a very short period of time, Beulah went through several men and several misadventures. She married her first husband in Owensboro, then divorced him and moved to Chicago and married auto mechanic Albert Annan. Soon she began having an affair with a Laundromat worker named Harry Kalstedt, but that apparently didn't work out well for her, because in April 1924 she shot him to death.

Beulah told multiple versions of her story—that she murdered Kalstedt in cold blood for no reason, that she murdered him because he was leaving her, and that Kalstedt tried to attack her and she shot him in self-defense. Whichever version is true, what IS common to all stories is her admission that instead of calling for help immediately, she sat around for two hours, drinking cocktails and watching him bleed to death while playing a record by Sophie Tucker called "Hula Lou" on automatic repeat the entire time.

Despite her waffling and inconsistencies, she was ultimately acquitted. It was a decision that shocked and outraged many. Albert Annan had supported his wife throughout the trial and nearly bankrupted himself paying her legal fees. The day after she was freed, she made the announcement that she was leaving him. "He is too slow," she told the press.

Next she fell madly in love with a boxer named Edward Harlib, whom she married once the divorce from Annan was finalized. Three months later she divorced Harlib as well, claiming "cruelty" on his part and demanding thousands of dollars in a settlement. A couple of other men crossed Beulah's erratic path after that, but tuberculosis put an end to her journey in 1928. She was buried at the Mount Pleasant Cumberland Presbyterian Church Cemetery in Owensboro.

But though Annan is gone, she is not forgotten. She lives on as the fictionalized "Roxie Hart" in the play *Chicago* by Maurine Dallas Watkins.

# Buckhorn

*One of central Kentucky's* most endearing and beloved characters, Pete Gross (known to all simply as Buckhorn), was a fixture of the Madison County scene for years.

Small-town fame came to Buckhorn on many levels. He hosted an early morning radio show on Richmond's WEKY-AM (his atonal and ear-splittingly loud rendition of "Happy Birthday to You" was a notorious local hit of sorts and kept the vu meters lying in the red). He was well known among Richmond's downtown pool sharks, drunks, and college students as the de facto custodian at several local bars, but also was a friend to bankers and businessmen. He was also known for zipping all over town on his motorcycle (and often ignoring all traffic laws).

However, Buckhorn's true glory lay on two other fronts. First and foremost, he was the quintessential wheeler-dealer. He always had something to sell and sold something every single day. He would open up his coat to reveal an entire store inside, like a bad old movie's "Wanna buy a watch?" street hustler. He had watches, coins, pocket knives, collectible cigarette lighters, antique silver cigarette cases, and so forth. All day long Buckhorn sped on his cycle from flea market to bar to junk store to pool hall, endlessly buying and selling like a one-man pawn shop a-go-go.

Secondly, Buckhorn had a special place in his heart for radios. He loved to fix, repair, and restore antique radios, and he repaired them quite well, even though he knew little or nothing about the fundamentals of electronics except what he had taught himself through trial and error. He had little formal education and, amazingly, could not read or write.

"I just wuk on 'em till they do right," Buckhorn said of his repair technique. He had a huge collection of old tubes and parts, but his methods for choosing appropriate replacement ones for radios were a cryptic, mysterious, spiritual matter, the mechanisms of which were known only to Buckhorn. He usually polished his tubes until the serial numbers were worn off. And yet he conjured and coaxed new life into the dead gadgets. How he did it remains a mystery. "Wal, I reckon it's got that Buckhorn Quietus on it," he would say when a piece was finished.

For those who did not have the opportunity to hear Buckhorn's voice, it was a powerful thing: a Deep South Louisiana-like upwardly lilting drawl utterly out of place for someone who'd never left Kentucky in his life. Add to this a delightfully squeaky and childish laugh that clashed with his rough, grizzled appearance.

Buckhorn died on his motorcycle in an accident in 1997. Those whose path he crossed will never forget him.

## William Branham

***Nowadays*** the name William Branham may not mean much, but it wasn't that long ago that it was recognized in almost every household. Branham ran a religious sect (some would say cult) whose exploits were legendary.

He was born in 1909 near Burkesville, in a log cabin with dirt floors. His father was only eighteen years old, and his mother was fifteen. Mr. and Mrs. Charles Branham had nine children in total, with William as the firstborn. They were a very superstitious family, but not particularly religious. Technically they were Catholic, but rarely attended church except for the occasional Christmas Mass.

As Branham describes it in his autobiography (cleverly titled *My Life Story*), a supernatural beam of energy or light accompanied his birth, shining in through the cabin window nearest the bed even though it was the middle of the night. Also according to Branham, after he bathed in this ray of light in his mother's arms, a halo spontaneously appeared over his newborn head.

As a youth, Branham had a promising career ahead of him as a boxer, having won fifteen bouts. Instead, in the late 1920s he abruptly quit boxing and chose to become a minister. He was ordained in a Baptist church and immediately began making a name for himself with his peculiar but charismatic stage presence. Before long, he had his own church and congregation, called the Branham Tabernacle, which grew by leaps and bounds.

As his fame grew, however, so did his boldness. Branham's proclamations from the pulpit grew progressively fringier and weirder, with apocalyptic predictions and supernatural phenomena playing a greater role. By the 1940s, he had aligned himself with the Pentecostals and gone full-scale into faith healing. In fact, he is said by many historians to have created the concept as we know it today. According to Branham, he was commissioned by angels to heal the sick. An allegedly undoctored photo of him with a halo over his head while preaching helped to keep the curiosity seekers coming.

**An allegedly undoctored photo of him with a halo over his head while preaching helped to keep the curiosity seekers coming.**

Whatever you might think of faith healing, it must be said that during these years no one considered Branham a fraud. His popularity and success as a healer spread nationwide, and he soon found himself on a worldwide tour playing stadiums and other enormous venues. Not bad for a Kentucky boy raised by illiterate parents in Cumberland County.

However, by the 1950s, the faith-healing preacher was pushing the limits of his audience. He began declaring that the Holy Trinity—a mainstay of Christianity—was a false concept, "of the devil," and not scripturally sound. He opined that hell was only a temporary punishment and that it was very likely you could get yourself out of it once you were there. He also insisted that Adam and Eve had omnipotent powers similar to God's, and that Eve had a little hanky-panky going with the serpent, who was actually Satan incarnate and was more like an upright-walking reptilian snake-man.

Toward the end of his life, Branham's philosophy, like Edgar Cayce's, had grown so bizarre as to completely alienate the majority of his already dwindling following. He claimed to be the prophet Elijah and to have personally witnessed firsthand all the major events of the Old and New Testaments. "I was with Moses at the Burning Bush," he claimed. "I was at the Red Sea when I seen the spirit of God move down and part the water."

Though Branham also claimed the God-given psychic ability to predict the future (usually in terms of news and world events), he was unable to predict his own tragic death on Christmas Eve 1965, from injuries sustained in an auto accident. He was laid to rest in Jeffersonville, Indiana, directly across the Ohio River from Kentucky. Many different offshoots of his followers still exist today, some of whom believe Branham will rise from his tomb like Christ on an Easter Sunday in the near future.

## The Hatfields, the McCoys, and Other Feuding Hillbillies

***There's a character trait*** possessed by old-time denizens of Appalachia that's all too lacking in humanity today: stubbornness.

This stubbornness is what used to be known as integrity, character, principles. These too are apparently an outmoded concept in twenty-first-century society. Of course, as with all things, there comes a point where it can get too extreme. One example is the concept of the "hillbilly feud."

Although blown out of proportion and exaggerated comically by the media, there really were hillbilly feuds in the good old days, and sometimes they really did span generations. Curiously, such flared-temper shotgun grudge matches were just as commonplace in the Old West, yet Hollywood regards such situations as somehow nobler than the hillbilly variety.

The most famous hillbilly feud is, of course, the one between the Hatfields and the McCoys. The Hatfields lived on the West Virginia side of the twisted Tug Fork River, while the McCoys dwelled on the Kentucky side. Contrary to the popular myth that they were poor and living practically like savages, both sides owned huge tracts of land and were well respected in their communities. However, both families were also in the moonshine business.

The feud began, some say, when one family's pig was found on the other family's land. (Although there was also some earlier unpleasantness during the Civil War, when a McCoy defected to the Union cause.) Anyway, the pig incident led to a property dispute, which naturally led to decades of kidnapping, arson, and murder as each side defended its family's honor. Before it all ended, around 1891, the death toll numbered thirteen. Interestingly, the family patriarchs, Ole Ran'l McCoy

and Devil Anse Hatfield, went unscathed during the bloodshed and lived to fine old ages. Their descendants went on to live respectable lives as doctors, teachers, farmers, and ordinary citizens. One of them, Henry D. Hatfield, served a term as governor of West Virginia.

Also famous in Kentucky was the Martin-Tolliver feud in Rowan County. It began in 1884, when John Martin killed Floyd Tolliver in a gun duel in a hotel in Morehead. A few days later Martin was assassinated while waiting to stand trial. The friends and families of these two men, eager to avenge the death of their loved one, escalated the violence in a series of murders between 1884 and 1887.

In Jackson, the Ku Klux Klan and a group called the Red Strings continued fighting the Civil War for years after it was officially ended. One of the leaders of the Red Strings was Captain Bill Strong, who figured heavily in other Kentucky feuds such as the Hargis–Callahan–Cockrell dispute.

In Perry County circa 1882, seventy-four men died in the French–Eversole feud, which ended in a bloodbath, during which time feuders commandeered and occupied the Perry County courthouse in Hazard. No one is one hundred percent certain what started the war. The popular myth is that it was over a woman's affections, but the more likely version is that it was over land and mining rights.

Who the heroes and the villains are in these disputes isn't always clear, but that they had the stubbornness to fight for what they believed in is, we maintain, indicative of some sort of heroism, however misguided.

# Personalized Properties

Luckily for seekers of the weird, Kentucky is a place where many people have unique ideas about how their world should look. Many of these people are true artists, though they may never have had the money, time, or luxury of formal training. Their own lives, families, and experiences, rather than a vast knowledge of art history, influence their work.

Others are driven by more than artistic hunger. Dotted across the state are people who use their property to express their religious, philosophical, or political viewpoints. Those of us who can't get television time or newspaper columns to air our beliefs need a forum as well, right? Other personalized properties are commercial in nature, a relief to see in a time when chain restaurants and bland corporate headquarters are being progressively shoved farther down our collective throats. So the next time you're on a long drive, keep your eyes peeled. Kentucky is full of these unique environments and landscapes. We here at *Weird* headquarters salute them all.

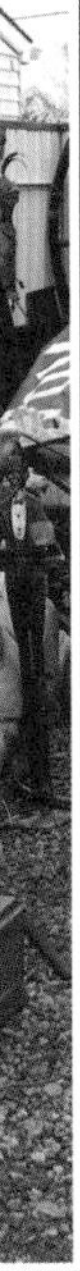

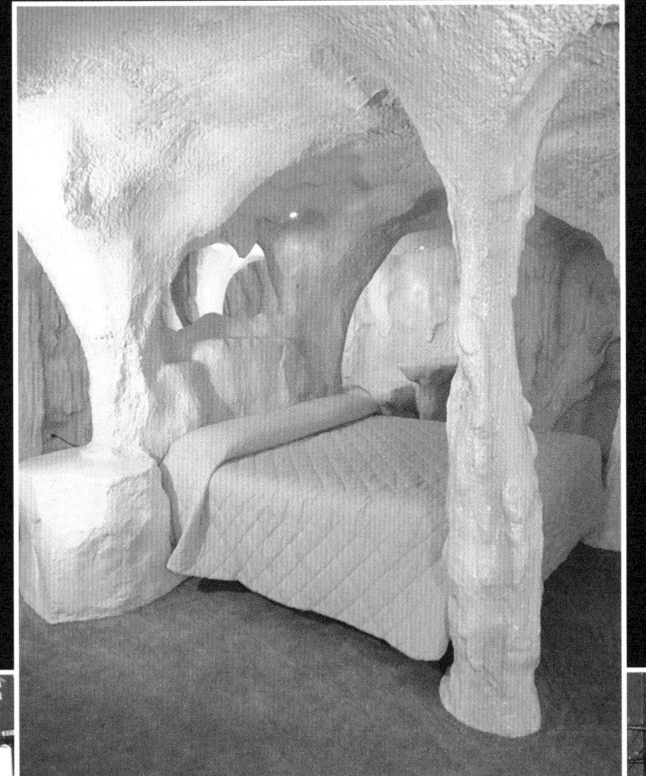

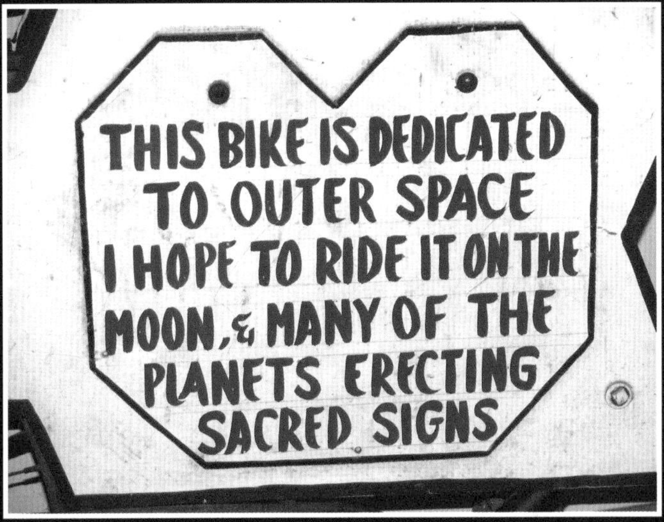

THIS BIKE IS DEDICATED
TO OUTER SPACE
I HOPE TO RIDE IT ON THE
MOON, & MANY OF THE
PLANETS ERECTING
SACRED SIGNS

SUPER-SONIC SPACE BUGGY
MELLWOOD

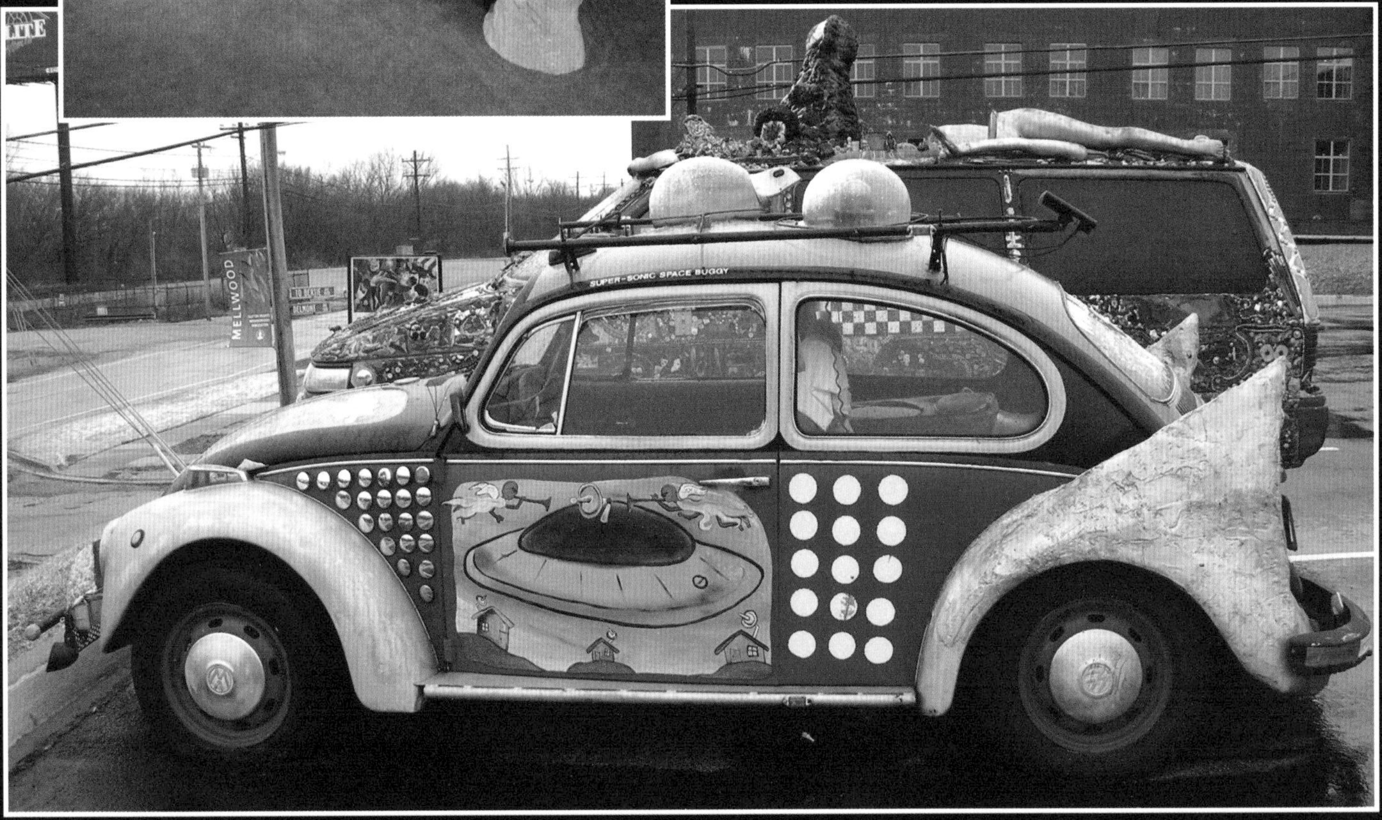

## Henry Harrison Mayes Says, "Get Right with God"

***Faith*** truly is a great motivator. In some individuals, faith expresses itself quietly. In others, though, it can be the impetus to do something that many would say is as extreme as extreme gets.

In the case of Henry Harrison Mayes, faith in God led to a lifelong mission, a creative drive, and a tireless work ethic that saw one man's quiet efforts reach around our nation. His base of operations for the bulk of this gargantuan seven-decade crusade was the tiny town of Middlesboro right here in Kentucky.

Born in 1898, Mayes was just a young man when he endured an experience during which, he thought, he came as close to being face-to-face with God as mortal man can. While working in a coal mine as a teenager, Mayes suffered a horrific accident. He was pinned against the mine's wall by an enormous piece of mining machinery. While pinned, and realizing he was dying, he begged God for his life. Furthermore, he promised that if he did indeed survive, he would dedicate the remainder of that life to spreading the Lord's work.

Live Mr. Mayes indeed did. And, starting in 1917, he made good on his promise—and didn't stop making good on it until his death sixty-nine years later, in 1986. Mayes dedicated his days to spreading the Lord's message

using the means at his disposal.

The bulk of Mayes's work came in the form of constructing concrete sculptures of crosses and hearts that bore messages on their flat faces. The two most prevalent messages were Get Right With God and Jesus Saves. In six decades, many other phrases popped up, among them Where Will You Spend Eternity?, Advertising God Since 1918, and in his personal case, the very literal Thanks to God Forever for Landing Me Safe Through the Cross of Jesus Christ. These signs were quietly placed, without fanfare, along the roads of both Kentucky and the nation at large. Before his death, signs designed, built, transported, and erected by Mayes stood in forty-four states.

Mayes created all his signs personally and shipped them all over the world at his own expense. In his later years, when age meant that the materials became too difficult for him to manipulate, Mayes began drawing his messages out on paper, putting them into glass bottles, and placing them in bodies of water throughout the world. All told, the man sent over 50,000 bottles into circulation. Many are invariably lost to time, some have been found, and undoubtedly many more will find their way into the confused hands of beachcombers in the future. Mayes just wanted that word spread! He even donated a few signs to NASA before his death, in hopes that his mission and his signs could make their way to the moon.

Mayes clearly lived his mission. But he also lived IN his mission. His house was shaped like a cross, and the roof was painted with religious slogans for passing planes to see. In his final years, Mayes moved to Tennessee, where he built his largest project, a rock garden that passengers passing by in airplanes could see from the sky.

Mayes has left a lasting impression on the people and culture of Middlesboro. One writer remembers his childhood impressions of this quietly pious man at his personal Web site, www.kywordman.wordpress.com:

"Among those of us who grew up in that mountain-rimmed valley, Mayes was known as 'the Sign Man' or 'the Cross Builder.' He lived near the valley's center in a cross-shaped house. He kept its lawn filled with cross-shaped signs. I never saw him in a car or truck. Instead, he rode a bicycle onto which a religious message board was attached."

Mayes's effect on the town was physical as well as psychological. He also built a gigantic cross of electric lights that still shines vibrantly at the base of a mountain in Middlesboro. While he has been gone from the town for over two decades, his effects still literally shine down upon it today.

Many of Mayes's roadside sculptures still remain. Be sure to find the ones you can—as highways expand, buildings develop, and time runs its course, more and more of these unique American roadside icons are falling by the wayside.

And the next time someone tells you that something is impossible, do as Henry Harrison Mayes did and find your own faith.

## Lasters Art Shack—Crofton

***Both C. M. and Grace Kelly Laster*** hail from rural Kentucky, and both share similar life stories. So it's not surprising that they have found each other and become two of Kentucky's most influential and outlandish folk artists.

Due to dysfunction in their home lives as children, both C. M. and Grace struggled with addiction. C. M. found himself in Chicago in the early '90s, and it was there that he decided to finally get clean. He also experienced a spiritual awakening and a newfound dedication to the world of art. He started Chicago's Recycled Art Project, which took refuse and junk and encouraged kids to turn it into something beautiful. To help in this ambitious undertaking, he enlisted the aid of his old Kentucky friend, Grace Kelly. She joined him in Chicago, and there they toiled away, both staying sober and dedicating themselves to art.

Eventually, while on the job, the two friends fell in love. They decided to marry and move back to Kentucky, where they continued their artistic endeavors. Over the years, the Lasters have dedicated themselves to using art to spread many messages—among them the power of Jesus and the dangers of drugs (based on their own experiences as well as on the death of C. M.'s brother from an overdose).

Now residents of Crofton, the Lasters are immersed in art every day, because they don't just produce artistic works, they live within them. Their workshop is known as Lasters Art Shack. There, the couple has produced hundreds of paintings, sculptures, and other works of art that capture their interests and spit them out at the world. The Art Shack stands on the same property as the Lasters' home, a live-in piece of art they appropriately refer to as the House of Two Million Objects. The couple live here with their daughter, Ruby Elvis. Visitors who come by are blown away by the strange adornments that cover the entire property. The most striking feature of their eclectic house is a painting of Elvis Presley that stands an impressive nine feet tall. This tribute to the King is the centerpiece of an ever-revolving set of artwork that surrounds the house.

Besides the myriad amount of assembled art, the yard features the World's Greatest Outhouse (with an air-cooled seat), Old Hank's Tool Shed, James Brown's Funky Junk Barn, the JunkYardArts project, which changes regularly, and more, depending on when you visit. While most artists restrict themselves to one or two mediums of expression, the Lasters have found ways to use everything to present their art—even the property on which they live.

C. M. and Grace Kelly go further than most in their public artistic pursuits. While most artists of this fashion put their art out for the world to see, the Lasters actively invite the world to come into their art. Visitors who stay with the Lasters often find themselves invited to sleep inside one of the couple's very own creations. On the Laster property stand two rooms where people can stay for short periods—the Itty Bitty Bed and Breakfast and the Outside Inn.

The Itty Bitty Bed and Breakfast is a tiny one-room building that can fit one person, or one person along with his or her pet. Slightly larger than the Itty Bitty is the Outside Inn, a cottage the Lasters built next to their garden. This rustic little cabin has a futon inside, as well as a small table where food can be eaten. The nearby garden offers a fire ring where visitors can brew their own coffee in the morning.

The term "outsider art" gets tossed around a lot, and the Lasters fit the mold. But with not one but two different guest domiciles on their property, the Lasters have to qualify as the most accommodating outsiders in the world.

If the Lasters' home didn't already show their above-and-beyond dedication to folk art, their car should be able to convince anyone. Dubbed the Rockin' Holy Roller, the car has paintings of Jesus on the front, the devil on the back, and in between are images of Johnny Cash, Elvis, Al Green, and a number of other singers. There are, in total, seventy-one pieces of art painted on the surface of the car. Besides visual art, the Rockin' Holy Roller also delivers art of the auditory variety: Gospel music blares from the minivan's intense sound system wherever it goes. The Rockin' Holy Roller has toured the country and been presented in dozens of music, art, and folk festivals throughout the nation.

C. M. and Grace Kelly Laster still teach workshops to children involving recycled art, just as they did back in their Chicago days. With their work, their home, their car, and their tireless devotion, these two visionaries are determined to carry on the best of the folk-art tradition.

# Martin Castle

***One of the most unique properties*** in all Kentucky is the Martin Castle, outside Lexington. The structure is not only unique architecturally, but is the subject of many heart-wrenching stories and myths about its desertion.

Rex Martin had the amazing castle built along U.S. 60 in Versailles during the 1960s. For decades, a legend about how the castle came to be was told so often that it was generally accepted as truth. And like many legends, the truth behind the matter is not so far away from the fiction.

As the story was told, Rex Martin was an eccentric millionaire who fell in love with a woman and promised he'd build a castle for her if she would accept his hand in marriage. The legend says she agreed, and he happily set out to work on a medieval-style structure worthy of his

queen. But as the castle neared completion, the woman got cold feet, and ultimately left him. Heartbroken, desolate, and hopeless, Martin moved to Florida, leaving his castle as it stood, a work in progress set back off a lonely country road. He never completed the building but also couldn't bear to sell the property, even though he was bankrupt. It was the last vestige of his former love, and thus, he tortured himself by keeping it even though, it is rumored, celebrities such as William Shatner and Lee Majors offered huge sums for it. Apparently, love, even the memory of a lost love, was worth no amount of money to the jilted, heartbroken owner of this mysterious place.

The truth is a little less dramatic, although still rooted in a love lost. After Rex Martin and his wife, Caroline, visited Europe in 1969, they returned to Kentucky with an ambitious plan—to build an estate reminiscent of the impressive architecture they had seen on that continent. They planned a home featuring fountains, a tennis court, seven bedrooms, and a whopping fifteen bathrooms. Set on a vast amount of acreage, with the actual house blocked from outside view by a rampart and four turrets, the entire castle complex would look more like something from a Disney fairy tale than anything from reality.

Unfortunately, the fairy tale came crashing down in 1975, when Rex and Caroline decided to get a divorce. In the course of worrying about rebuilding their lives, neither had time to think about finishing their dream house. The couple went their separate ways, and the castle sat abandoned in the Kentucky countryside. It's been that way for decades, and today is a mecca for visitors from far and wide who come to look at the stunning structure and to ponder the story behind it.

Probably the most famous visitor to Martin Castle was no stranger to castle life, England's Queen Elizabeth II. Upon visiting, Her Majesty sized

it up against her own royal digs by declaring it an "Americanized Mickey Mouse Castle."

After Martin's death in 2003, the property became available for the first time. Thomas Post, an attorney in Miami and a University of Kentucky graduate, purchased it for $1.8 million. *Weird Kentucky* had a chance to speak with Mr. Post at that time, and he excitedly talked about his ideas for the place, which ranged from the world's largest bed-and-breakfast to a winery to a cultural showplace for theater productions, live music, and other events.

Unfortunately, on May 10, 2004, an enormous fire consumed the entire castle. According to the Lexington *Herald-Leader,* a local resident said, "It was like a huge fireball. Honestly, it was like something from a huge movie set." The fire must have reminded many of a medieval siege gone wrong. In fact, it was a tragic setback for a dynamic property that had only recently been granted a new lease on life. It is suspected that the blaze was a result of arson, although the motive behind such an act remains unknown. For years before the incident, break-ins and thefts had occurred regularly at the castle, so it was no stranger to crime.

While the burning of the castle is undoubtedly a tragedy, the curiosity, dismay, and ultimately the support that the general public showed in light of the event is an encouraging sign that this magnificent place will ultimately come back to life. Mr. Post is doing his best to make sure that's true. The center structures of the castle are being rebuilt, bigger and better than ever. Mr. Post's dream of finally opening the castle to the public is close to being a reality.

The fantasy building that Rex Martin began has been many things throughout its history: a source of whispered rumors of lost love, an abandoned mystery on a hillside, and the tragic victim of a fire. Now, as time moves forward, this strange, storied castle may finally get a chance to serve as something healthier and happier than all of those: the majestic centerpiece of a community, open to all.

## Wildwood Inn—Florence

***Few industries*** rely on a cookie-cutter formula more heavily than the hotel industry. The differences between rooms at a Days Inn, La Quinta, Red Roof Inn, or any of the other numerous chains are slight and hard to spot. Even higher-end hotels throw few surprises at their visitors, instead relying on tried-and-true nonthreatening formulas that ultimately come off as bland.

Most travelers prefer it this way—why risk a bad night at someplace unpredictable when the old standby formula of bed, bathroom, and television has worked so well for so long? This is not to mention, of course, the effect the movie *Psycho* has had on people's desire to avoid staying in smaller, more individualized, family-run hotels off the beaten path. Best to give in and stay at a chain rather than get discovered by the next Norman Bates.

The owners of Florence's Wildwood Inn have rallied against these attitudes of conformity and fear. Their hotel offers each guest the opportunity to have a completely unique experience in one of their "fantasy suites." These magnificent theme rooms transport the traveler from the roadside not just to comfort, but to an out-and-out alternate reality.

And the Wildwood doesn't go halfway in offering guests these fantasy options. They have not one, not

five, not even ten, but a whopping thirty-one different selections of suites. There are few who can't find their expectations fulfilled in this strange hotel.

Some of the suites are what you might expect: fancy rooms with a romantic bent. The King Spa Room, for example, features a king-sized bed and a heart-shaped Jacuzzi, while the Cupid Room features a red bed with a heart above it, a red couch, and a red Jacuzzi. They're the sorts of rooms you'd expect to find in a place like this. But don't be fooled—the majority of the accommodations here aren't anything predictable. In some cases, they're more than you can probably even imagine.

The Arctic Cave, for example, allows visitors to feel as if they are sleeping inside a block of ice, and they are encouraged to bathe in a warm melting glacial waterfall as part of that process. The bed in the Speedway Suite is checkered, but more importantly, it is surrounded by a number of race cars, all surrounded by a facsimile of stands. This allows hotel patrons to actually feel as if they are sleeping in the middle of a track during a car race. Now there might not be too many of us who harbor a fantasy of sleeping in the middle of a racetrack, but for the minority who do, the Wildwood Inn provides!

Fans of rock climbing and spelunking should rejoice.

You can spend the night in a Tennessee Cave, a Kentucky Cave, a New Mexico Cave, or a Utah Canyon. A night in a tree house or on a safari should whet the appetite of any outdoorsman who happens to be indoors for the night. If you want to visit New York City, you've got two options. Try the patriotic and traditional Statue of Liberty Suite or sleep in Central Park, as many a genuine New York City homeless person has done for decades. If you're a water lover, go for the Nautical Suite. If that's not specific enough for you, there's always the Pirate Ship. The Happy Days Suite takes the visitor back to the idyllic '50s, when everyone slept easier at night anyway.

Staying in some of these suites isn't necessarily easy on the wallet. Some of the rooms are so elaborate that the hotel charges over $200 for a single night's stay—but to live out one's fantasy, this seems like a paltry sum. Traveling to the real New York and sleeping in the real Central Park would cost you more than that in airfare anyway, and you'd have to worry about muggings and the like in the process.

There's something to be said for this very quirky place. We all spend too many nights in drab, plain hotels that offer no variation from the everyday. The Wildwood Inn is on a one-hotel mission to change all that (well, a two-hotel mission if you count their sister location in Gatlinburg, Tennessee). And that's a mission we can all gladly support.

# My Old Kentucky Home Is One Strange Place

***Federal Hill,*** in Bardstown, is the ancestral home of the Rowan family and the purported inspiration behind Kentucky's state song, "My Old Kentucky Home." Stephen Foster, the composer of that famous piece, was a cousin of the Rowan family and was inspired to write the song while visiting Federal Hill. This is documented in dozens of books and brochures on the history of both Kentucky in general and this site in particular.

What those guidebooks leave out in their flowery depictions of Bardstown is the strange relation this house has to the number thirteen. Its structure is linked to the number in dozens of ways: Its walls are thirteen inches thick, ceilings thirteen feet high, the front of the house has thirteen windows, and each floor is separated by thirteen steps. Originally, the home had thirteen rooms. Each landing has thirteen railings, and the home has thirteen earthquake protection bars. There are thirteen mantels spread throughout the place.

The man responsible for this odd numerical obsession was none other than John Rowan, the builder of the house and the patriarch of the Rowan family. A very active politician in the nation's early years, Rowan served in the Kentucky legislature, United States House of Representatives, and the United States Senate.

Some stories say that Rowan infused his house with references to the number thirteen because of his patriotism. His home, these theories say, served as his live-in tribute to the thirteen colonies that originally broke free from British rule. This would make sense for someone with as much love for his country as the politically motivated John Rowan clearly had.

Other stories say that Rowan simply had a personal affinity for the number and considered it a source of good luck. His obsession had nothing to do with politics or patriotism, but more to do with his being convinced that the number would do wonders for his life if only he could work it into his everyday routine.

# Lynn's Paradise Cafe

***You'd have to want*** some serious caffeine in order to take advantage of this eight-foot-tall coffeepot out in the parking lot of Lynn's Paradise Cafe in Louisville. It's big, red, and a working fountain—all key to making it a roadside attraction of its own. But there's a lot more to Lynn's than this pot.

Every city needs a restaurant like Lynn's Paradise Cafe. It's one of the most deliberately and delightfully tacky, garish, loud, colorful, and fun places to eat you could imagine. Who can say it isn't beautiful? Festooned inside and out with hipster folk art, it provides plenty to look at while waiting to be seated and then while waiting for your food. (We recommend their pancakes.)

Lynn's features a huge outdoor cement zoo, with animals that both kids and adults are encouraged to climb upon. Toys are left on tables to be used before, during, and after meals. Dozens upon dozens of lamps are found scattered throughout the restaurant—many of these are participants in the annual World's Ugliest Lamp contest that Lynn sponsors each year at the Kansas State Fair. She brings back the ugliest of the ugly to decorate her café. Perhaps most notably of all, a huge mural made of corncobs makes up one wall—its theme is changed each year, but it's always composed of a number of multicolored corncobs.

The gift shop inside the lobby offers a

selection of strange products and souvenirs, Archie McPhee-style. Cracker Barrel it ain't. Any restaurant owner who's willing to post her macaroni and cheese recipe on her Web site is okay in our book.

White

# Frankfort Avenue Art House

***In the Louisville suburb*** of Clifton stands an amazing house completely encrusted with all manner of bric-a-brac from the twentieth century: statues, skulls, dolls, clowns, signs, toys, antiques, train memorabilia, and artwork.

Generally referred to as the Art House by locals, the place is indeed a work of art and should be protected as a national treasure. Not everyone agrees, unfortunately. We've heard rumors that city officials have made failed attempts in the past to "do something" about the Frankfort Avenue "eyesore." This is where the battle lines between us and them are drawn.

The owner declined to go on record or be interviewed for *Weird Kentucky,* but welcomed us to take all the photographs we liked and to spread the word about his wonderful creation.

# Studies of Studios

***More and more*** these days, a popular "road tripping" experience for many seekers of the weird is to tour the studios of eccentric outsider and folk artists. It just so happens that Kentucky is blessed with a preponderance of them, and all are happy to show their work to curiosity seekers. Interaction with these oddball artists is often just as fascinating and bewildering as their artwork itself, and their studios are always a Cabinet of Dr. Caligari–esque labyrinth of strangeness.

**J. T. Dockery**—Born and raised in the woods of Jackson County, Dockery is one of the most genuine southern-eccentric personalities Kentucky has to offer. Although color blind, he executes colorfully raw and savage paintings in acrylic. He is beset with sometimes agonizing arthritis, but manages to ignore the pain without the use of major pain relievers. He welcomes visitors to his studio in Lexington and often gives them free samples, such as CDs of his surrealist garage bands and his disturbing stream-of-consciousness comic books.

**Kathleen Lolley**—Like a quaint old children's book turned mysterious and foreboding, Kathleen Lolley's paintings are a mythical landscape populated by cute but disturbing creatures, bottles of blood, science experiments, ships, trees, and houses. As have many Kentucky artists, Kathleen has done her stint in the big city (she lived for a time in Los Angeles and did some work for the popular SpongeBob Squarepants animated cartoons), but the magnetic vortex of Kentucky always pulled her back in the end. Lolley's studio is located at a collective shop called Kopilot, on Bonnycastle Avenue in Louisville.

**Minnie Yancey**—This beloved Kentucky folk artist, popular for whittling colorfully painted grinning animals from wood, holds a yearly open house event called A Day in the Country on her rural farm in Isonville.

**Adrian Wright**—A tattoo artist in Brandenburg, Adrian Wright is quickly making a name for himself as a fine artist as well. His colorful paintings dwell on classic horror monster subjects such as Frankenstein, Dracula, the Wolfman, the Creature from the Black Lagoon, Zombies, and Skulls. Not surprisingly, Wright's studio is frequently a pilgrimage destination for hipsters of all ages.

## Cafe 360

***Jefferson County's*** Cafe 360 is adorned with trippy and oddly disturbing murals by Kentucky artist Noah Church. Besides the large amount of art that makes this place unique, it's also the home base of the 360 Party Van, a strangely painted van with an amazing sound system. The café itself doubles as a hookah bar and has spearheaded an antismoking ban movement.

The bar embraces its weird side on its home page, www.cafe-360.com. "American food, with a dash of international flavor. Eclectic art with a touch of the amazing by local artists, Hookah elegance and musical diversity, and internet access. . . . In other words: perfect."

## Ferrell's Metal Man

***This eye-catching*** life-size robotic man, composed primarily of metal ductwork, can be found greeting passersby along Highway 60 in Clay Village. He's the mascot for Ferrell's Air Conditioning and Heating, which operates in a historic old schoolhouse.

## Pink House

***Ask anyone*** in Old Louisville where the Pink House is, and chances are good you'll be directed to this tasty candy-looking bright pink mansion in St. James Court.

Many in this community see the Pink House as a landmark and source of local pride. Others think having a bright pink house plunked down in the middle of an otherwise quaint neighborhood is an eyesore and a distraction. It has stood for years, and the debate rages on.

## The GWAR Car

***What finer tribute*** could you give to the metal band GWAR than to paint its name in big smudgy letters across the side of your car, which you then drive around northern Kentucky? We're sure that this strange band, with its elaborate costumes, space exploring back story, and outlandish concerts, would enjoy a tribute such as this.

## Supersonic Buggy

***A personalized*** "art car" is parked in Butchertown. This strange ride didn't come straight off the assembly line! The Super Sonic Space Buggy Volkswagen is by Scott Scarboro, of the techno-hillbilly band Monkey Boy.

## Gus Ballard's Incredible Backyard

***In the Germantown section*** of Louisville stood one of the most magnificent personalized properties of all time. While it was unfortunately dismantled in the mid-1990s, it's still worth writing about due to the level of infamy this place garnered during its existence.

The home of Gus Ballard, this site looked normal from the street. But those in the know would make their way to the back of Ballard's house, where they were met by a cornucopia of color, mostly in the form of plastic objects.

From large flowers to laundry baskets to thousands of children's toys, there were seemingly endless items nailed to the surface of Ballard's home. Hubcaps and ceiling fans ran around the border of the property, further giving it the appearance of the fantasy of a child on a sugar high.

# A Man's Home Is His Castle

***After Everhart Maupin's wife*** passed away, he decided that rather than just sit and look at the walls of his Lexington home, he'd do something to them. That something was a folk-art wonder that would eventually draw people from all over the country to visit him.

Maupin, a stonemason, covered his wooden home with a brick shell that he painted blue, yellow, and terra-cotta, and he created a low courtyard wall in the front. There were plenty of oozing mortar joints everywhere, which in 1995 he told the Lexington *Herald-Leader* were called "weeping willows" by masons because of the way the mortar ran.

In a 2000 article for the Knight-Ridder *Tribune News,* a reporter noted that the mortar was studded with dolls, a bowling ball, other found objects, and "so many other things that the utility poles and wires out front look like part of the creation." The article went on to say that Maupin's efforts extended to "behind his house and alongside the porch," which was decorated with "the top part of a porch light, cans, buckets. . . ."

Big concrete slabs with University of Kentucky logos adorned the front of the house. The concrete slabs and mortar were pretty much the only things Maupin ever bought. The rest of the items he found along the streets and brought home in his pickup truck.

Maupin started his castlelike creation sometime in the 1980s. At some point, a magazine (he couldn't remember which one) did a story on the house. The publicity it generated increased the number of visitors who came to appreciate his work. Maupin told the *Tribune News,* "I haven't seen anybody who didn't like it."

Maupin became a mason after coming home from World War II. He did work all over the area, including at another *Weird Kentucky* location: the Martin castle on Versailles Road. In 1995, he told the *Herald-Leader,* "I don't know what they're ever going to do with that place. Just like this house here. Seems like I'll never get through."

In November 2001, the *Herald-Leader* reported that there was a fire at Maupin's home, which damaged much of the house and the brick façade. We're assuming that the building survived the fire, but sadly, it no longer exists, at least as Maupin created it. He died in March 2007 at the age of eighty-three, and the house was sold to a new owner a month later. One man's folk-art legacy is gone.

# Claudia Sanders Dinner House

***Colonel Sanders*** may have sold out his fried chicken empire and even his name and likeness in 1964, but he was no dummy. He'd already been laying the groundwork for Sanders 2.0, by way of his wife. Unable to use his own name anymore, he quickly rolled out a new restaurant in Shelbyville marketed under her name, and the Claudia Sanders Dinner House was born!

With all respect to our good friends at Yum! Brands (current marketers of KFC) who have done a fantastic job with the franchise in recent years, it still must be said that the chicken of today isn't necessarily the same formula as it was in the 1950s. But old-timers say that Claudia's chicken still has that good old-fashioned taste, with all seven secret herbs and spices. Mmm mmm, finger lickin' good!

You can get to Claudia's by taking exit 32 off I-64.

## Smitty's Trading Post

***More than any*** other entry in this book, perhaps, this antiques and collectibles store in Frankfort exemplifies what this great state is all about.

Taken individually, many of the items on open-air display out front may or may not dazzle you. But taken as a whole, each bit of bric-a-brac forms a part of an exquisite mosaic, making this no ordinary flea market but a cathedral of discarded Americana, a shrine to the human condition and all its follies and foibles.

It's also like a Rorschach test of aesthetic aptitude. As William Blake said, "The fool sees not the same tree the wise man sees." And not everyone sees the same thing when they gaze at this secondary-market museum of earthly effluvia that the elusive Smitty has nobly archived for the inspection of us all.

We've never actually been able to catch Smitty during business hours, but we'd like to shake his hand for making the Commonwealth of Kentucky a more interesting place to live. Smitty's "junk store as art installation" is far more important than anything found in any art gallery, and for those who listen, Smitty's store tells us volumes about where we've been and where we are headed.

And to think, some see it as nothing more than a yard full of rained-on furniture, rusty farm implements, and fast-food kids' meal toys!

# Roadside Oddities

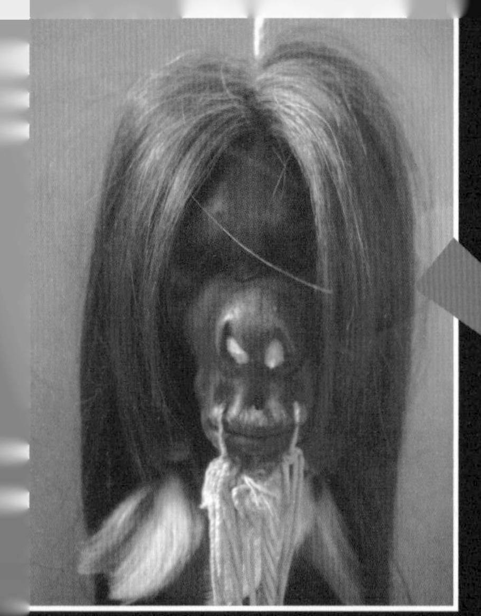

*You want roadside oddities?* The entire state of Kentucky is a roadside oddity. Road tripping through Appalachia isn't just about retro motels and diners. It's about the abstract peculiarities to be found all around us as we travel the highways and byways of our home state.

Want to ride a triceratops that survived the great Flood? See some nightmare-inducing dummies? Contemplate a real shrunken head? Kentucky's got it covered. Or perhaps you'd like to play some Bible-themed miniature golf and then mingle with the coed undead at Transylvania University.

Who needs a visit to Mammoth Cave after all this? In Kentucky, if it's the weird you seek, ye shall be richly re-weirded.

CRY
OUT!

## Museum for Dummies

***Do you experience*** unexplainable tension, anxiety, and fear around a ventriloquist's dummy? If so, how would you feel about three buildings filled with these guys? A place where you are surrounded by miniature humanoid simulacra with flapping mouths, floppy unarticulated limbs, and bulging, staring eyes that burn holes into your very soul at every turn. Sound like fun? Then read on!

Fort Mitchell is proud to be the location of the Vent Haven Ventriloquism Museum: the world's only museum dedicated to the noble art of throwing your voice and making it seem to have emanated from a small, corpselike doll sitting on your lap. The place will overwhelm you with its jaw-dropping array of dummies and give you a crash course in this enduring vaudevillian tradition.

Charlie McCarthy—probably the world's most famous ventriloquism dummy—is here. So is Paul Winchell's Knucklehead Smiff, Farfel the Dog (from the '50s-era Nestlé's commercials), and Gutters, the alcoholic dummy.

Also appearing is the dummy who started it all: Tommy Baloney, a Billy Childish–looking figure with a deerstalker cap and a smugly enigmatic smile. Museum founder W. S. Berger's collection began with Tommy Baloney in 1910.

The most horrifying-looking dummy is called Granny. She really does resemble a rather ossified elderly woman, albeit in miniature. Made in 1850, she was fitted with a device that made her capable of smoking cigarettes by herself.

If wooden dummies don't sufficiently creep you out, consider this: In ancient Egypt and Greece, ventriloquism began as a necromantic practice. It was believed that through concentration, skilled practitioners could summon up the actual voices of the dead, speaking through them (rather like New Age "channeling" today). But by the superstitious medieval ages, ventriloquism was considered tantamount to witchcraft. Only with the advent of vaudeville and burlesque did the modern-day idea of ventriloquism as entertainment take root.

Each summer Vent Haven holds a "conVENTion" at Fort Mitchell's Drawbridge Inn. It's the world's largest and longest-continuing gathering of ventriloquists, be they professional, amateur, or aspiring. It provides continual encouragement for the followers of this arcane practice and ensures ventriloquists a place in generations to come.

Vent Haven Ventriloquism Museum is located at 33 West Maple Avenue, Fort Mitchell, in Kenton County. It's open to the public by appointment; the recommended admission fee is $5. (But don't be a dummy: Give a little more if you can spare it; they've got a smokin' Granny to support.)

## Getting a Head (and More) Here

***Next time*** you're in the vicinity of Covington, head on over to the Behringer-Crawford Museum. Small but amazing, it features all sorts of natural wonders and curiosities. There's a hairball taken from the stomach of a cow, a striking two-headed calf in all its taxidermic glory, a giant elk, and a stuffed specimen of the now extinct miniature breed of English terrier.

What really packs 'em in, however, is the museum's exhibit of a real shrunken human head. Such heads seem to be only in the hands of private collectors or museums these days, so take advantage of this rare opportunity to see eye to eye with a legitimate freak of nature.

The museum is located at 1600 Montague Road in Covington. It was expanding both space- and exhibit-wise at the time *Weird Kentucky* was being written, so before you show up, make sure to give them a call to find out what's open.

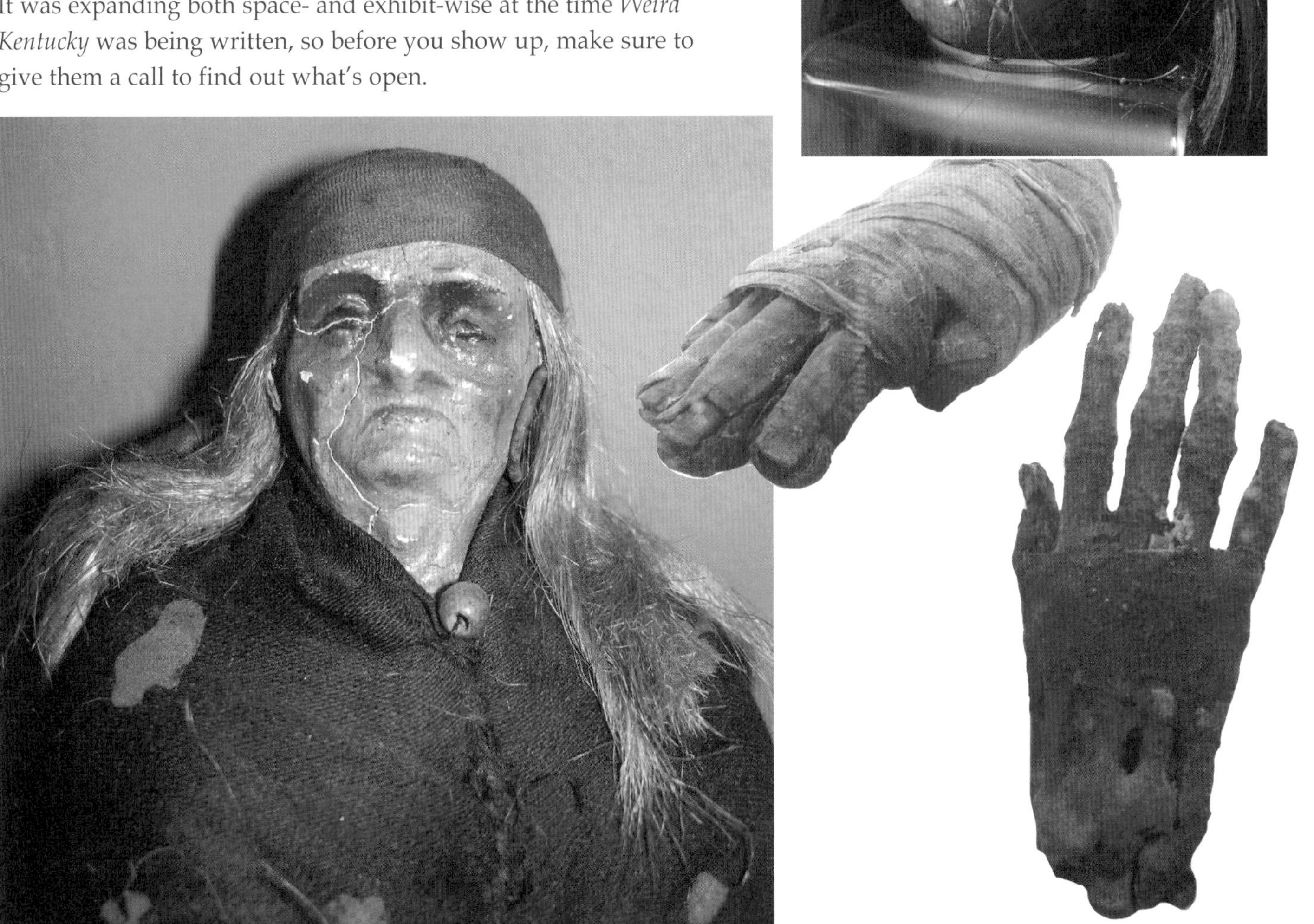

# Darwin Beware: The Creation Museum

***In the summer of 2007,*** the world's news media were abuzz about Kentucky's latest dubious achievement: the biblical Creation Museum in Petersburg. Here's a museum that presents a literal interpretation of the Old Testament Book of Genesis as absolute truth, alleging that geologists, anthropologists, and paleontologists are wrong about practically everything science suggests about evolution. According to its Web site, "The Creation Museum presents a 'walk through history.' Designed by a former Universal Studios exhibit director, this state-of-the-art 60,000 square foot museum brings the pages of the Bible to life."

This fundamentalist viewpoint makes for a fascinating—if confusing—journey, all for a mere $19.95 admission fee ($14.95 for seniors, $9.95 for children).

Among the controversial information set forth in the museum's exhibits:

- The earth is only a few thousand years old, not 4.5 billion.
- Adam and Eve are presented as Caucasian.
- Dinosaurs were in the Garden of Eden and made it onto Noah's ark. They not only survived the biblical Flood, but coexisted with humans, who could fit them with saddles and ride them like horses (ye ha!).
- Internet pornography and abortion are a direct result of believing that the earth is millions of years old.

Although much of the museum's presentation is done in a pseudo-scientific fashion, there are little or no reputable source citations provided for its claims. Some assertions don't even make internal sense, and non sequiturs such as "a single ash cloud cools the Earth a fraction of a degree" are presented apropos of nothing.

An article in the *Cincinnati Enquirer* reported that employees at the Creation Museum are required to sign a statement attesting to their unwavering belief in the teachings of the Answers in Genesis Ministry, the organization that founded the museum. This includes such statements as "no apparent, perceived or claimed evidence in any field, including history and chronology, can be valid if it contradicts the Scriptural record."

During the course of the tour, *Weird Kentucky* spent just as much time observing the museumgoers as the exhibits themselves—they seemed to be there to marvel at the strangeness of it all. Whatever you believe, one thing is certain: These folks have gone to enormous lengths to pursue their vision, and spent $27 million to sculpt their own version of creation and reality. For that audacity and self-determination alone, we say more power to them. As the old German cabaret song goes: *I'm all through with logical conclusions; / Why should I deny myself illusions?*

Moses

## Road Fair

***The Kentucky State Fair,*** held each summer at the Kentucky Exhibition Center in Lexington, has an old-school rural charm replete with 4-H awards, vast displays of corn and hay, and absolutely no reason for going other than for the sake of looking at corn and hay, sheepshearing, goat-shaving, cow-polishing, and pig-racing.

However, there are sights within the fair for those who appreciate roadside attractions, though you'll have to pay for parking and admission to see them. Like the immense seated (and talking) statue of Freddy Farm Bureau. He has entertained the masses every year in much the same way that the Muffler Man "Big Tex" entertains the crowds at the Texas State Fair.

Freddy got his start as a promotional "insurance man" statue for Kentucky Farm Bureau Insurance, but he's become a beloved statewide institution who has literally taken on a life of his own. He "speaks" to passersby through a hidden speaker and is always referred to as a living person in the media and even in casual conversation among locals. When *Weird Kentucky* first started to take photos of Freddy, he said, "Oh, can you take that again? I think I blinked." Wonder if he has a good side?

And then there's the portable ice-cream stand that sets up its sweet business every year at the fair. The "cone" is metal (try selling ice cream from inside a metal enclosure in 102-degree heat), and the soft-serve part of the structure is an inflated balloon that wobbles in the wind, creating a surreal but soothing sight.

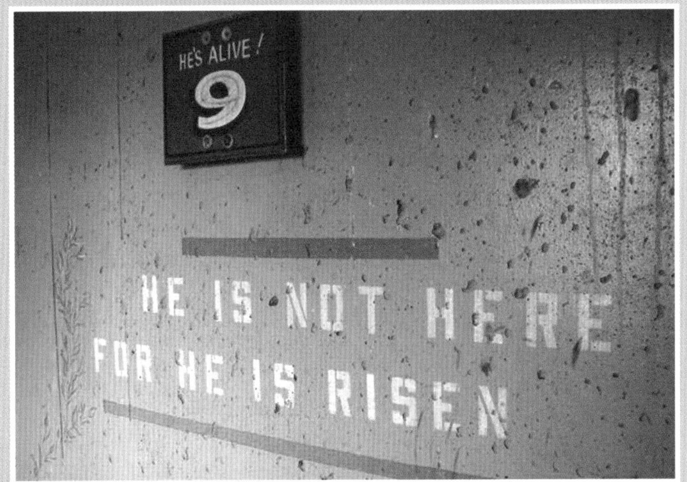

## Golfing with God in Lexington

***You're dying*** to spread the Gospel to the youth of today, but all the tried-and-true outreach methods just don't seem to be getting through to these punks. In a moment of deep contemplation, you ask yourself, What would Jesus do? And then the answer comes to you in a brilliant flash of insight: Of course, open a miniature golf course!

That's the revelation that one man in Lexington had, anyway. Since 1988, his Bible-themed putt-putt attraction at the Lexington Ice Center & Sports Complex has astounded, mystified, and anointed many an impressionable miniature golf enthusiast. It offers fifty-four holes of educational-like info-tainment, taking you on a green-felted journey through the Bible.

Each of the first seven holes represents the seven days of creation, and since God rested on the seventh day, the seventh hole is a gimmie. But the final holes represent the miracles of Jesus and are therefore extremely difficult.

More disturbing is Jesus' tomb, which you have to play through. We're told that there used to be a recording of Jesus' voice talking to you while you putted in his tomb, but it can no longer be heard. It was probably too distracting for the golfers. When Alexandra Pelosi came here to interview the owner for her documentary *Friends of God,* he said that this was the part of the course he was most proud of.

The center's Web site states that it strives "to create a Christ-like atmosphere." We're not entirely certain what that means, especially in this context.

All ribbing aside, as miniature golf courses go, this truly is one of the best in the nation. A lot of thought and creativity went into the planning and execution of each of the holes, and even the most jaded and seasoned professional miniature golfer will find himself challenged by the miracle holes, especially putting the Red Sea.

# Golgotha Fun Park, R.I.P.

***Kentucky's*** other biblically themed miniature golf place for the pious putter was Golgotha Fun Park in Cave City. Unfortunately, however, according to a recent report from *Weird Kentucky* reporter Debra Jane Seltzer, the attraction has been closed and for sale since around 2001. In 2007, it was announced that the property would be transformed into a dinner theater and, ironically, a haunted mine attraction.

Golgotha's first eighteen holes represented the Old Testament, while the other eighteen showed Christ's toughest miracles. (In the Bible, Golgotha was the hill where Jesus was crucified.) The holes were very tricky due to steep hills and other natural hazards. The difficulty of the course probably discouraged repeat business as well.

## Southeast's Religious Billboards

***When you get down*** to southeast counties like Estill, Lee, and Wolfe, there's a curious and delightful phenomenon there: The roadside billboards are often three-dimensional, with the lettering and graphics being cut from wood or foam and applied to the board.

Not only is this low-budget way of advertising charming and unique, it's also really handy for when you want to change your billboard's message. You can just rearrange the appliquéd letters as you would those plastic letters some people have on their refrigerators. The letters are usually nailed on with just one or two protruding thin finishing nails so as to be easily pulled out for the next advert.

Our favorites are the highly eye-catching religious billboards. Their messages change often and can range from the merely puzzling to the positively impenetrable. A particularly favorite example was an election-time posting several years ago that said GOD VOTES FOR MEN OF GOD.

## Back to the Grind

***It's easy to imagine*** that some patrons of Bondurant's Pharmacy in Lexington may feel a little off before picking up their prescriptions from its convenient drive-through window. Not many would guess that the building's shape—a giant mortar and pestle—is an example of mimetic architecture. That's a fancy phrase for "it does what it looks like." You see, a mortar and pestle were once a pharmacist's most used tools. Like Lexington's old root beer stand shaped like a giant mug of root beer (long since torn down), it's nice to have this lovely piece of distinct architecture around.

Bondurant's was the first drive-through pharmacy in Lexington, and according to www.bondurants.com the man behind the building was Joe Bondurant, who got the idea after visiting Las Vegas in the early 1970s ('nuff said!). It can be found at 1465 Village Drive.

## Transylvania University

***It scarcely makes locals blink an eye,*** but outsiders are generally stunned to find out that a university with such a name exists. Lesser known is the fact that some people originally wanted to call Kentucky Transylvania. A large portion of Kentucky (as well as part of Virginia) was briefly called Transylvania when founded as a colony in 1775 by Richard Henderson. Transylvania does have an ominous ring to it, but its literal meaning is really quite benign: trans meaning "across" and sylvania meaning "woods," so Transylvania means "across the woods."

Henderson's short-lived colony was already defunct by the time the university was completed (opened first in Danville in 1780, then moved to Lexington in 1789), but the name remained. Today most Kentuckians call it Transy for short.

Transy's gift shop does a bustling business with vampiric-minded visitors, and it's alleged that the university's attorneys once had to send a cease-and-desist letter to a West Coast manufacturer of gag gifts who had created a gothic-fronted and blood-spattered TRANSYLVANIA UNIVERSITY T-shirt, completely unaware that such a college actually existed!

Discover a natural place like Mammoth Cave and the roadside attractions will pile up near it just like bat guano (but nicer, of course). Nearby Cave City is resplendent with many places where you can pile up on your kitsch fix.

## Sleep in a Wigwam!

***So says the sign*** in front of the Wigwam Village Inn #2 on the Dixie Highway. Technically, these structures are teepees—wigwams are actually dome-shaped. But we'll use the term "wigwam" since that's what Frank A. Redford, their creator, called them. There were seven of these Wigwam Villages built in the Southeast and Southwest between 1937 and 1949. Only three of these remain today (Cave City, KY; Holbrook, AZ; and Rialto, CA).

Redford's fascination with Native American culture began when he was just a boy. After traveling out west and becoming inspired by different teepee establishments, Redford returned home to Kentucky to build a wigwam restaurant in Horse Cave, where he also housed his huge collection of Native American artifacts. In 1933, he decided to add fifteen teepee-shaped cabins for tourists. This would become the model for the six other Wigwam Villages. Unfortunately, Wigwam Village #1 was torn down in 1981, but a Wigwam Gulf station still stands across the street as a reminder.

The village layout had the largest wigwam as office-restaurant-souvenir shop with gas pumps out in front. To the side of the main wigwam were two smaller wigwams as restrooms, labeled BRAVES and SQUAWS. The cabin wigwams were laid out around these in a semicircle. Each cabin was about twenty-five feet in diameter and had two diamond-shaped windows. Swastikas, an Indian symbol, were painted on the tops of the wigwams, but they were painted over during World War II because Hitler used the swastika symbol. The cabin interiors were ten-sided and decorated in southwestern style with tiled baths, hickory bark, and cane furniture. Indian blankets were used as bedspreads, and Indian rugs were placed on the floors.

Redford patented his Wigwam Village concept in 1936 and built his second one in 1937 in Cave City. The main wigwam housed Redford's collection of Indian artifacts.

New owners in the 1990s stripped the museum and rooms of their Indian relics and auctioned them off through Sotheby's. The motel was then put on the market and purchased by a local preservationist who restored the property.

The central wigwam is fifty-two feet high. Advertisements in the 1940s bragged about its being "the largest wigwam in the world." It originally contained a restaurant and gift shop, but in the mid-1960s the restaurant closed. The fifteen cabin interiors have been restored with hickory and cane furniture. Each cabin has a bathroom, air-conditioning, and color TV, but like a real wigwam, no phone.

*—Debra Jane Seltzer*

## Experience Rocktical Illusions

***An ancient creature*** sits in front of Big Mike's Mystery House, and it's not a tourist. It's a replica of the extinct mosasaur nicknamed Big Mo, which looks like a combination of a monitor lizard, alligator, and porpoise. There's a fossil of it somewhere at Big Mike's, hence its concrete presence out front.

Mike's is billed as Kentucky's largest rock shop, but the Mystery House has other delights for the adventurous. Visitors are encouraged to walk up walls and perform other seemingly impossible, gravity-defying feats. And there's an optical illusion room where you and a friend can take turns at appearing bigger or smaller for the camera. All this fun for just a buck for grownups, fifty cents for kids. If you're itching to defy gravity, Mike's place is at 566 Old Mammoth Cave Road.

## Scamper with Dinosaurs

***You can't have*** a roadside mecca without a dinosaur or two, and Dinosaur World fits the bill nicely. You can even see some of the dinosaurs lurking in the Kentucky woods and fields as you come off the Cave City exit from Interstate 65. Around one hundred dinosaurs of both the bluegrass and meat-eating varieties loom over visitors as they walk along paths on the grounds.

## Burlesque Dancers and Country Ham

***Guntown Mountain*** is a Cave City Wild West attraction that has some historical claim to its shtick. It's located near where Jesse James, who spent a lot of time in Kentucky, maintained a hideout. Smith's Country Store is actually a real general store that predates the theme park, having existed on the site since 1906.

Gunfights are reenacted in the streets of Guntown Mountain, and "authentic" western entertainment can be found in the saloon. (Who knew they had steel guitars and "illusionist" magicians in the Old West!)

In a way, it's unfortunate that Guntown Mountain is located so close to Mammoth Cave, because both attractions are best enjoyed as all-day excursions. If you travel any significant distance to come to Kentucky specifically for the purpose of visiting Mammoth Cave, take some time out and head over to Guntown Mountain as well. Even if you think you don't care about cowboy-themed entertainment, the Miss Kitty–esque burlesque dancers and the tasty country ham are worth the side trip.

## Crestwood Radiator

***A frightening sign*** for an automotive repair shop in Oldham County, done in the vein of R. Crumb's underground comics.

## Coca-Cola Spaceship

***A lovely example*** of 1950s architecture, this Coca-Cola plant in Fayette County looks for all the world like a gleaming UFO.

## Rooster Run's Cock of the Walk

***Rooster Run*** is a small community in Nelson County that's built up a reputation over the years as a must-visit Kentucky destination. Why? Well . . . just because, that's why.

There really isn't much in Rooster Run, in fact, but there's a great general store that contains a sort of Rooster Run museum in the back—lots of newspaper clippings and items of historical interest, and an extensive line of souvenirs.

Among these souvenirs, the baseball caps have been extremely popular, and some would cite these caps as what has propelled Rooster Run into the meta-consciousness of the nation. For some reason, the hats, bearing the image of a chicken with the words Rooster Run, have struck a resonant chord in hundreds of thousands of people who have ordered and worn said hat even if they've never been to Kentucky at all.

Most popular with us, however, is the giant fiberglass chicken statue that welcomes citizens to Rooster Run. There's a whole subculture of people who obsess over giant chicken statues—hey, someone's got to do it! The Rooster Run giant chicken wears a kerchief, but not a hat. Similar blue-kerchiefed chickens have been identified in Atlanta and in Pigeon Forge, TN, but they wear cowboy hats, making the Rooster Run specimen unique according to researchers of giant fiberglass fowl.

Historically, it's said the place got its name from having once been a watering hole for men—roosters—to run to and party. (And, sometimes, run from the angry wives who were looking for them.) Although Rooster Run never had a post office and was never registered with the government as an actual town, it has come to be so recognized in recent years and now even appears on many state maps.

## One Mother of a Goose

***The people*** of Hazard aren't sure why George Stacy chose this fowl motif for his home, but they are certainly proud of it. According to the hazardkentucky.com Web site, he didn't even have an affinity for geese. His wife said he just came up with the idea for a home shaped like a goose one day. A live goose was sacrificed to figure out its bone structure for building purposes, and construction proceeded, lasting from 1935 to 1940. The Stacys lived in the house for years and later added a store onto it. Mother Goose serves as a private residence today.

## World's Largest Baseball Bat

***Another surreal*** "world's largest" claim for Kentucky! We had no idea this monumental baseball bat even existed until we happened to run into it on Main Street in Louisville. No photograph can do it justice: Until you've been there, you can't know what it's like to be at the foot of a baseball bat that's as tall as a building.

The bat, a giant replica of Babe Ruth's famous Louisville Slugger, which he popularized in the 1920s, is over 120 feet tall, which is taller than the five-story building it leans against: the Louisville Slugger Museum and Factory.

The museum itself is definitely worth checking out, so don't just stand outside and gawk. The Louisville Slugger has been a baseball standard since 1884, and there's a lot of history here. You can even check out the colossal baseball mitt that's located inside.

Farther down the street you'll find Caufield's Novelty Shop, which created its own answer to the Slugger Museum's bat: the world's largest vampire bat. This bat hangs upside-down on the exterior wall of Caufield's building, and its eyes glow red at night!

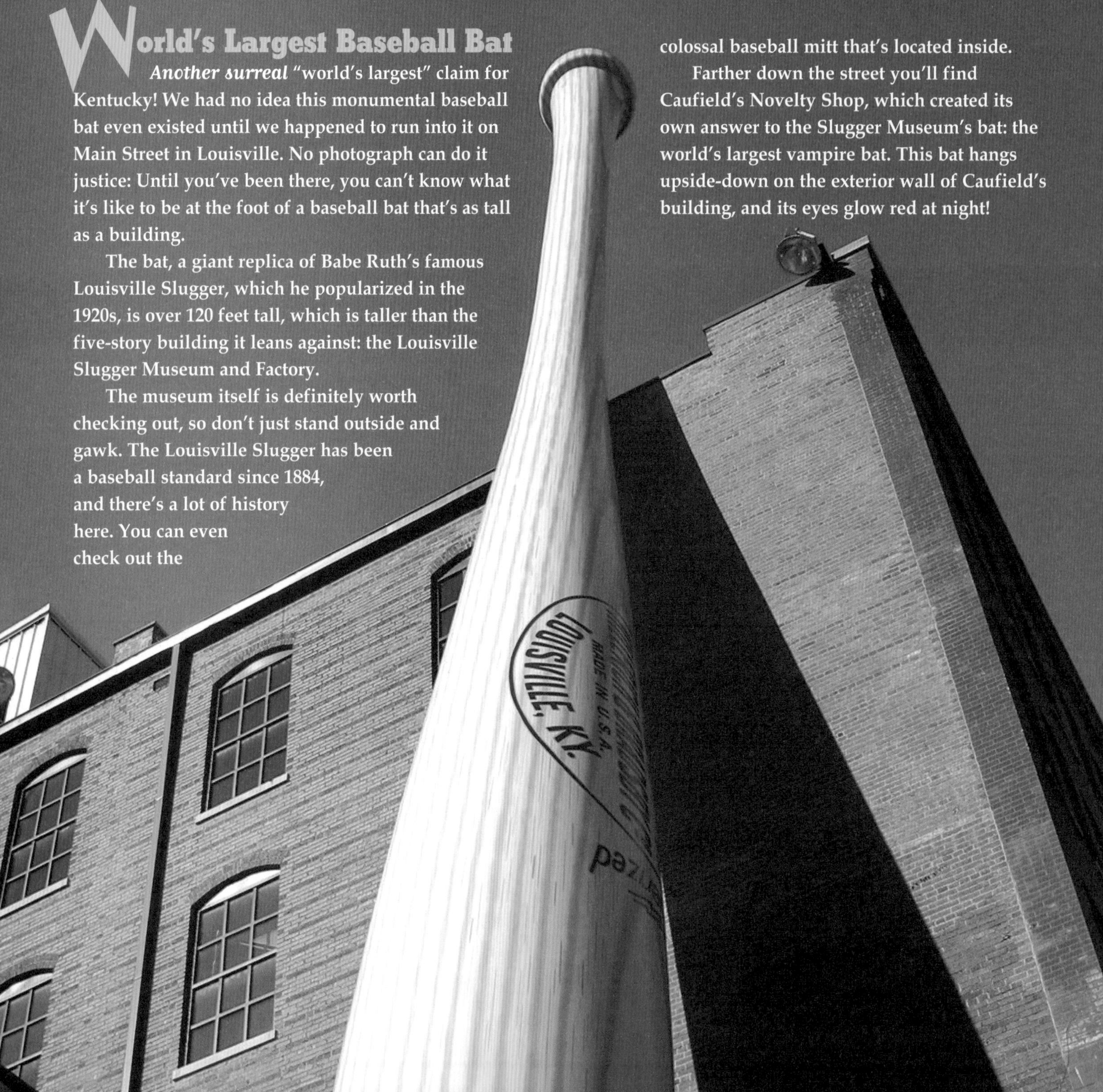

## Ollie's Trolley

***During its heyday*** in the 1970s, Ollie's Trolley chain of burger stands numbered in the hundreds and dotted Kentucky and surrounding states. Today very few survive, but there's still one in Louisville at 978 South Third Street. Along with Bondurant's Pharmacy in Lexington (also built in the '70s), Ollie's is part of the final vestiges of the great twentieth-century wave of American mimetic architecture.

The Ollie's chain was the brainchild of John Y. Brown, the politician who bought out Colonel Sanders and his Kentucky Fried Chicken empire. Brown clearly thought he had a sure thing here: small kiosks designed to resemble trolley cars, offering "gourmet" cheeseburgers cooked rare and slathered in a mysterious sauce instead of the traditional ketchup and mustard. Alas, it just didn't catch on, and today the few remaining Ollie stands have tweaked the menu somewhat since the early years.

But are the burgers any good? Emphatically, yes. We recommend the Ollie Burger with bacon.

## You're Not in D.C. Anymore

***An anonymous*** *Weird* fan tipped us off to one of those strange "Where am I, again?" experiences you can have while driving along Highway 68 East outside Fairview. A gigantic obelisk looms over the gently rolling hills in the area, and you'd swear for a moment that you were seeing the Washington Monument in D.C. But you aren't.

Fairview is the birthplace of Confederate president Jefferson Davis, and it is his towering monument at which you are gazing. At 351 feet, it is two thirds the height of the Washington Monument and is otherwise—at least on the outside—an exact replica. It was built by the Daughters of the Confederacy and finished in 1924.

# Tombstone Junction

***It took not one,*** but two fires to destroy Tombstone Junction, a Wild West–themed amusement park outside Corbin. It's gone, but remains branded into the memories of those who experienced it.

Oddly enough, Tombstone has an unusually strong following today, especially among railroad buffs, because of the actual functioning steam trains and tracks that were part of the park. They weren't little kiddie trains or trolleys; they were the real deal.

Karl Lusk, retired executive director of the Kentucky Railway Museum, told *Weird Kentucky* that there "were two small steam switch engines, with cars that were converted from either flatcars or cabooses" and "another locomotive, a larger switch engine from the Morehead and North Fork Railroad in Rowan County."

Live-action performances of gunfights and train holdups were constantly held on the grounds, with actors who never broke character and helped to convince one and all that they were in a genuine Old West town, although the presence of electricity (especially the PA system used by the modern country bands that would perform there) sort of detracted from that.

Rumors and contradictory stories about the demise of the place abound. There were reports that someone used an acetylene torch to attempt to salvage steel from the old wooden rail cars, which caused the second fire. Karl Lusk said this wasn't accurate and that most of the cars survived the second fire. Some buildings, including the shop building for the railroad, also remained. All the railroad equipment, including the locomotive engines, was auctioned off in 1996, but the cars were in bad repair and likely scrapped.

You can still visit the spot where Tombstone Junction once stood, and many do, even though there's really nothing there to see. A growing number of people have talked about the possibility of bringing it back. If so, it would be great to see this junction rise from its tombstone.

## Mystery Blasting Sign

***In the hills of Knott County*** this BLASTING ZONE sign has been a source of befuddlement among locals for several years now.

Why? Well, as far as can be seen, there is no blasting work going on here and never has been. No construction site. No roadwork. No quarrying. No nothing.

And yet this sign has not only remained here for years, it's seemingly permanent, mounted on steel posts in the ground like any other road sign.

One person suggested it's about blasting going on underground for construction of secret subterranean military tunnels and bunkers. The more likely explanation isn't so exciting. It was probably just a simple mistake that's slipped through the cracks of bureaucracy, which someone's forgotten and/ or been too lazy to fix. (Still, the secret CIA tunnels are not an unreasonable theory.)

## Roadside Memorial Markers

***The tradition*** of erecting a roadside memorial marker began in the South, and Kentucky was one of the first states to take it up. Grieving friends and relatives place some sort of marker by the side of the road near where a loved one died in a car accident.

Some particularly bad stretches of road are so dotted with these sad memorials that they reinforce the danger of the location. We don't know for a fact that anyone has died because his attention was diverted from a bad curve while checking out a roadside memorial, but odds are it has happened.

Some argue that the memorials are a public nuisance that should be removed quickly. Others feel that families have a perpetual stake in these spots. When it comes to accidents, where a loved one died can be far more important and powerful than where they're buried.

To some, it may seem grisly and macabre to document them, but these memorials are not much different than tombstones. And regardless of how one rationalizes one's interest, they are quite fascinating and speak a lot more about the human condition than any cemetery.

## Museum Plaza

***This futuristic*** skyscraper doesn't exist—yet. But by the time you hold this book in your hands, dear reader, the Museum Plaza construction will be under way.

Designed by the acclaimed architect Joshua Prince-Ramus, this avant-garde structure will soon change the face of the Louisville skyline. Its shape resembles a giant letter H with a square protrusion coming off the side, and it has a diagonally angled elevator shaft that is external to the building. Although its peculiar and radical architecture puzzled many locals at first, the design ultimately won their hearts and minds.

The space-age edifice will contain museums, artist studios and galleries, shops, offices, condos, and restaurants, making Museum Plaza an amazing place for the area's artists to live, work, and play.

Once completed, Museum Plaza will be the tallest building in Kentucky and taller than any in many midwestern and southern states as well.

*Old Forester bottle in Louisville.*

*The* Clasped Hands *stands in front of the Insight Training Group building in Louisville.*

*Cardinal Motel, Bowling Green.*

*This tin teepee is a former gas station attendant's booth in Hilltop.*

# Roads Less Traveled

Normal people buy a map, get into the car, and stick to the biggest, brightest, most logical roads of choice. Simply put, this gets them where they want to go as fast as possible. It's sensible behavior—but sensible is often not fun.

Weirdos, on the other hand, know that it's not the destination but the journey that counts.

For most Americans, passing through Kentucky along I-75 is their sole experience traveling within the state. That's a shame, because a beautiful and bewildering world, more surreal than any imagined on *Green Acres*, lies just off the beaten path, not far from any exit. To find the truly interesting places in life, one must look for the unpaved, rocky terrain that we call the roads less traveled. The stories that drift around on lonely streets and avenues are oftentimes the most amazing tales you'll ever hear. You've just got to be willing to hit the brakes long enough to hear them. We encourage all weird travelers to take their time, make random turns, and find the roads less traveled.

## Crybaby Lane

***In the woods*** behind my grandparents' Kentucky farm was a prime horse trail I usually rode with my teenaged uncle. The trail followed, for a mile or so, some power line towers, then turned away from the towers and wandered back into the woods. After a while, we'd spill out of the woods onto a godforsaken stretch of dusty dirt road named Rebel Ridge.

Rebel Ridge was a failed attempt to bring a housing development to the area, but there were only a couple of sad, run-down doublewides stuck out there in yards that were more like unkempt fields. It was at best a wide dirt path that cut through unused pasture land and was surrounded by woods.

The trail dead-ended after about half a mile, but there was one place that kept us coming back: a short trail off to one side called Crybaby Lane. It was a dismal trail, lined with trees that grew at awkward angles, like crooked fangs exploding from the gums of some horrible beast's gaping maw. The branches arced toward the sky, then plunged earthward again into what looked like bony, knobby claws just waiting to pluck you out of the saddle.

**Satanists took the babies when their parents' backs were turned. Then they'd drive out to the county line, hike back to the pond, and sacrifice the innocents to Satan by drowning them in its waters.**

And then there was the pond itself, at the trail's end. The water was black, seemingly unable to absorb any of the light above it. No wind caused a ripple or wave. Just black. "You know why they call this Crybaby Lane?" my uncle asked, in a way that told me I'd probably be better off not knowing. Which meant I had to know, so he shared the story with me right there by the pond.

Back in the 1950s, Oldham County was plagued by a rash of kidnappings. Babies—newborns to about age two—were disappearing, and the police were stumped. It turns out that a group of Satanists were involved. They took the babies when their parents' backs were turned, in parks, or right from their cribs in the middle of the night. Then they'd drive out to the county line down near Butler, hike back to the pond, and sacrifice the innocents to Satan by drowning them in its waters.

This went on for a while, until one night when the Satanists were at the pond, a storm blew in. Most of them called it a night, but two stayed behind to clean up, just in case a hunter stumbled upon the place and got suspicious about charred inverted crosses and piles of old cloaks.

It started to rain hard, and the guys were almost finished when one caught his cloak on something along the pond's bank. He tried to pull the cloak loose, but it was stuck fast. When he reached back to unhook himself, he felt cold, clammy flesh. In a flash of lightning he could see it was an arm: a baby's arm, caked with pond scum, emerging from the water and holding onto his cloak.

He stumbled back and screamed, yanking himself free but also slipping and falling face first in the mud. He turned over and wiped the muck from his face, only to see in the next flash of lightning dozens of babies crawling out of the water and wallowing through the mud toward him. He screamed for his friend, who had noticed what was happening but was frozen with fear a few feet away.

As the babies reached the fallen Satanist, they began screaming and shrieking and crying. They grabbed the Satanist's feet and dragged him into the water. The last thing the other devil worshipper ever saw of his friend was his face, which was contorted in terror as tiny little fingers clawed at it and pulled him beneath the black surface of the pond.

The surviving Satanist stumbled into the county sheriff's office at 5:00 a.m., wearing a cloak and ranting about how a bunch of vengeful dead babies just dragged his friend into a pond. The police thought he was nuts, but they investigated. When they dragged the bottom of the pond with a net, they found the body of the Satanist, as well as dozens of pieces of ragged children's clothing, but that was it. They never found any of the kidnapped babies' bodies that had been allegedly thrown into the water.

The Satanist stood trial for the murder of his friend as well as for multiple kidnappings. He could never finger any of the other Satanists because they all went by code names. He was incarcerated in the Luther Luckett Correctional Facility's ward for the criminally insane, where he lived with a lifelong fear of water and toddlers.

**My uncle told me that if you listened real close on moonless nights, you could still hear those babies howling and crying.**

It didn't matter to me that there was no record of a wave of baby murders for which a lone, raving Satanist was imprisoned, or that a small-town guy wouldn't know who his fellow Satanists were. That can all be explained away with stories of media cover-ups and attempts to protect local families. What did matter was that my uncle told me that if you listened real close on moonless nights, you could still hear those babies howling and crying. And if you were unlucky enough to be in the area, especially during a storm, they'd come up from the pond's bottom and pull you in with them.

After my uncle made like he was going to throw me in a couple times, we rode on. I vowed never to return anywhere near Crybaby Lane, but of course, a few weeks later I took some friends there, told them the story and made like I was going to push them into the water. We all laughed until we realized it had become silent at the pond, broken only by the occasional frog croak or sudden chorus of grasshoppers. We hauled ass away from the water as fast as we could without looking like we were scared.

Years passed and my grandfather eventually sold the farm. I forgot about Crybaby Lane, until I was a junior in high school and fell hard for a girl I'll call "J." I found out she lived on Rebel Ridge, which must have been built up in the years since I'd been there. When I told her the grisly story, her mouth twisted into a sly smile and her beautiful, dark eyes brightened. "You know what we have to do?"

I did, and it pained me to think about it. We were going to spend the next new moon night on Crybaby Lane.

The afternoon of our campout was cloudy and overcast, but rather than being dark, the whole world was cast in a sickly silver light. When we arrived at the trail, the light grew increasingly ashen, and the trees seemed a lifeless brownish-gray. "It didn't seem this freaky the other day," I heard J say.

We set up camp on the banks of the pond with two companions: a stoner guy named Scott and his girlfriend. We built a little fire, passed around a couple of cans of beer and generally had a good time. Even when I trotted out the story of Crybaby Lane to remind everyone why we were there that night, it didn't seem as horrifying as it did quaint.

Campfire dying, beer exhausted, and the mood properly set, J and I excused ourselves to our tent. Time passed well, and I was thinking everything about the night had turned out perfect.

Then I froze. The woods, which had been filled with the sounds of the fauna in the area, had gone completely silent.

"You awake?" I heard J whisper to me. "It's so quiet out tonight."

"Yeah, I was noticing that."

And then it wasn't quiet any more. There was a tremendous plop as something leapt into the pond. And then another plop. And then a third. I did my best to remain calm, but I could tell that J had gone rigid lying next to me.

I could hear Scott and his girlfriend whispering to one another in their tent.

"Scott, you awake?" I said in that strained manner I guess you would call yelling in a whisper.

"Did you just hear that?" his voice called back.

"Probably frogs," I said.

There was another splash, and then a weak gust of wind that carried on it the foul smell of death. It may have just been sulfur, but isn't Hell supposed to smell like sulfur?

Then I heard footsteps in the dry bed of leaves that coated the ground. J and I did our best to get dressed without making a sound, as if that would fool anyone into thinking our tent was empty. The footsteps got louder, and I put my hand on the hilt of my folding camping knife.

Whatever was there was right outside our tent, shuffling through the leaves. Then something brushed against the thin fabric of the tent. It was low to the ground, just about baby height. And it wasn't alone. There were several somethings out there, and I could hear them scrounging about and splashing in the water.

One of the somethings let out a terrible, inhuman yip, and though I'd heard that yip before, years ago, and other ones answering in the woods, my mind snapped right then and there into a determined, if not entirely sane, decision. I grabbed J's hand tight and leaned close to her.

"We're getting out of here. Together."

If she disagreed, she didn't voice it loud enough for me to notice.

A something now leaned against the tent and left a couple of imprints in the nylon that looked to be just the perfect size for baby hands. They were up a little too high, but that didn't matter at this point.

"Scott!" I yelled suddenly. "Get the hell to the car now!"

The four of us tumbled out of our tents and ran blindly down the trail at top speed, dove into the car, and collapsed, out of breath and completely free of wits.

Whatever had been at our campsite either didn't follow us, or was maintaining a wary distance. I heard what I thought was just me laughing half-hysterically. And then I realized it wasn't me at all. It really was the woods, or something in them, laughing at us in high-pitched, raspy yelps.

We ended the night driving to our friend's house and spent about an hour banging on her window before she opened it up and let us in. Our tents and assorted gear sat back at the pond for three days before we went back to collect them.

I hear Crybaby Lane is nothing more than a memory now, a victim of human expansion. There are no more ancient trees or black water ponds full of murdered babies seeking revenge. There are a lot more houses back on Rebel Ridge now, though I hear they're still having problems with wild dogs.—*Keith Allison*

## The Middle Bridge Ghost

***Many rumors exist*** regarding the Middle Bridge in Warren County. All of them concern the ghostly spirit of a young woman returning to the bridge after tragedy befell her there.

The details of the stories have much in common. People driving across the bridge find that their cars malfunction and stop halfway across. At this point the wind picks up and a fog forms. Out of this mist emerges the hazy image of a young girl. This specter makes its way around the disabled car, staring into its windows with glowing, ghastly eyes. After a few moments of exploring the car and its riders, the woman fades away, the fog dissipates, and drivers find that their cars again function normally.

While these aspects of the legend are mostly agreed upon by those who tell the story, what's not as cut-and-dried is the reason this cursed young woman haunts this spot in the first place.

Some stories link the ghost's presence with young love. The woman was once a teenager in love. One night she and her beau were out on a date and lost track of time. Knowing that they were mere minutes from curfew, the woman's lover raced home. By the time they reached Middle Bridge, he was going at a dangerous speed—and paid the price for it. He lost control of the car, crashing and sending his young love hurtling through the windshield and over the bridge into the river.

Those who ascribe to this version of the tale claim that the ghostly reappearance of the girl is motivated by her concern for her boyfriend. While peering into cars, they say, she is looking for him—to make sure he is all right and to see if he has returned to her after all this time.

A darker, more twisted version of the tale leaves love out of the equation and replaces it with evil, fear, and the base nature of society. In this story, the young woman was not in love at all—but instead was being pursued by a few drunken young men who planned on taking what they wanted from her. These nefarious creeps managed to corner the girl on Middle Bridge in the dead of night. Knowing the fate that awaited her, she jumped from the bridge, choosing to kill herself rather than give up her innocence.

The ghost, it is said by those who believe this twist on the tale, is looking for vengeance. As she stares into cars, she's searching for her tormentors in order to exact swift

revenge on them. She also checks to see if there are any other males on the prowl who can't take no for an answer so that she can make their lives a living hell as well.

No matter which version of the story they believe, most who have visited this place agree that there is something otherworldly, something just plain off about it. Beware if you encounter the young woman whose soul is trapped here. Her motivations remain unclear.

## Child's Creek Bridge

***I grew up in*** Georgetown, near Closplint, which is off of Route 38. There is a bridge in Closplint where many accidents have happened. It crosses over Child's Creek. Many of the drivers who have crashed their cars there have had similar stories of why the accidents happened. They have nothing to do with drinking or recklessness, but instead, with a ghost!

The drivers all swear up and down that while crossing the bridge, a woman appeared out of nowhere. Strange, intense, and unexpected, the woman stares directly into cars. Drivers find her mysterious presence hard to look away from. It is during these interactions that drivers will find themselves so distracted by the woman that they crash their car. Needless to say, when the shock wears off and they look to find the woman to be a witness in their accident reports, she is nowhere to be found.

Supposedly, this woman died herself on this bridge many years ago. She returns periodically to try to get others to join her in her misery. From what I have heard, cops have heard the story so many times that they no longer roll their eyes at it when distraught drivers claim the woman distracted them on the road.—*Glen Clements*

## Ghost Bridge

***Teenagers*** who find themselves bored in my town of Winchester often pay a late night visit to Ghost Bridge. This quiet, spooky site is regularly visited by the ghosts of four teenagers who leapt off the bridge to their deaths years ago, or so the stories say.

I have visited the bridge, and in the silence of the night heard footsteps running around underneath us. I was completely convinced at the time that they were the footsteps of the four boys, although it could have just been my mind playing tricks on me.

What I find really interesting is that older people react to the story by telling us how dangerous it is there—and yet the ghosts don't serve as a warning at all. In fact, they just attract more people out there.—*Brigitte Gun*

# Cody Road Bridge

***In Independence*** is a railroad bridge with many strange legends attached to it. It's said that a woman was killed while driving her car across this span after a bad storm. The car died and was washed into the raging creek below. If you park on the bridge at night with your lights off, the story goes, the woman will appear; this is said to occur frequently during storms or when the creek has flooded.

## *My Incident on Cody Road Bridge*

I grew up hearing stories about a ghost at the Cody Road Bridge, but I was never easy to scare. I have two older brothers who delighted in doing anything they could to make me freaked out. I was a veteran of the ghost story game when I was barely out of diapers. So when I was of driving age, and I could borrow my brother's car, it never occurred to me exactly how scared one dumb old bridge could make me.

I had been out with my friends one night, driving around, mostly bored. I dropped them all off. The quickest way home once I was on my own involved going across the bridge—and quick was necessary, as I was very tired. As I came across the bridge, it was about 1:30 in the morning and it was drizzling. About halfway across, the car stalled out. I freaked and figured I had run out of gas. I looked at the gauge, though, and there was over a quarter of a tank. Then, I realized where I was.

Just as it registered with me where I was, I heard a scream. It was loud, clear, and distinctly that of a woman in distress. I instinctively screamed as well. I turned the key a number of times and nothing happened. It seemed like hours, but must have been about thirty seconds. I screamed again. I turned the key one more time, and the car turned on. But as it did, there was an intense, bright, white flash of light. It wasn't like lightning, a flash on the horizon. Instead it was right there, all around me, almost like it came from inside the car with me.

I was sufficiently terrified. With the car started, I gunned it and got out of there. I had been tired before, but now I was wide awake. I didn't get much sleep that night, needless to say.

I didn't see any ghost woman, but I heard and saw some very inexplicable stuff. Since that day, I have been less of a cynic. I am less quick to dismiss scary stories I hear, as I will always remember my own personal incident on the Cody Road Bridge.—*Greg Heiler*

## Ghosts Along Highway 25

***My husband and I*** grew up in the mountains of Eastern Kentucky, in a town called London. There is some weird stuff in this area. A ghost appears at midnight on a sharp curve along Old 25 South, close to Livingston. It is a woman who appears on the side of the road, hitchhiking. If you stop and pick her up, she'll ride in the car with you as you negotiate the curve and she even talks with you. But once the curve straightens out, she disappears. This actually happened to a friend of mine: one minute, the woman was there, and the next, my friend looked over at the passenger seat and nobody was in it! The girl was supposedly walking to a dance at a nearby school and was struck and killed by a car.

My brother, who has been on the Lexington police force 32 years, saw another roadside ghost. He was driving home late one night along Bowman's Mill Road. As he drove past a culvert where a creek runs under the road, he saw a completely wet, naked woman with long black hair. She was sitting on the culvert alongside the road. He stopped his car and backed it up, to see if she needed help. He asked her three or four times, but she kept her head down and would not answer, so he drove off. When he got to work the next day, he told his story to the other officers. They told him that he had seen a ghost, and that there was a story around the woman.—*Jean N. Smith*

### U.S. 25

Many of the places featured in this book can be found on or near U.S. 25, which is probably our all-time favorite road. Running straight down the center of Kentucky for the entire vertical span of the state, it truly is the Route 66 of Kentucky weirdness.

Highway 25 begins in Covington, right at the Cincinnati, OH border. From there it winds its way to Florence, then spends the next couple of hours running alongside I-75, as a sort of rural companion, passing through Crittenden, Dry Ridge (where it becomes the Skeeter Davis Highway for a stretch), Williamstown, Corinth, Double Culvert, Georgetown, Lexington, Clay's Ferry, White Hall, Richmond, Berea, Conway, Wildie, Renfro Valley, Mt. Vernon, Livingston, London, and Corbin.

In Corbin, U.S. 25 splits into two, one leg going east (25 East), one going south (though for some reason they call it 25 West). 25E takes you to Barbourville, Pineville, Middlesboro, and Cumberland Gap, at the juncture of the KY–TN–VA borders, before continuing on into TN. Meanwhile, 25W takes a long deviation out into the middle of nowhere, eventually winding its way to Williamsburg, where it rejoins its parallel path with I-75, and then goes on into TN (where it again wanders away from the interstate and heads deep into the mountains). Both 25E and 25W have their points of interest, but it's 25E that has that good ole weird feeling all the way to the border.

## Lost Branch Anti-Gravity Hill

***I was born*** and raised in the small town of Sparta, in Gallatin County, which is basically one huge holler. For you non-country folks, a holler is formed at the spot where two extremely steep hills meet at the bottom. The hills leading up from Sparta's holler are outrageously steep and sometimes hard to get up in a little car or truck. There's a legend involving these hills that takes place in a half-mile section of Highway 465 that's nicknamed Lost Branch.

A small tribe of American Indians once thrived on the very grounds where Lost Branch is today. When a group of European settlers moved onto the land, the Indians weren't happy, and they would sometimes attack the settlers when they left the safety of town. It was rumored that the victims were scalped.

Unfortunately for the settlers, they had to leave town frequently in order to get water from Lost Branch Creek, which was no easy trick, as they had to climb the steep hills of the holler to get to the creek. One day, a young boy and girl took a small, single-horse wagon to the top of the hill to get water. Along the way, they broke a wheel, and the boy struggled to push the wagon the rest of the way up the hill. Indians surprised the children near the top of the hill, and in his fear, the boy let the wagon go. As it slid backwards, it rolled over the boy, killing him. His body was never found. The girl was taken captive, tortured, and killed.

The legend says if you drive to the bottom of the first hill heading east on Highway 465, you will be truly freaked out by a strange gravitational experience! It has to be a summer night as the sun goes down. Drive your car to the bottom of the hill slowly and bring it to a stop at the bottom of the hill. Put the car in neutral and just hold your foot over the brake: do not apply your parking brake. Your car will slowly make its way up the hill, supposedly pushed by the spirit of the little settler boy.

I had to try this out once I got my license! I did exactly as I was told and made it almost to the top of the hill, no kidding. My car then rolled backwards down the hill for a few feet. At one point, it felt as if I had backed over something large. Then I heard a scream. Needless to say, I left the area fast.*—Letter via e-mail*

## Matchstick Bridge and Gravity Road

***I have two notable locations*** that come to mind from my teenage years. The first area is the Keno Bridge, in Pulaski County, in the Burnside area. The bridge is a very high one over train tracks and it is said you can drop an unlit match (wooden sticks, not paper from a matchbook) from the side of the bridge and it will light before it reaches the ground. I have seen this actually happen, and I was curious to how it occurred, what's the trick? I'm sure it has something to do with physics, and I seriously doubt it was fireflies amazingly lighting at the same time a match was dropped.

The second area is in Wayne County, the Gap Creek community, at the base of Poplar Mountain, heading towards Duvall Valley. Just as you start the steepest climb up Poplar Mountain, on the left side there is a dirt road only a few hundred feet long leading to a metal cattle gate and into a field. On that short "runway" is an uphill incline in the opposite direction of the paved highway going up the mountain. You can put a car in neutral and the inertia of the mountain will pull you up the gravel runway over the hump onto the road and down the paved road you go.

Back in my day, we used a '66 Plymouth, affectionately named Christine (I know, the real one from the movie was a '58 Plymouth Fury). No matter what speed you went, fast or slow, the speedometer bobbed at 45 mph. Anyway, we also tried this experiment with an '88 Honda Civic and a '71 Chevy pick-up truck, all with the same results.*—Lisa Bolton*

## Moved by the Spirit on Bowling Green Bridge

***Between Bowling Green*** and Richardsville is a bridge that is home to one of the most famous local legends in the area. With a wooden plank road and green metal, this distinctive bridge looks ominous. Those who know the stories and the mysterious phenomenon associated with the bridge know that this is not a place to be trifled with.

It's said that the spirit of a young lady has called this bridge home since her unfortunate demise here. Some say she jumped to her death from this span. Others say that an automobile accident took her life. Either way, it's agreed that the young lady's restless soul is concerned enough about modern crossers of the bridge to help them along in their journey.

Many drivers find their way to this bridge late at night to test the legend. They drive their cars to the end of the wooden crossing and turn around. Instead of parking, they leave their cars in neutral. To their astonishment, their cars are slowly dragged from one end of the bridge to the other. This is attributed to the ghost of the girl, who is said to push the cars off the cursed place that took her life.

Testing the bridge is a tradition among college students in Bowling Green. Hundreds have gone there skeptical and returned as true believers. The next time you are in the area, be sure to see for yourself if that girl's ghost doesn't drag you off this very strange bridge.

## Princeton's Gravity Hill

***Yet another*** Gravity Hill exists in Princeton. Early in the twentieth century a man and his sons were killed at this spot when a runaway ice truck plowed into them. Since then, visitors who brought their carts, and later their cars, to the site say the departed family's ghosts go out of the way to make sure no one else suffers a similar fate. Cars left in neutral roll uphill; it is said they are pushed by the spirits that guard the road. One of the most persistent legends is that if you put baby powder on the front of your car and are pushed uphill, you will find three sets of handprints after the phenomenon finishes—one large set and two smaller, more childlike ones.

# Meshack Road's Vanishing Hitchhiker

***There is an old road*** that runs along a small creek outside Tompkinsville that has long been called the Meshack Road. The small town of Tompkinsville itself is located in the south-central part of Kentucky, just a few miles north of the Tennessee border. It is an old and remote area where stories of ghosts and "haints" are common.

For many years, people have reported variations of a vanishing hitchhiker story associated with Meshack Road. The story goes that one evening two young men were on their way to a local dance when they picked up an attractive young woman along the road. She was wearing a formal dress, and they invited her to go to the dance with them. She accepted and danced with both of the young men that evening. She agreed to let the boys drive her home, but only if she could be let out at a certain spot. It was raining when they left the dance, and one of the boys offered her his coat. He told her that he would pick it up later.

They dropped the girl off at a small house along Meshack Road, and a few days later the boy went back to pick up his coat. He went up to the house, and a woman answered the door. But when the boy asked for the girl, the woman told him that she had once had a daughter but that she had died in an accident on the road. She told the boy where she was buried, and when he went to the churchyard, there was his coat lying beside the grave!

There is another tale of a phantom associated with this road, and it too involves a mysterious hitchhiker. It seems that for many years, travelers along the road have reported that an invisible presence can often be felt clinging tightly to the waist of a horseman or motorcycle rider. This specter holds on to the rider's waist for about a mile before it disappears. No one has ever been able to come up with an explanation for this phenomenon.

## Gates of Hell

*I'm sure you have heard* many tales of the Gates of Hell in Elizabethtown. This is a road (St. John's Road) that leads through a cemetery and is named the Gates of Hell because the place is so eerie you feel like you have driven straight into the underworld when you go there.

I have been there many times. I have heard the stories of ghosts, glowing tombstones, moving trees, and more. But what I have seen myself is even scarier than that—devil worship. Thank God you can stay in your car when visiting, or else I truly think I would have been a goner.

This story happened about six years ago, the summer before I went away to college, but I still remember it like it was yesterday. My two friends and I planned on visiting the Gates of Hell for the umpteenth time that summer.

Now the funny part of this story is, my friends and I weren't scared of the Gates of Hell at all. In fact, we were heading out there that night to try to scare other kids who showed up looking for frights. It was late summer, and a weekend night, so we knew there would definitely be carloads of thrill-seekers to chase and flash our high beams at. Ideally, these would be girls we could later hit on after scaring.

Unfortunately, our best-laid plans fell through fast. When we got there, someone had strewn a bunch of wood across the road. We didn't take it as a warning—instead, we just got out, moved it, and drove on in anyway.

The road and cemetery seemed particularly quiet that night. Even us seasoned travelers got pretty quiet. Then, we got scared. From across the cemetery, we saw it: the flashing of a car's headlights, one time, two times, three times.

We stopped and looked at each other. I myself didn't want to keep going, but kept quiet out of fear of looking chicken in front of my friends. I later found out that each of my friends went through the same exact thought process. Unfortunately, none of us expressed it, so we crept towards the car we had seen.

When we got close to where it had been, its lights came on again. This time standing in front of them were about five people dressed in black. We screamed and threw the car into reverse. As we did, we saw one of the people lift their arm and chuck something at us. It turned out to be a hammer. It bounced off the ground about three feet in front of the hood as we pulled away. We turned around and peeled out—behind us, those freaks were charging toward us. Luckily, we got out of there. It still goes down as the scariest night of my entire life.

When people ask about scary places, even all these years later I offer up the Gates of Hell in Elizabethtown. The stories—and more importantly the people—that hang out there should not be trifled with.—*Curtis Flynn*

## Alleys of Louisville

***Like many*** old American cities, Louisville is crisscrossed with an extensive set of alleyways for trash trucks and deliveries. Many have fallen into disuse and are barely traversable by car. However, they make for a fascinating glimpse into the past, since they've changed very little since the nineteenth century. Some even have the original cobblestones, under which lies soil that hasn't seen the light of day since the 1700s.

Most of Louisville's service alleys are easily navigated, though, and it never fails to amaze us how few people ever bother to go down them. If you're adept enough and know your way through them, you can avoid traffic and stoplights while getting to your destination. Not to mention that the scene is much more interesting here and you get to scope out everyone's garbage for potential treasures.

Two of the more well-known alleys even have names—and fanciful ones too: Billy Goat Strut and Nanny Goat Strut can be found downtown, shunting the driver on a side trip through a part of Louisville that few ever see.

## Ferry Cross the Kentucky

***Follow Tates Creek Road*** between Nicholasville and Richmond, and you'll find your route abruptly interrupted by the Kentucky River, with the road going right into it! This turn of events must come as quite a shock to out-of-towners who are just passing through or, worse, are lost. This spot in the road is known as Valley View.

At that point, the only way to get across to the other side without turning around and going forty miles out of your way is to board the Valley View Ferry. It's a paddlewheel ferryboat that you drive your car onto and let shuttle you across the river as you sit at the wheel. This has been the case since 1785 and apparently will be forever, since the landowners were granted a "perpetual and irrevocable franchise" to operate the ferry here.

After 210 years of service, the original ferryboat collapsed under the weight of snow and ice during a snowstorm in 1996. The new boat, called the *John Craig* after the original ferry operator, utilizes parts from the old ferry.

The ferry runs from six a.m. to eight p.m. weekdays, eight a.m. to eight p.m. Saturdays, and nine a.m. to eight p.m. Sundays. It is closed during the winter months, which must be a profound inconvenience for those who live in the area!

## What's in a Name?

***It seems like back in the day,*** people didn't put a whole lot of thought into naming cities, towns, or settlements. Some of America's oldest and tiniest spots in the road have extremely obtuse names whose original meanings (if there really ever were any) have been lost in the passage of time.

But Kentucky's town names can out-obtuse the best of them. In fact, the people who named these places must have been bold surrealists, possibly hallucinating on squirrel brains and 'shine. Ballard County's small town of Monkey's Eyebrow is one of the more famous examples, but there are also these.

### Rabbit Hash—Gone to the Dogs!

The tiny town of Rabbit Hash would be worthy of inclusion in *Weird Kentucky* based on its odd name alone. The fact that the mayor is a member of the canine species merely clinches the deal.

An unincorporated town, Rabbit Hash has a hazily

defined set of borders. Between four and forty people claim to be residents, depending on the popular conception of the border's location on any given day. The most notable landmark in the area is the Rabbit Hash General Store, which has stood since 1831. In 2002, the majority of the town was bought by the Rabbit Hash Historical Society and placed on the National Register of Historic Places. Sleepy by nature, the town butts up against the Ohio River and is in general a very quiet place.

One event that helped make a splash in Rabbit Hash was the 1998 mayoral election, which was won by a politically motivated dog. The election was documented in a film entitled *Rabbit Hash – The Center of the Universe*. In 2004, over three thousand people voted in the mayoral race and elected one Junior Cochran—another dog.

Mayor Cochran's duties largely involve making public appearances. He is known to have his photo taken with kids, to attend local festivals, and to take part in television shoots to promote Rabbit Hash. He is also the official mascot of the Northern Kentucky Women's Crisis Center pet protection program.

Rabbit Hash actively promotes itself as a tourist destination. At its Web site, www.rabbithashusa.com, the town promises that a visit will drop a visitor's blood pressure by twenty points. Tourists are invited to scratch the mayor behind the ear.

### Jugernot

Obviously named by someone who couldn't spell juggernaut. Local explanations in Pulaski County say the name came from some guy allegedly asking another guy if he wanted a jug or not.

### Bugtussle

The glories of Bugtussle were not unknown to the writers of the greatest rural trilogy in television history: It was referred to in the collective mythos of *The Beverly Hillbillies, Green Acres,* and *Petticoat Junction.* You can find it in Monroe County near the Kentucky–Tennessee border.

### Tiny Town

Todd County, near Guthrie. As longtime fans of the 1937 midget western film *Terror of Tiny Town,* we came here hoping to find diminutive blacksmiths and vampires on horseback but were bitterly disappointed.

### Tacky Town

In Harlan County. Actually, we found it to be rather tasteful.

### Lola

We don't know who Lola was or why a town was named after her, but we like to think it was named after Marlene Dietrich's showgirl character in *The Blue Angel.*

### Symsonia

Isn't that a great name? It was originally called Slabtown, but its name was changed to Symsonia in 1847, for reasons unclear to all then and now. It's in Graves County near the Clarks River.

### Freemont and Fremont

These two towns located in McCracken County, only a mile apart from each other, are listed as distinct entities on maps. Who knew a single vowel could make such a difference?

### Rugless

Downtown Rugless, such as it is, can be found in Lewis County. It's apparently a humorous misspelling of an early landowners' name, Ruglas (which itself is a misspelling of the name Ruggles, according to some genealogical sources).

### Pactolus

What's a pactolus? We may never know. This Carter County town is notable for having been the home of Roy Rogers's grandparents.

### Gap in Knob

This area's name refers to a topographic feature of the local terrain, but it's still hilarious to us. We're easily amused.

### Bobtown

In this Madison County location, there used to be a wonderful, huge white building with BOBTOWN written in giant letters across it, making us wonder just who Bob was.

### Tywhapity

Located on the Hancock–Daviess County line. Also known as "Tywhapity Bottoms" or "Tyewhoppety" to some old-timers.

### Overda

Blink, and you'll miss this extremely slight spot in the road (Route 828), way off the beaten path in Lawrence County, overda hills and far away.

### Ape Yard

Yes, that's right, Ape Yard. There's not much left here these days except for a grocery store with a small gorilla monument welcoming you to Ape Yard. Oh, to have been here in years past, when we could have visited the Ape Yard Baptist Church, Ape Yard Insurance, Ape Yard Farm Supply, and the Ape Yard Chamber of Commerce. The settlement is located near East Bernstadt in Laurel County.

### Kettle Island

The first thing you'll notice about Kettle Island is that it isn't an island. No one seems to know what that's about. Follow 221 west out of Pineville and you'll breeze through this tiny community in minutes.

### Lickskillet

This one's not quite as baffling as it sounds—the concept of licking skillets was something of a popular theme in rural America circa early 1800s–early 1900s. Other towns called Lickskillet, Skilletlick, Lick-a-Skillet, and Lick-the-Skillet popped up all over the country during the nineteenth century, and in 1918 a string band called the Lick the Skillet Band was formed, which eventually morphed into the classic old-timey band The Skillet Lickers. We just like the sound of it.

### Kingbee

In the world of actual bees, there are no king bees, only a queen. But they do things a little differently in Casey County.

### Penile

Who wouldn't be intrigued by a tiny town, listed only on the most detailed Kentucky maps, known as Penile. How does a town end up being called that? Was it a typo? A joke? Or did the word once have some other arcane meaning, now obscured in the swirling mists of time?

We had seen genealogical records that refer to a Penile Cemetery and set out to find it. Alas, our search was fruitless, for aside from a few homes, there really isn't much of interest in Penile except for the Penile Baptist Church and a great polar bear statue in someone's yard.

By the way, the locals don't pronounce their name as you might think, as if it rhymes with senile. They say *Pa-nilé.* Guess that makes a difference.

As if it's not bad enough to have a town whose name begs for puerile jokes, there are some unfortunate street names too. Located within the town is the corner of Penile and Manslick.

### Static

Straddling the border between Kentucky and Tennessee in Clinton County you'll find the town of Static. It's unincorporated, and therefore, not technically part of Clinton County (even though it obviously is). Don't ask us to explain why or how, that's just the way things are. Even stranger, by some accounts, Static is not even considered to be part of the state of Kentucky (even though it obviously is).

However, the Kentucky side of

Static follows Kentucky laws, and the Tennessee side follows its own. This leads to some interesting and abrupt contradictions. At the border, one gas station on the Tennessee side sells beer, while another gas station just a few hundred yards away in Kentucky cannot. Fireworks are legal in Tennessee but not Kentucky, so one could be fined if you legally bought them on one block and set them off in your yard a block away. Tennessee has no lottery, but Kentucky does, so this is an easy location for Tennesseans to buy tickets.

The town of Static runs alongside Highway 127 for a long stretch. You'll hit it just after passing through a town named Bug.

## Banana Republic

For many years, the humble town of Fulton billed itself as the "Banana Capital of the World." Why? Well, it's complicated, but the short version is that for reasons relating to rail commerce and train car refrigeration, seventy percent of the nation's imported banana supply stopped here regularly.

Now, we're not sure how that would make Fulton the Banana Capital of the World—at best, that would make Fulton the Banana Capital of the Nation, right? But we'll forgive them a little America-centric thinking, because it was a good excuse to throw a heck of a party: From 1962 to 1992, the town hosted what they called the International Banana Festival (although again it's unclear how many other nations took part). Best of all, the festival boasted the yearly creation of the world's largest (two tons!) banana pudding.

Although the banana train no longer passes through Fulton, we see no reason to let such a trifle spoil the festival. But what's done is done: The International Banana Festival has since been renamed to the less catchy Pontotoc Festival, after its historic railway station.

## Disputanta

Rockcastle County is a place where the air is thick with mysterious vibes and an uneasy feeling of spookiness, even when the surroundings are perfectly normal and pleasant. It seems to be something that comes directly from below, from the soil, perhaps from the very rocks for which the county is named. This cognitive dissonance is only heightened by locations like Disputanta.

On the face of it, there's really nothing to Disputanta: a cemetery, some farms and houses, rolling fields and forests, and an abandoned post office. But for the better part of a century, this territory has stirred the hackles of many a neck and sent the creep-o-meter readings off the scale for seekers of the paranormal.

There is an ancient legend that Satan himself dwells, or has dwelled, here. So prominent and persistent is this folktale that it became the subject of a theatrical production by Kentucky-born playwright Johnny Payne. Payne is currently head of the department of creative writing at the University of Texas El Paso, and his play *The Devil in Disputanta* has been produced on numerous stages to great acclaim.

The traditional explanation for the region's name is typically simplistic, specious, and dubious. Some claim that no one could decide what to call the town, so they called it Disputanta—y'know, because it sounds like "dispute." But we contend that the real source of the name probably is the preexisting town of Disputanta, Virginia. And when searching for the origin of that town's nomenclature, we find . . . the exact same unlikely "dispute" story.

*Weird Kentucky* made many visits to Disputanta in search of Satan and hasn't spotted him. Yet.

# Ghosts of Kentucky

As *William S. Burroughs says* in the film version of *Naked Lunch,* "America is not a young country. It's old . . . and dirty . . . and evil. Before the settlers, before the Indians, the evil was there."

Ghosts have roamed the rolling mountains and hills of Kentucky since before recorded history. When the earliest European settlers encountered the American Indian here, they were told that this territory was the "dark and bloody ground" and feared because of the ghosts of the ancient civilizations that existed here prior to those we call Native Americans.

Whoever these ancient people were who left their strange remains in Mammoth Cave and in caverns under Lexington and Augusta, their spirits linger on. That Kentucky is so populated by ghosts and legends, despite being only recently densely populated (as compared to, say, most countries in Europe) is a testament to its complicated prehistory.

Multiple ghost sightings, as opposed to simple and vague folktale anecdotes, can be found in every one of Kentucky's counties. The reports are of all manner of manifestations, from visual sightings to audible noises, objects moving, and disturbances of the senses. When next you travel through Kentucky—perhaps via I-75 or its evil twin, Highway 25—know that there are haunted sites literally within minutes of wherever you might choose to pull over and stop your car. Here's just a smattering.

# Hauntings of E.K.U.

***Eastern Kentucky University,*** located in Richmond in the central part of the state, is a lush and beautiful campus that conceals quite a few secrets within its quaint confines. Most universities have an old "haunted dorm" legend somewhere in their history, but from what we've seen, E.K.U. has far more than its share of paranormal hot spots.

## Keene Hall

Legend has it that a suicide that took place on the sixteenth floor of this men's dorm is responsible for hauntings throughout the building, but phenomena on that particular floor are said to be even greater. Witnesses have seen and heard doorknobs moving by themselves, music seemingly coming from inside walls (and no, not the guy in the next room blasting The Misfits), and other disturbances. When you walk around this dorm, strolling through its '60s–'70s-dull ceramic-tiled hallways, you definitely get a sense of bleakness, desperation, and despair. Then again, maybe the same could be said for dorm life in general.

## Sullivan Hall

Another suicide is the basis for the rumor here, this time of a female nursing student who allegedly killed herself in the 1970s. We spent many hours in the library trying to track down any reference to this suicide in old newspapers and came up empty-handed. However, we did find a reference to a nursing student's death in a nearby dorm, which has no reports of haunting. Either the story is attributed to the wrong dorm, or Sullivan Hall's specters have nothing to do with the other suicide. Our vote is the latter, since *Weird Kentucky* has experienced some ghostly activity here and spoken to many residents and former residents of the dorm who report the same. Many had their experiences before they learned of the legend.

## Moore Building's Naked Ghost

The specter of a naked female has often been seen in the Moore building, which is a huge and sprawling edifice housing E.K.U.'s science program. However, the descriptions given of this ghost vary wildly—tall to short, young to old, blond to brunette. So are there more than one of these free-spirited spirits padding around the building's weird old halls? We're on the lookout for a firsthand gander at this supernatural streaker!

## Keen Johnson Ballroom

Said to be a "Blue Lady" in an evening dress, this is the most famous of E.K.U.'s ghosts. Though the tale predates the '70s, the same story of the suicidal nursing student is often heard in reference to the Blue Lady. In truth, the earliest recorded sighting of a ghost here (that we know of) is in the 1950s. Unlike in the dormitories, there's nothing stopping visitors from walking in and having a look around, so this is your best bet for ghost-hunting if you should find yourself on E.K.U.'s beautiful campus.

The Blue Lady of Keen Johnson has also been seen in the nearby bell tower, reportedly singing. A bluish mist has often been said to be a manifestation she takes. The bell tower is off-limits to the general public.

## Model Laboratory School

Ghostly activity, moving objects, and "anxiety zones" have been experienced here in the elementary wing, the underground maintenance tunnels, the band room, and the auditorium. Although some people attribute these hauntings to Model's high incidence of students who met tragic deaths in recent decades, anecdotal evidence seems to show that many of these reports of ghosts predate those premature passings.

## Ghost Dog

Behind the amphitheater in the ravine there's a grave for a dog called Mozart, who was the music department's mascot in the 1960s. It's said that Mozart can be seen walking about—sometimes in the ravine and around the nearby music building.

It's interesting to note that with the exception of Keene Hall and Model Laboratory School, these haunted locations all face each other in the same area of campus. And complicating the suicidal nursing student rumor is the story of a sorority girl who accidentally fell from a tenth-floor window at Telford Hall in 1991, which some also point to as an impetus for E.K.U. hauntings, but strangely, not in Telford Hall itself. A rash of other recent deaths in dorms will probably eventually also add to the speculation and confusion.

## Aunt Polly of Renfro Valley

***Just as you enter*** the little resort town of Renfro Valley, there's a beautiful ancient cemetery with ornate and interesting grave markers. One of those graves belongs to Aunt Polly, an early resident of the area and proprietor of a general store–gift shop just across the street from where she's currently interred. According to one legend, her original wish was to be buried on the property with her home and her store, but for various reasons she was laid to rest in the cemetery across the street instead. This, according to legend, didn't exactly please her, and her spirit keeps wandering back across the street to oversee what's going on there.

A few years ago we chatted with employees of the store, who prefaced their stories with disclaimers about being good Christians and not believing in ghosts, and then went on to say things like "and yet, there's been times when you definitely feel her presence here" and remarking on odd sounds from upstairs, cold spots, and things being moved around, disappearing and reappearing elsewhere.

At the risk of sounding like every other self-styled sensitive and would-be ghostbuster out there, we must admit that when we visited, we did sense something amiss in the air that made us feel that creepiness was going on just under the veil of reality. Then again, this feeling tends to extend to the general area, not just Polly's house, and whether the house is the cause or a symptom of this weirdness remains to be seen.

# Whitehall

***Madison County,*** just outside Richmond, is home to the mysterious old mansion known as Whitehall, former home of Cassius M. Clay. Clay's a pretty interesting character in his own right. His exploits include murders and duels, fighting in the Mexican-American War, publishing an abolitionist newspaper called *The True American,* and helping to engineer the U.S. possession of Alaska. He married a fifteen-year-old girl when he was eighty-nine, and even in the final years of his life was still a sharp marksman, defending his home from burglars by chasing them out with a rifle. (And yes, he's the namesake of the father of boxer Cassius Clay, better known as Muhammad Ali.)

Whitehall has long been regarded as a haunted house, with many sightings reported over the years by sober, level-headed people who don't otherwise go for ghost stories. Some say the ghost is of Cassius Clay himself, while others suggest that there are several ghosts and that at least one of them is one of the men Clay shot and killed in the library of the house. Other possibilities are Samuel M. Brown, whom Clay killed in a duel at Russell Cave in 1843, and Cyrus Turner, whom Clay stabbed in a fight in 1849. Most recently, it has been suggested that Clay's wife and daughter are the place's most commonly occurring apparitions.

Though I haven't personally seen a ghost here myself, I was affected by the place. Once while taking the guided tour (given by women dressed in period costumes), I began having severe feelings of anxiety just as we were about to go up to the third floor. The anxiety was pronounced enough that I excused myself from the rest of the tour, simply saying that I didn't feel well. Suddenly the tour lady seemed very agitated and said that actually she didn't feel well either, and, trembling, excused herself and went to go call for another guide to replace her for the rest of the tour!

Whitehall is on U.S. 25, just outside Richmond, as we said. Or you can get there by taking the Winchester–Boonesboro exit off I-75 and follow the clearly marked road behind the Shell station.

# Liberty Hall and the Vanished Opera Singer

***This historic Frankfort mansion*** was built in 1796 by Kentucky senator John Brown and was the residence of his family until 1937. There are numerous ghosts said to be inhabiting the property. To our mind, the most interesting is a vanished opera singer from New Orleans. Seems she was attending a party at Liberty Hall in 1805. At some point during the proceedings, she wandered out alone into the backyard garden—and then never returned. As the story goes, she was never seen again and no trace of her was ever found. Many fanciful and conspiratorial theories have been advanced in an attempt to explain her strange disappearance, but at this late date it's doubtful that we will ever really know.

Another ghost is said to be that of a dead soldier who had a crush on one of the Brown family members. He mopes around the grounds, pining for the young woman and peeking through windows, much to the consternation of those who happen to see his face looking in on a dark night.

The most famous specter of Liberty Hall, however, is the Gray Lady, said to be the ghost of Margaret Varick, a member of the Brown family who came to live there in 1817 but died only three days later. She was buried in the garden, and although her body was later moved to a cemetery, her ghost seems to remain. Many direct sightings of the Gray Lady have occurred over the years and continue to the present day.

Some have suggested that the ghost of John Brown may be lurking around, but most researchers doubt this. Go sniffing around for yourself and check it out—it's at 218 Wilkinson Street, and tours are given on every day but Mondays. Even when the home itself is closed, the backyard and the garden where the opera singer mysteriously vanished are open to the public.

# Central State Hospital

***Most people*** driving by Central State Hospital today probably give it little thought as they zip past. It's simply a small, clean, and modern one hundred and twenty bed mental health facility located on a modest parcel of land in Anchorage.

All looks fine to the naked eye, but hints of the way things once were can still be glimpsed and understood. The Anchorage area has always had a pronounced vibe of creepiness, and ghost sightings are higher than average here, as well as in surrounding areas of Lyndon and Middletown. At one time, the original grounds of the hospital extended for hundreds of acres, with rolling hills of dense forest and fertile farmland, providing the perfect atmosphere for spirits—and perhaps patients—to roam free.

In 1873, the place was the Lakeland Home for Juvenile Delinquents, which soon thereafter expanded its purpose to become an insane asylum. No asylum of that era was ever a friendly place to be, but this one takes the proverbial cake when it comes to hellish conditions. For decades, improper care, senseless deaths, and unchecked madness lent a continually grim patina of very bad karma to this land.

Think of every horror story you've ever heard about psychiatry and it's all here: overcrowding, abuse, insulin "therapy," freezing cold showers as "treatment," crude lobotomies, electroshocks, you name it. According to Jay Gravatte of the Louisville Ghost Hunters, wards with a capacity for 1,600 patients held more like 2,400. In 1943, a Kentucky grand jury discovered that Central State was unfairly committing and imprisoning people who were not even mentally ill! Although there were indictments for malfeasance in the 1950s, it wasn't until the 1970s that the hospital truly became more of a proper hospital and less of an Abu Ghraib.

Today all the original buildings have been demolished, and a new complex occupies an area closer to the highway

than the original hospital's site. For years, the crumbling old hospital with its sinister-looking twin towers was a mecca for ghost hunters and seekers of the unusual, and the grounds where it once stood are still as haunted as ever by the ghosts of those who endured its purgatory.

Some of these specters include mysterious ghostlike persons that have been seen shuffling around the area of Lakeland Road and the nearby railroad track, appearing, disappearing, and reappearing again.

Shadowy figures and deep anxiety have been reported by joggers and walkers on the nature trails of E. P. Sawyer State Park, which now occupies land where the former Central State Hospital was located. Voices, apparently of the dead, have been tape-recorded late at night by ghost hunters in the hospital cemetery, which is also now part of the park grounds. *Weird Kentucky* heard the tape, and, for what it's worth, voices are clearly heard, although it's hard to make out just what they were trying to say. Most of the stones in the graveyard are now missing, and the ones that are still extant are misplaced and piled haphazardly around nearby trees. You can still tell where the graves are, however, by the prominent sinkholes that dot the landscape. It's incredibly neglected and poorly maintained, a sad place for people who were unhappy enough from the get-go without having their final resting place so shoddily treated. No wonder they wander around complaining about it.

Some who have visited this forlorn yet hallowed ground have reported a sense of being pulled downward—not strongly, but always perceptibly—a feeling of being drawn to the soil, of wanting to drop to one's knees or lay on the ground. This same sensation has been reported by persons on completely opposite ends of the vast property.

## Lock & Key Coffeehouse

***Memories*** of a checkered past linger in the building now occupied by the Lock & Key Coffeehouse at 201 Main Street in Georgetown. Built in 1899, it was originally John McMeekin's Furniture and Funeral Parlor, then went through a number of permutations over the years, including a bank, a food stamp office, and an antiques mall.

In 1929, during its incarnation as the Georgetown National Bank, President George T. Hambrick committed suicide in the bank's restroom by placing a pistol to his head. The bullet exited through his skull and lodged in the wall, where the hole is framed today as a historical curiosity.

Hauntings and odd phenomena are fairly common here, including unexplained sightings of a man upstairs. The ghost had been jokingly nicknamed George, on the logical assumption that it might be the ghost of the bank president. However, a local spirit medium who frequents the establishment is convinced that the ghost is from one of the dead who were embalmed on the premises in its earlier tenure as a funeral parlor and mortician's office.

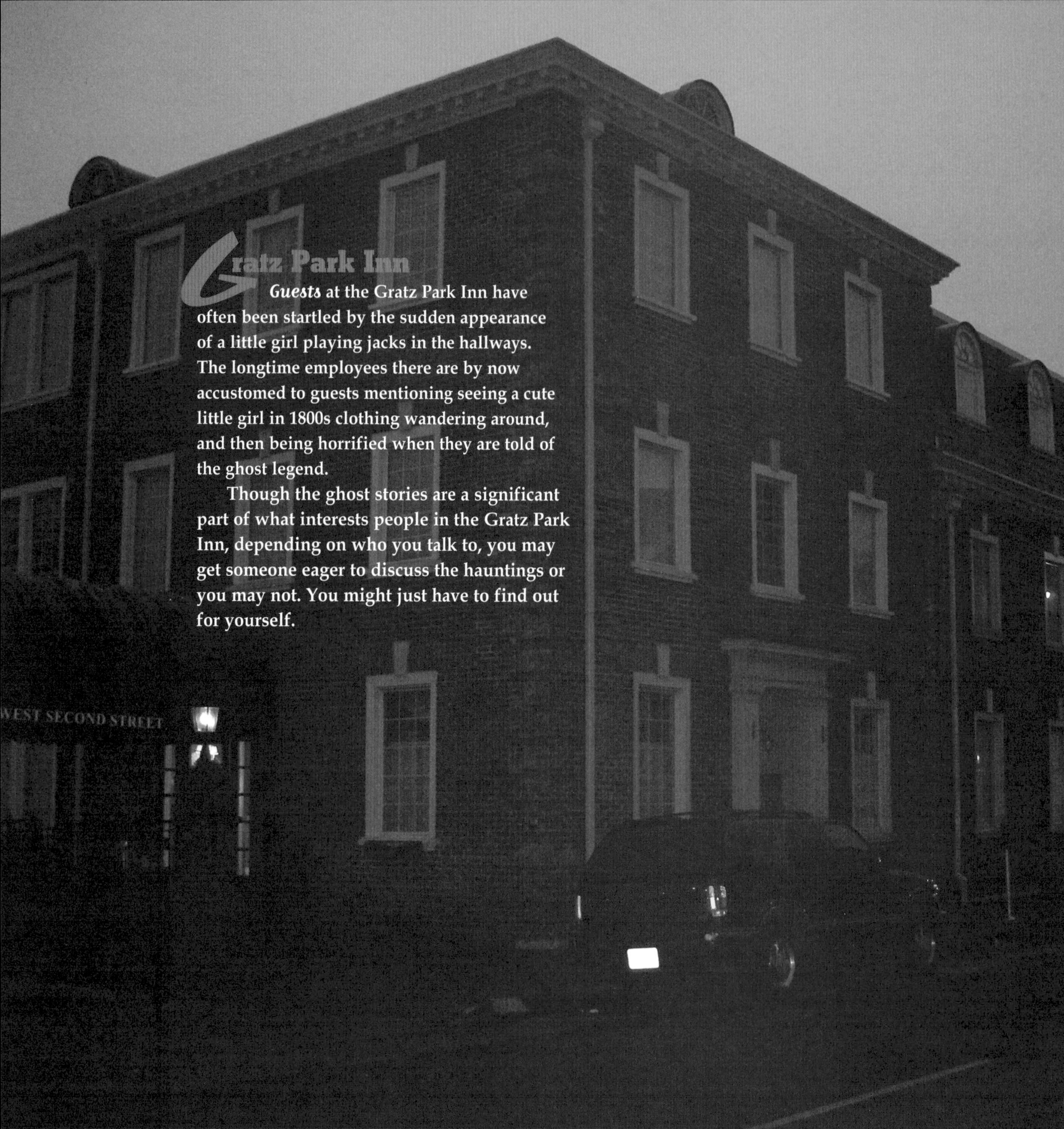

## Gratz Park Inn

*Guests* at the Gratz Park Inn have often been startled by the sudden appearance of a little girl playing jacks in the hallways. The longtime employees there are by now accustomed to guests mentioning seeing a cute little girl in 1800s clothing wandering around, and then being horrified when they are told of the ghost legend.

Though the ghost stories are a significant part of what interests people in the Gratz Park Inn, depending on who you talk to, you may get someone eager to discuss the hauntings or you may not. You might just have to find out for yourself.

## Does Jesse James Haunt the Talbott Tavern?

***Here's a real slice*** of Americana, and a severely spook-ridden one to boot. The Talbott Tavern in Bardstown, built in 1779, is the oldest stagecoach-stop tavern and hotel in the United States. This building was well known as a must-visit place for anyone who happened to be passing through the area. Because of its central location at the junction of major stagecoach dirt roads, it was visited by practically everyone who traveled cross-country or to the frontier.

The main tavern area is preserved, looking mostly as it did then, with only a few modifications and modernizations. Everyone from presidents to kings to outlaws made camp here: Abraham Lincoln, Andrew Jackson, Henry Clay, William Henry Harrison, King Louis-Phillippe of France, Jesse James, Daniel Boone, and many more.

Although Jesse James's ghost is claimed by some to walk these halls, we see no reason to believe that he should haunt a tavern just because he used to drink here. Ghostly activity predates his death, and in fact, James himself may have had a paranormal experience at the tavern. One night he claimed that he saw the murals painted on the walls of an upstairs room coming to life, and in his panic he shot the walls full of holes. Then again, he may just have been hallucinating on a bad batch of bourbon.

Ghosts of children have been prevalent here over the years, as well as ghosts of mysterious old men in antiquated clothing and of a woman said to be a suicide victim. She hung herself with a rope suspended from the main tavern's chandelier. Although that chandelier, which once held candles, has since been retrofitted with electricity, it is still in use today.

The eerie upstairs hallways have had so many ghost sightings that the staff have become accustomed to them. Manager Jonathan Mattingly noted one guest who complained about the children laughing and running in and out of the room next door. "I had to break it to him that there were no other guests in the hotel that night," says Mattingly, "and certainly no children in the building." A small display in the upstairs foyer alerts guests to the potential for such hauntings, so caveat emptor: Don't ring the front desk if you hear the pitter-patter of little (dead) feet!

Aside from the woman who took her own life, who's responsible for all these spirits shuffling around the tavern? Although it's almost a certainty that people died of illnesses and were murdered on the premises in the violent and chaotic frontier days of the eighteenth century, the most likely answer lies within two nearby buildings:

## The McLean House

This handsome old circa-1812 brick building was once a post office and also a hospital that no doubt saw a lot of suffering, pain, and death, especially during the Civil War. Today it's a bed-and-breakfast.

## The Jailer's Inn

The city jail was conveniently located right next door to the tavern, and nowadays you can sleep here too. The structures of the jail cells have been left in their rustic and grim state, but fixed up somewhat and made into a very unusual inn. Original jailhouse graffiti still exists in some spots (including an elaborately painted winning poker hand). There's definitely a frightening and oppressive air to the building. You can't forget that you're in a jailhouse where many troubled souls lived and died over the span of two centuries. The Jailer's Inn is owned and operated by a local attorney who's happy to give tours to the curious. Like the Talbott Tavern, the inn is increasingly popular for "ghost tourism."

A fire broke out upstairs at the Talbott Tavern in 1998, and destroyed the old wall murals that Jesse James shot with lead. Though the paintings may be ruined, the bullet holes are still there in the wall for all to see. It has been speculated that the fire could have been supernatural as well. Renovations are still ongoing, but whoever is working there will usually be glad to take you up to what is now called the Jesse James Room for a peek at the outlaw's handiwork.

## *A Noisy Night at the Talbott Inn*

Recently my friend and I took a trip to Bardstown, and stayed for one night (and thankfully only one night) at a beautiful but haunted old stagecoach inn from 1779 called the Talbott Tavern & Inn (Court Square, 107 W. Stephen Foster Ave.). I had absolutely no idea the inn was haunted when I booked my stay there. (If I knew it was, I wouldn't have made the reservation; a ghost tour is one thing, spending the night with them is another.) I merely liked the idea that I could stay in a historical place where Jesse James hung out.

Well, the evening before we were scheduled to stay there we decided to have a drink at the tavern inside the inn. I started talking to the bartender, who after some discussion, told me that my friend and I were the only two people staying in the inn that following night, and that, "the ghosts will have someone to keep them company." I just shrugged off his comment as an attempt to scare us (my friend and I are both women). We checked into the Talbott in the General's Quarters at about 6 p.m., and I immediately felt as though someone was watching me, especially when I was taking a shower. After the Innkeeper left (at about 7 p.m.) my friend went to grab our luggage as I got ready. I heard all kinds of banging noises outside the door to my room, but when I went to investigate (I used to be in law enforcement), there was no one there. My friend was still outside by the car. . . . I went back into the room and out of the corner of my eye I thought I saw a shadow move into the bathroom. I sat down in a chair in the room, but felt as though there was someone there with me. It's difficult to explain, but suffice to say it was uncomfortable enough that I had to get up and move.

After my friend brought the baggage up to the room, I saw yet something else strange, like a light coming from an upper corner of the room, across from the bathroom. At this point I decided to take out my contacts, and we went out to dinner—me with my hair still soaking wet, and without any makeup. I just didn't want to have to go back into the bathroom.

As it turned out, my friend ran into the Innkeeper as she was outside gathering our luggage, and asked her if she could see some of the other rooms in the place, since she's a history buff too. The Innkeeper just handed her a bunch of keys, and

said that after she's done to leave them on the front desk—that they'll collect them in the morning. When we came home from dinner, the inn seemed to take on a more ominous feel. There were a lot of noises—banging, doors slamming shut, water turning on and off in unused rooms, the toilets flushing on their own, etc. So we decided to check out the other rooms in the "newer" (I think about 1815 or thereabouts) section of the inn. I found one room that had a very calm feeling to it, and was toasty warm (our room was warm, but very cold in spots, as was the Lincoln Room next door to the General's Quarters).

The minute we turned off the lights in our room, I heard the sound of a door slam shut loudly, a man sneeze, and then loud footsteps going down the hall. Then the door to our room banged a few times, as if someone grabbed the doorknob and tried to push the door open. Then I heard all kinds of noises throughout the rest of the inn—from a bell chiming eleven times (I counted) at 4 a.m., to horses' hooves clomping outside the window to our room, to what sounded like three men talking and laughing (all night long and into the morning), to footsteps going all over the entire inn (again, all night long). It was so noisy that I didn't get to sleep until after about 5 a.m., when I finally put cotton in my ears. Then when I fell asleep, I had a terrible dream of a man being hanged right outside the window to our room, which overlooked a courtyard, which I later learned was the site of many hangings.

The next morning I said to the staff, "So, this place is haunted. . . ." They related to me that they've learned to live with the ghosts. They said that they're just playful and noisy spirits, but never hurt anyone. But they also informed me that their other property, called the McLean House (105 W. Stephen Foster Ave. in Bardstown), was seriously haunted. That the maids don't even like to go in there, and that often guests leave in the middle of the night.

So, both of these places would seem like great investigations—and you may want to check them out. The McLean House in particular, as it was supposed to be used as a Civil War hospital, and one maid recounted to me that she's had things thrown at her by ghosts, and that she's cleaned the entire house (an 8-hour job) in just under 2-hours! She said she'd stay in the Talbott Tavern alone anytime overnight, but never at the McLean House. She also said there's a painting of a little boy in particular that seems to change while you look at it.—*Hannah Cwik*

## Phantom Monks

*A ghostly monk* is often reported seen wandering South Sixth Street in Jefferson County's "Old Louisville." Generally the source for this haunting is attributed to the proximity of the St. Louis Bertrand Catholic Church at the corner of Sixth and St. Catherine, although the vision of the monk has been seen wandering far afield from there, as far as Belgravia Court, a significant distance away. With the large quantity of alleged haunted houses in the multi-block radius, it's almost certain that some ethereal overlap is taking place here, and also quite possible that, given the traditionally Catholic neighborhood, more than one monk's ghost might dwell locally.

Thomas Merton's ghost has been alleged by some to walk around the environs of New Haven in Nelson County, where his beloved Trappist Abbey of Gethsemane is located. What makes anyone think this is specifically Merton's ghost, however, is something we've always been curious about, since there is no shortage of monks who have lived and died in the vicinity.

## Bobby Mackey's Music World

***Just across the Kentucky border*** from Cincinnati, in the town of Wilder, lies Bobby Mackey's Music World, a country-western bar and nightclub that some have called Kentucky's most haunted location.

The structure was built in the 1850s as a slaughter-house and meatpacking plant. The well in the basement, where blood from the animals was drained, can still be found there. After the slaughterhouse closed, the building became a ritual site for satanists who supposedly sacrificed animals there. The occult group's activities were exposed in 1896 during a spectacular murder trial that made national headlines.

A young woman named Pearl Bryan had an unwanted pregnancy by the son of a minister and sought help from a Cincinnati medical student named Scott Jackson. Jackson, allegedly a member of the Wilder occult group, knew very little about how to terminate her pregnancy and ended up only mutilating the girl horribly. He and the minister's son, Alonzo Walling, wound up murdering the girl near the abandoned slaughterhouse—by severing her head, which then disappeared. When the poor girl's body was found, she was identified by her shoes.

The men were eventually caught but never revealed what they had done with the head, though police had their suspicions about the old well in the slaughterhouse basement. The two were offered a deal to avoid being executed if they would reveal its location, yet strangely, they refused and took the secret to their graves.

Apparently, they were far more afraid of the consequences of displeasing Satan than of any threat a mere mortal could make.

During the Kentucky organized crime heyday from the 1920s to the 1970s, the site was inhabited by a number of delightfully sleazy nightclubs, and several other deaths took place there over the years, including that of a stripper named Johanna who committed suicide on the premises in the late 1930s. In 1978, it became Bobby Mackey's Music World.

Not surprisingly, people have had every type of ghost experience here, from hearing noises and screams to objects being moved and actual sightings. One ghost is apparently especially fond of playing the "Anniversary Waltz" on the jukebox, which plays by itself without coins—sometimes even without electricity!

**People have had every type of ghost experience here, from hearing noises and screams to objects being moved and actual sightings.**

Music World has an honored place in the sphere of ghost lore. In his book *Sinister Forces: The Nine,* occult researcher Peter Levenda reports that "in 1991, there was an exorcism of a nightclub in Wilder, Kentucky. . . . Claude Lawson claimed that the owner of Music World, Bobby Mackey, was running a haunted establishment and that he had been attacked by evil spirits during the time he worked (and lived) there as a caretaker." Another author, Douglas Hensley, has self-published a book about Mackey's called *Hell's Gate,* and has in his possession at least twenty-nine sworn affidavits of witnesses (including clergy and police) to ghostly phenomena. And still another book, *No Rest for the Wicked,* by Troy Taylor, makes a connection between this case and that of a haunted house in Greencastle, Indiana, where the unfortunate Pearl Bryan grew up.

At least one person has claimed to have become possessed himself after visiting the place, and another filed a lawsuit claiming to have been attacked by a ghost in the restroom.

## Hauntings in Butchertown

***It's the crumbling*** and ancient buildings that make for that good ole Butchertown feeling. This was the first part of Louisville to be settled and inhabited, and contains the city's oldest structures, even older than the so-called "Old Louisville." As the town's center evolved, this territory was used in the nineteenth and twentieth centuries primarily as the stockyard district, and therein lies the real reason for Butchertown's decidedly vertiginous vibe: Billions of animals—and that's billions, not millions—have met very unpleasant deaths here. It's a PETA activist's nightmare!

The main remnant of the blood-spattered pork-scented olden days of Butchertown is the Swift & Company plant on Story Avenue. Local residents have long complained of the stench that wafts from its greasy walls, day after day, presumably the smell of snouts and hoofs boiling in their own unrendered fat. Pig blood can often be seen leaking from trucks in their lot, trickling out onto the sidewalk. Mm-mmmm! It's ALMOST enough to make me think about giving up bacon.

Most of the other old livestock-processing centers are gone now, but some say they have left an indelible psychic trail. The former site of one meat-processing plant is now a park, with lovely lush grass, trees, and swing sets, and a charming view—overlooking the Swift plant. It is without a doubt one of the most unpleasant parks we've seen; it's not just the tacky view or the hot dog-scented atmosphere. People have reported dizziness, feelings of panic, chills, and a sense of not being alone in the park. There is of yet no documented case of a ghost sighting here, but we are confident it will happen and even more confident it will be the ghost of a farm animal.

Meanwhile, down the road, there's the former Fischer meatpacking plant, which has recently been somewhat spruced up and made into the Mellwood Arts Center,

with flea market-style cubicle booths for local artists and craftspeople to sit and paint watercolor begonias in, trying to forget that they're in the heart of an abandoned baloney factory whose floors are still stained with decades of blood (literally stained, this is not flowery figurative talk).

The story is oft repeated about how Buddhist monks were brought in before the renovation to try to cleanse the factory of evil spirits and bad vibes. It is said that they recoiled in horror and panic and had to send out for reinforcements. They performed quadruple-whammy versions of their customary blessing ritual but were never really satisfied that the place had been cleansed of its karmic stench. *Weird Kentucky*'s been in there both before and after the art-colony renovation, and we can tell you that all the hauntedness that was there before is still right there the same as ever, lurking in its girders, clinging to its discolored tiles.

Don't let that discourage you from visiting the Mellwood Arts Center, however, by any means, and we suspect that if you're the type of person to be reading a book such as the one you now hold in your hands, you're probably not likely to be scared off anyway. There's another source of haunting in the area. Thomas Edison's ghost is sometimes said to walk the halls and streets surrounding his former home on Washington Street in Butchertown.

## Haunted Radio Station

***On Court Street*** in downtown Cynthiana, you'll find WCYN radio, an oldies station broadcasting at 1400 on the AM dial. According to some reports, the building is haunted with visual, audio, and kinetic manifestations. It's the oldest building in Cynthiana and in all of Harrison County in general. The ghost could be that of David Sheely, who was executed in 1847, apparently wrongly, according to the book *Chronicles of Cynthiana,* by Lucinda Boyd, published in 1894. Some believe that Sheely's ghost wanders Cynthiana still, looking for retribution for his unjust hanging.

## Haunted Hazard Hospital

***I live in Perry County,*** just a few miles outside of Hazard. We have a lot of legends of haunted places in and around Hazard—like the old Hazard Miners Memorial Hospital. It was closed in 1987 after 30 years serving the area. It is part of the college today. Many weird things go on there, like the sound of footsteps in the basement hall. The elevator will go floor to floor by itself, and voices and the sounds of footsteps walking in halls can be heard when no one is there. Doors open by themselves. A security guard told me a lot of guys quit their jobs at the hospital because of all this.*–Darth*

## Crybaby Bridge

***In Shelbyville*** there's a bridge known as Crybaby Bridge that has a myth attached to it regarding a baby who was allegedly killed there. The story goes that if you sprinkle baby powder all over the roof of your car and drive very slowly across the bridge, you'll hear a baby crying and sometimes you'll find a baby's footprints in the powder when you get to the other side.

Like the guys on the TV show "Mythbusters," a friend and I decided it couldn't hurt to put this strange-sounding legend to the test. We covered the roof of a 1999 Oldsmobile Intrigue with baby powder and cruised as gently as possible across the bridge, so as not to blow it all away. As it turns out, that's difficult to do. The vibrations and air currents inevitably mess up the powder, and if you flog your sense of disbelief sufficiently, you might be able to convince yourself that some of the patterns look like baby toes. (And since when do babies walk, anyway? Once they walk without help, aren't they then, by definition, no longer babies, but toddlers?)

Again some suspension of disbelief is needed to hear a baby crying, just as with the Singing Bridge in Frankfort,

which at least makes a grating sound as your tires cross it, but I wouldn't exactly call it singing.

Incidentally, there are Crybaby Bridges in many states, such as New Jersey, Alabama, South Carolina, and at least a dozen in Ohio alone! Most have similar legends associated with them.

## Brothers in Arms Share a Spooky Ride

***One night in 1994,*** as I made my way back from a bar in Louisville to the Army base at which I was stationed, I took a spectral hitchhiker for a short ride.

I didn't even know he was a ghost at first. I saw him on the side of the road in my headlights, stopped a little ways past him, reversed my car to where he stood and offered him a ride to the base, which was a good four or five miles off the highway. As he got into the car, I saw that he was wearing what I thought was an old Civil War outfit, complete with a sword. Since people in the area love the Civil War, I assumed he was part of a re-creation event and his outfit didn't bother me. It didn't even think it was odd that this was happening at three or four in the morning.

We drove not more than a mile or so. About 100 feet after we crossed an overpass, the soldier picked up his sword and asked me to stop. I asked him if he was sure, and told him it was too cold to be walking the rest of the way to the base, which is where I assumed he wanted to go. Plus, I explained, if he was regular Army he would have to be getting up in a few hours like the rest of us, and it was better if he just let me take him where he needed to go on base. He said no thanks, and that he appreciated the ride. He told me to have a safe trip.

So dressed in Confederate garb with hat, sword, and all, and very polite besides, he got out of my car. I looked in the passenger side mirror to see where he went and saw nothing. I looked on the other side of the car and saw more of the same. I put the car in reverse to use the backup lights and still saw nothing. I turned the car around and tried to use my headlights to see what I could see . . . nothing. There was nowhere else for the soldier to go and short grass for acres around the road, but he was gone.

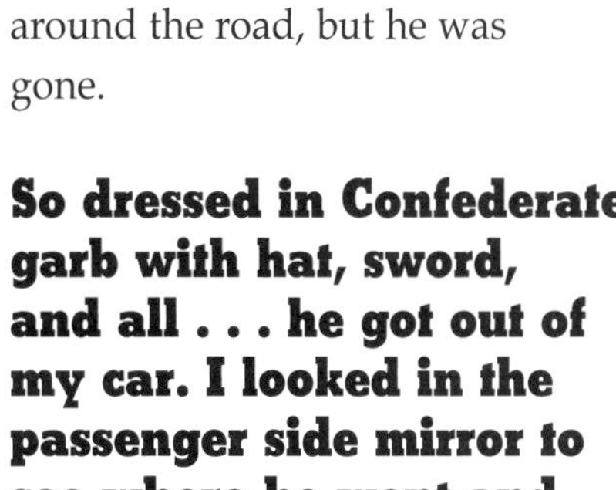

**So dressed in Confederate garb with hat, sword, and all . . . he got out of my car. I looked in the passenger side mirror to see where he went and saw nothing.**

I went home to my barracks and didn't think anything about it till the next day when I told my friends about what happened. They said I must have been drunk, but I'd only had a few drinks earlier that night and knew that I wasn't. And even though the drive from Louisville to the base took over an hour, I wasn't tired. I never ever thought that seeing a ghost would be something I might experience, but that's what happened to me.—*Lee Jorgensen*

## The Speed Museum

***This museum*** in downtown Louisville is said to be inhabited by a white-gowned female apparition in its basement, and some hold theories about the ghost being "Miss Hattie" Bishop Speed, the museum's founder. Supposedly, a lot of activity has occurred near a portrait of J. B. Speed's first wife, which has led many to speculate that Miss Hattie, his second wife, is jealous.

However, we're inclined to believe the place is teeming with all manner of ghosts, not just Miss Hattie's. The building is filled with paintings and sculpture, and we are convinced that such artwork has a great potential to hold a spiritual "charge" because of all the psychic energy that is put into its creation. The building also holds collections of antique furniture, textiles, and kitchenware, as well as cultural exhibits such as ancient African items and Native American artifacts. In fact, there have been reports of a ghost near the Native American culture display that do not match the "woman in white" believed to be Miss Hattie.

Let the ghost stories be the reason to get yourself into the Speed Museum if you haven't already been there. It's an amazing collection that demands repeating viewings by the living as well as the dead.

## Harrodsburg Spring Park

***A gravestone*** in the Harrodsburg public park, dedicated to a young woman—name unknown—bears this simple but chilling couplet:

> HALLOWED AND HUSHED BE THE PLACE OF THE DEAD.
> STEP SOFTLY. BOW HEAD.

The bits and pieces of her story are sketchy, but what is known is that she drifted into town in the late nineteenth century and checked in to the Graham Springs Hotel (later called the Harrodsburg Springs Hotel), which once stood where the park exists today. During a dance held that night, she came down from her room to take part in it, dancing with many men and generally being the life of the party. As was customary for most dances at this time, the lights were dimmed during most of the evening's festivities.

At the end of the evening, when the lights came back, the man she had been dancing with found she was dead in his arms. An attempt to notify her next of kin was fruitless, as it was determined she had checked in to the hotel using a falsified name (Virginia Stafford) and information. For some reason, rather than taking the Jane Doe to the nearest cemetery, she was buried right in the hotel's backyard. Even by nineteenth-century standards, displaying the graves of your unexplainably dead tenants on the lawn wasn't exactly good PR!

Then came a mysterious fire, which completely destroyed the building in the 1920s. The hotel's fiery end has been often attributed to the unknown dead woman's ghost. An unfortunately popular embellishment to the tale is to claim that the fire occurred "one hundred years to the day" of her death, which is not only impossible if you do the math, but presumes to know the date she died, which has not been determined.

If the woman's ghost was already haunting the premises between her death and the fire, we have no knowledge of it. But shortly after the hotel was immolated, reports starting popping up of people seeing the ghostly figure of a woman dancing in the area of her grave and the nearby springhouse. Once the park was established on the grounds and more people had a reason to be there, the sightings dramatically increased, making it one of the more popular and enduring ghost legends of Kentucky.

You can visit the park and its phantasmal guest by heading out Highway 63 in Monroe County. Ask a local if you can't find it; practically everyone there knows the ghostly tale.

## Ghosts of Mammoth Cave

***Perhaps*** the only location in the state more obviously haunted than Bobby Mackey's Music World is Mammoth Cave. In and of itself, the cave is a scientific anomaly, with a system of caverns that goes on for hundreds of miles, most of which has yet to be explored. It is still unknown where the cave ends. Many believe it connects to the Carlsbad cave system out west, and still others are convinced that it is the gateway to the deep subterranean "Hollow Earth" civilization that many have theorized about in the last century. Prehistoric man used Mammoth Cave as a burial site. Some of humanity's earliest funerals were held in this very spot, and it was apparently extremely sacred to this ancient civilization, no doubt seeming even then like a portal to another world.

In the eighteenth century, the area that would later become the Commonwealth of Kentucky was a sparsely populated, mysterious place. The local Native Americans were wary of it, using it as a place for hunting, but not for settlement. There was something dark, something sinister, something far more ancient than their own civilization, inhabiting this territory, it was said.

When deposits of saltpeter, which is used in gunpowder, were discovered in Mammoth Cave in the late eighteenth century, it created a reason for the area to become settled and populated. The property where the cave is located changed hands several times as it became a major source of this compound. Colonial settlers used at least seventy slaves at a time in the complicated saltpeter operation, and many died during the grueling and miserable labor. This too is thought to be a potential reason for the cave's ghostly activity.

After the War of 1812, the bottom fell out of the saltpeter market and Mammoth Cave's mines were forced to shut down. But by then the cave had become something of a tourist attraction in its own right, partially because of the bizarre mummified humanoids that were found by workers and slaves deep in some of the most remote cavernous passages. It was at this time that the name Mammoth Cave stuck and became official.

A later owner of the cave, Dr. William Croghan, set up an experimental clinic for tuberculosis patients in the cavern, under the misguided notion that the moist underground atmosphere would be curative. The experiment failed, and many of the patients died. They were buried near the entrance of the cave.

*Floyd Collins*

By the twentieth century, another tragedy created yet another haunting legend: that of explorer Floyd Collins. Collins entered a pit known as Sand Cave in an attempt to discover if it was connected to the Mammoth Cave system. We now know that Collins's hunch was right, and that it was indeed a branch of Mammoth Cave he was entering, but he never got to make that discovery for himself.

On January 30, 1925, Collins's foot was crushed by a giant boulder and was pinned under its immense weight. Before long, his lantern went out, and he was alone in the dark, in intense pain, and had the horror of knowing that he was in a place where no human had set foot in centuries. As he lay there, wedged under the rock in an uncomfortable sideways position, he no doubt thought of his mother's premonition before he left on his exploration: She had experienced a vision of poor Floyd dying in the cave and his soul being carried away by angels.

Sooner or later, people realized that Floyd wasn't coming back up, and a rescue mission was mounted. Although searchers did eventually manage to locate the injured man, they were at an utter loss as to what to do. Days were spent mulling things over as Collins lay there, his foot no doubt becoming increasingly necrotic. A reward was offered for anyone who could figure out a way to free him, but no one came forward, at least not with an idea anyone else considered viable. Why no one simply cut off Floyd's leg at the knee is a question that has never been answered. A gruesome solution, yes, but it beats dying—and that's exactly what happened to Floyd while everyone stood around mumbling, "Golly gee, there orta be some other way."

*Floyd Collins cave burial*

For years after his death, Floyd's body had even more adventures. Originally, he was given a burial inside the cave, but his brother Homer decided this was not a proper resting place. He had the body exhumed and transported to the family farm for burial. But a few years later, after Floyd's father sold the farm, the new owner dug up Floyd's corpse and placed it on display for tourists!

But wait, it gets even weirder. In 1929, unknown persons stole Floyd's corpse. An APB was issued to be on the lookout for Floyd Collins's dead body, and sure enough, it was eventually found in a cornfield, with one horrific (and somewhat ironic) difference: His left leg had been removed.

Floyd's corpse was returned to its post as a greeter for the tourists. His posthumously amputated leg was never recovered. Later he was reburied inside Crystal Cave, and then in 1989, he was moved yet AGAIN to the Flint Ridge Cemetery, where he remains today—as far as we know, anyway.

Many people are convinced that Floyd's ghost is still lurking around the area, inside and outside the cave. Those who believe in Floyd's ghost say his is a spiteful spirit, angered at the triple indignities he suffered in the bungled rescue, the multiple disinterments, and the theft of his leg.

Modern-day employees and visitors at Mammoth Cave still report paranormal phenomena on an almost daily basis: Lanterns inexplicably go off and on, apparitions of people appear and then disappear, and unexplained voices and other sounds echo through the subterranean labyrinth. If you visit only one haunted location in the state, make it Mammoth Cave. We guarantee it will not disappoint.

NEELY
1815

# Cemetery Safari

*Cemeteries are everywhere* you look in Kentucky. They're even in places you DON'T see. For instance, a few years back, South Hill Station, a Lexington shopping center, closed its doors and the building was to be converted to condominiums. When the workmen began digging out the foundation, they found buried skeletons. They eventually figured out that the shopping center had been built over a forgotten cemetery.

The South Hill Station story is perfectly exemplary of Kentucky in general: There's always something creepy and unknown going on underground!

Being so finely chopped up into small counties (one hundred and twenty of them: third-most counties of any state in the union), Kentucky naturally contains a higher number of official county cemeteries than many other states. And because of our dense mountainous and rural areas there's also a very high quotient of private family cemeteries, often on private property and just as often lost, forgotten, or bulldozed over. In fact, we could do an entire book on Kentucky's burial grounds, and one day we just might. In the meantime, here's just a smattering.

## Tent Girl

***In May 1968,*** a man named Wilbur Riddle happened to be collecting old glass telephone-pole insulators from the roadside of I-75 near Georgetown and, in so doing, made a ghoulish discovery.

He came upon a large bundle wrapped in green tent tarpaulins. Curious, he gave it a kick, and sent it rolling down the roadside embankment. As it went, the outer tarp came off and revealed a second tarp—shaped like a human body.

Riddle rushed to a nearby gas station and called the sheriff, who came out and cut away the tarp. Inside was a badly decomposing female body stiffened into a position seemingly of escape from the wrappings. She was white, sixteen to nineteen years old, with short, reddish brown hair, and no identifying scars, tattoos, or marks of any kind.

Because the Jane Doe was wrapped in tent tarpaulins, the press dubbed her Tent Girl. The police waited for someone to come forward to identify her, but no one did. False hopes were raised when a mother of a missing teen thought the body might be that of her daughter, but it wasn't.

Tent Girl was buried in Georgetown Cemetery in 1971 and received a headstone etched with the police sketch and description, in hopes that someone still might step forward to identify her. Months turned to years. Years turned to decades. All hope was lost of determining the identity of the girl who had become something of an icon as one of America's most troubling unsolved mysteries. Her grave site and the location in which her body was found both became part of something called "legend tripping"—destinations for curiosity seekers.

Then along came private detective Todd Matthews, who became fascinated with the story when he began dating Wilbur Riddle's daughter. He threw himself headlong into the case, devoting thousands of hours of research and travel to finding more information about Tent Girl. In 1998, his efforts paid off. Using the Internet, he met a woman who was seeking the whereabouts of her sister, Barbara Ann Hackmann-Taylor, who had been missing since 1967. Because Barbara was thought to have been living in Florida at the time of her disappearance, no one had connected her to Tent Girl until Matthews put the pieces of the story together and had the body exhumed. Sure enough, DNA evidence indicated that Tent Girl was indeed Barbara Ann Hackmann-Taylor, and the decades-long mystery was put to rest. A second grave marker, this one bearing her name, was placed underneath the original Tent Girl headstone.

But the mystery of what happened to her still remains, and we may never know the true circumstances of her death. Barbara's family last knew her to be in the company of her husband, a traveling carnival worker named George Earl Taylor. Prior to Tent Girl's identification, Mr. Taylor insisted that he hadn't seen Barbara in years, and that she had simply left him for another man without seeking a divorce. By the time Tent Girl was discovered to be his wife, he had long since died of cancer.

## Long Run Cemetery

***There's a lot of history*** in this obscure cemetery just east of Middletown, even if it's of a tangential sort: Abraham Lincoln's grandfather lies here, as does Harry Truman's great-uncle, and an acorn taken from a tree under which Abraham Lincoln once gave a speech is now thriving here as a full-fledged oak. Okay, maybe that's not exactly something that makes you leap from your chair yelling, "Honey, start the car!" but somebody else reading *Weird Kentucky* probably is doing just that.

The foundation of a demolished church is also on the grounds, and this adds to the peculiar yet peaceful vibe this place has. You'll find the cemetery on Old Stage Coach Road.

# Eastwood Cemetery

***There is a small cemetery*** in Eastwood with quite a few interesting stones, most notably:

- Nora Deadman's homemade concrete marker has no exact death date listed, even though the person who made the marker (seemingly by etching the dates into the wet concrete with a finger) had plenty of room for it.

- There's a stone with an arrow calling the visitor's attention to a mass grave believed to be located in a sinkhole next to the cemetery. It's said to contain the remains of pioneer settlers killed in "Floyd's Defeat" (also known as the "Long Run Massacre"), by a tag-team of Indians and British soldiers working in cooperation with each other. One of the few to escape the massacre was Squire Daniel Boone. So far, no one has mounted an archaeological expedition to confirm who in fact is buried in the sinkhole or to give them a more fitting burial.

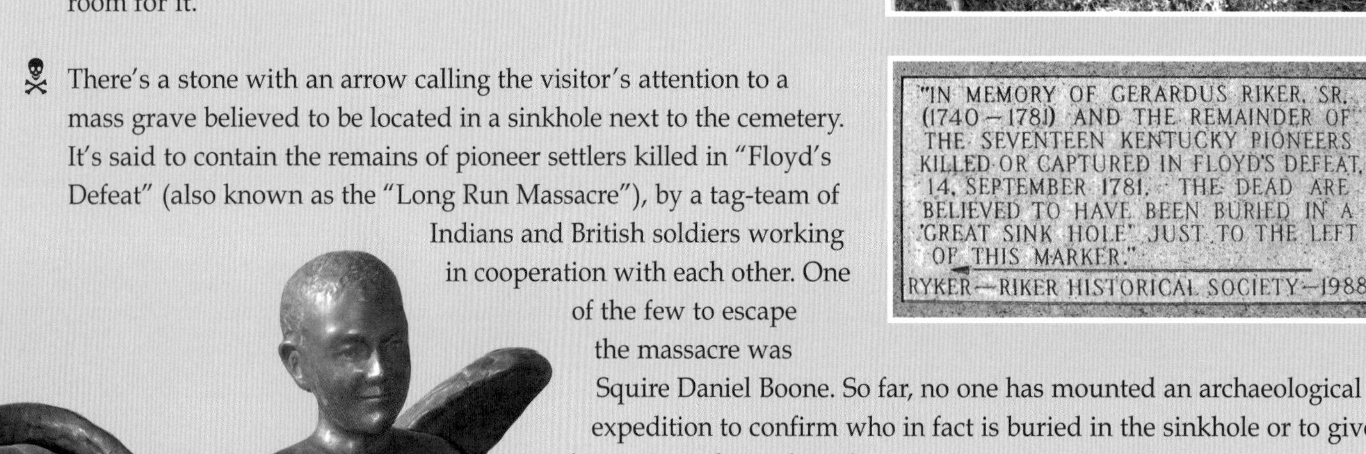


- A homemade marker for one "O. Mitchell" was apparently made by using a drill or another crude electric engraving tool on a slab of slate.

- A curiously striking bronze cherubic figure kneels in an odd pose, with hand extended, almost like he is at the end of a vaudeville dance routine. An ever-present collection of coins lies at his feet.

## Fred's Final Resting Place

***Many interesting*** and ornate nineteenth-century graves can be found at Simpsonville Cemetery, but the primary reason to visit it is to pay your respects to Fred Purnell.

Who's Fred Purnell? He's the man behind the world-famous Purnell's Sausage, whose plant still operates within a stone's throw of the cemetery and turns out over 100,000 pounds of country sausage each day.

Fred, a railroad engineer who didn't care for that weak city-boy sausage, started making his own country-style sausage at home. Its popularity grew, and before long, Fred was a sausage tycoon. In 1956, he purchased land in Simpsonville for a new sausage factory and never looked back. Purnell's was, and continues to be, the leader in the field of authentic old-style, whole-hog country sausage.

And even in passing, Fred was an innovator: This may be the only gravestone out there with a picture of a pack of sausage on it—not to mention a smiling, happy piggy!

## Bardstown Cemetery–St. Joseph's Cemetery

***Standing side by side*** in Bardstown, these twin graveyards cover a huge expanse of land with hundreds and hundreds of graves, ranging from the Revolutionary War era to the present day.

What we like most about this place, however, is the number of wonderful grave statues that have the color and overall appearance of milk chocolate. No matter how many times you look at them, you can't help imagining that these figures are drenched in hot chocolate fudge coating.

One of our favorites is the one that uses this Jedi inscription: MAY THE FORCE BE WITH YOU, ALWAYS. Considering that the *Star Wars* Jedi religion created by George Lucas has actually taken on a life of its own, claiming thousands of followers, we'll probably be seeing more graves like this one in the years to come.

## John Rowan's Toppling Tombstone

***A beloved figure*** in Bardstown history, John Rowan served as a judge, a United States Senator, a chief justice, and a Kentucky secretary of state. Such a great man with a lifelong string of accomplishments deserves a monumental gravestone, wouldn't you say?

Well, Rowan himself didn't think so. He made it clear in his final arrangements that he wanted no grave marker at all—not even a tiny one. (He felt that it would be disrespectful to his parents to have a grave marker that was superior to theirs—and they had no markers at all.) But then, as now, relatives have a bad habit of ignoring their loved ones' final wishes. The body was barely cold, and his family was already making arrangements for a headstone in Bardstown Cemetery. And not just any headstone. This would be an enormous and ostentatious obelisk—exactly the opposite of what Rowan had wanted.

Shortly after its installation, Rowan's stone fell over twice and was damaged. The stonemasons came back to repair it and stated they could find no reason for it to have fallen over. A couple of months later, they were called to reinstall the gravestone a third time, for it had toppled over again! Local stonemasons began to refuse to reerect it, cognizant of Rowan's final wishes and convinced he was sabotaging his own monument—from beyond the grave!

All sorts of rationalizations were made. Maybe the ground underneath was settling; maybe tree roots were interfering (even though there were none in sight). Thinking that for some reason this burial plot was unsuitable for an obelisk of this size, it was decided to dig Rowan up and transplant him to the Federal Hill Cemetery in Bardstown. But the stone kept tipping over there too, on an increasingly regular basis. Sentries were posted to make sure vandals were not responsible, and they saw the strange phenomenon with their own eyes. The marker just kept falling over completely by itself and for no visible reason!

The original stone was so damaged from all of its falls and patching up that it had to be replaced, and that is the current gravestone. To this day, they say it still won't stay upright.

# Whistlin' Dixie at Cave Hill

***One of the nation's*** most elaborate and prestigious cemeteries is Cave Hill, located at 701 Baxter Avenue in Louisville. Among its notable residents:

- Colonel Harland Sanders, the fried-chicken king
- Patty Hill, composer of "Happy Birthday to You"
- Jim Porter, the seven-foot-nine Kentucky Giant
- Louis Seelbach, co-founder of the Seelbach Hotel
- John Colgan, inventor of modern chewing gum
- William Shakespeare Hays, believed by many to be the true author of the song "Dixie"

Cave Hill's most amazing and beautiful monuments, however, aren't those of its celebrities. Take a day to explore the grounds and you'll be bombarded with sensory overload from the most diverse and striking collection of tombstones you're likely to find anywhere. And yes, take an entire day—this place is so huge, it's possible to get lost in it. There's a white line and a yellow line running through two roads to help you find your way out of the labyrinth. (Tip: The yellow one will take you directly to Colonel Sanders's grave.)

And for the genealogy researchers among you, Cave Hill has a superb burial database archive, which is searchable both on computer and on hard copy in their offices.

J.S.
LAMPTON
BOUCHE

COL. HARLAND SANDERS
COL. HARLAND SANDERS

## Black Cat of Bardstown

***The old stone jail*** at Bardstown has been there for 200 years. A coffee tree grows beside it, the only one known in the state of Kentucky. Also located beside it is a very small, old cemetery with some aboveground crypts that are in disrepair, the bones they contained having long since turned to dust. No inscriptions are readable on these crypts.

A large and very unusual black cat haunts this cemetery. Larger than an average housecat, it always appears from the biggest of the old crypts. A chill wind will always begin to blow, even on the hottest summer day. It follows you with large eyes that seem to glow with an intelligent, supernatural light. If you glance away, it will disappear and reappear in another part of the cemetery, without any noticeable movement, always watching.

Some people say it is the ghost of a woman who was hanged for witchcraft in the early 1800s. Others say that it is the guardian of the family that are (or were) buried in the crypts. It has been seen for years, and I have personally seen it myself several times over a time span of 25 years. It always disappears as you leave the cemetery. It always looks the same, no matter how many years have passed since I have been there. I like to pay occasional visits to this cemetery, just to see if the cat appears, and he has always done so. If he is just a regular ol' cat, he sure has aged well!–*Karen Drake*

## The Frito-Lay Magician

***All but forgotten,*** Harry Collins of Glasgow is known today for the striking and slightly eerie larger-than-life-size statue of himself that stands over his grave in Cave Hill Cemetery. Some people have reported hearing music coming faintly from his grave. Each day, a fresh flower appears in his statue's hand, along with a penny in his lapel, baffling the cemetery caretakers.

For decades, Collins was known as the official traveling magician for Frito-Lay, entertaining shoppers in live supermarket appearances and on television commercials. And of course, whenever he performed his feats of prestidigitation, instead of "voila" or "alakazam" he shouted, "Frito-Lay!"

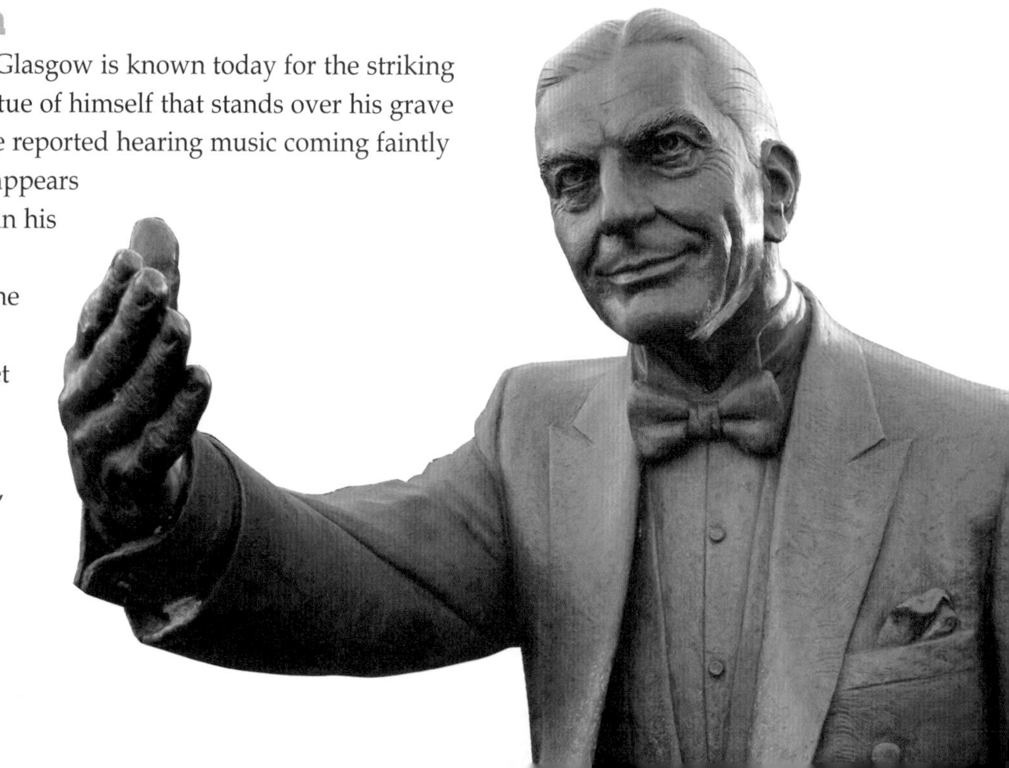

## Montgomery Cemetery

***This cemetery*** is not accessible by car, and if you blink you'll miss it when driving down Highway 150 in Bullitt County. It's ensconced in the middle of a cow pasture, which, at the time *Weird Kentucky* visited, was very muddy, very cowpie-laden, and very full of livestock. It's a nice feeling to be in a cemetery and yet surrounded on all sides by curious, mooing cattle. Such a nice feeling, in fact, that we didn't want to leave once we'd made the trek out there. Someone in a nearby home told us that it's generally considered okay to climb the gate and slog your way across if your purpose is to visit the cemetery.

## Charles "Speedy" Atkins

***Maplelawn Park Cemetery's*** most famous resident might be Charles "Speedy" Atkins of Paducah. Just as Floyd Collins's fame came after his death and largely as a result of what happened to his body afterward, so did Atkins's claim to fame arrive posthumously. Atkins, born 1875, was a migrant tobacco-farm worker from Tennessee who earned the nickname Speedy due to the haste with which he performed his tobacco labors. In 1928, he drowned after falling overboard into the Ohio River from a fishing boat while drunk and was subsequently mummified by his friend and funeral home embalmer A. Z. Hamock. Yes, that's right, we said mummified.

It seems Hamock, who was the director of the town's only African American funeral home, had been working on developing an experimental new formula for preserving bodies and was eager to try it out. It worked so well that the corpse was transformed into a solid statue. Atkins had no relatives and few friends, so there was no one around to object, although Hamock reportedly did obtain permission for his experiment from the McCracken County coroner.

So impressed was Hamock with his handiwork that he abandoned his plan to bury Speedy in the nearby Oak Grove Cemetery. Instead, Hamock chose to prop up the mummified body in the lobby of his funeral home and display him there for all to see (though Speedy did take a holiday for a while when he was temporarily washed away in the Paducah flood of 1937). Even though Hamock died in 1946, Speedy remained on display until 1994, when he was finally given a proper burial by Hamock's widow, Velma. Mrs. Hamock, who now runs the funeral home, told *JET* magazine before the funeral services, "It was all an experiment, but it was a success. Speedy's never been duplicated, he's the only one that we know of. He's not stinking, nothing. The amazing thing is he really hasn't lost all of his features. He doesn't look like a corpse laying up in the casket for sixty-six years. I never saw a dead man bring so much happiness to people." Speedy's funeral, steel casket, flowers, and burial plot were all donated by local businesses.

Before his burial, Speedy had plenty of adventures: He had been featured in numerous publications, including *Ripley's Believe It or Not!* and the *National Enquirer*. He was even the star of an episode of the television program *That's Incredible!* Incredible indeed!

## Return to Sender

***Weird, but true:*** This peculiar cemetery, which apparently consists of one mass grave, is located in the front yard of the post office in Berea. Brings new meaning to the term Dead Letter Office.

As far as we can tell, they must have built this post office on the site of an old graveyard and either moved all the bodies to the front, or just built on top of them and placed a marker with a list of names up front as a sort of gesture of goodwill. One of the entries has ___ where his first name should be, indicating that these names were most likely transcribed off old, hard-to-read tombstones.

Whether the bodies were moved or not, it still seems a rather ignominious end for people who once had individual graves and markers of their own but now are lumped together for all eternity.

Another theory: Perhaps this is the original site of the cemetery, but when the post office bought the property, they decided that it didn't look right to have all these scary old tombstones laying around in their front yard and did away with them in favor of this nice, white, clean, tasteful, simple, single monument that doesn't look so spooky. Either way, we still think it's a rotten deal for the residents.

And, oh, yeah, it should go without saying that all of this is clearly a warning sign that this post office is probably haunted. Stay alert while you're buying your stamps.

## Cemetery in the Louisville Zoo

***Another cemetery*** whose hallowed ground is now surrounded by civilization can be found at the Louisville Zoo. It's an odd feeling to be taking in the giraffe exhibit one moment and staring at someone's grave the next.

The cemetery—and the zoo—now occupy what was once a vast tract of land owned by Jenkin Phillips, an early surveyor of Kentucky and a Revolutionary War soldier who fought alongside George Washington.

## Valley of Rest

***It's a lovely name*** for a cemetery—although it's not really in a valley, and we're not sure how restful it is, being surrounded by gas stations and fast-food joints in the town of La Grange. There are many interesting headstones here, but Valley of Rest's most notable occupant is Rob Morris, whose marker proclaims him the poet laureate of Freemasonry.

Morris is quite revered for his numerous books and other writings in the secretive and spooky world of Freemasons. But even more importantly, he is the founder of the Order of the Eastern Star. The OES is a Masonic organization that is open to males and females but is largely operated by female relatives of Master Masons. Their insignia consists of an upside-down pentagram with various items inside it, such as a candle and a chalice.

Morris was also grand master of the Grand Lodge of Kentucky and president of the Masonic College.

## Polly Want a Tombstone?

***Located*** on Main Street in downtown Richmond, Richmond Cemetery is a very large and beautiful graveyard filled with a variety of interesting stones:

- James McCreary and his pet Polly—Former governor of Kentucky. Not many locals are aware that a former governor is buried here, and even fewer realize that McCreary's pet bird, Polly, is buried in her own grave beside him. As far as we know, Polly is the only animal buried in Richmond Cemetery.

- Keen Johnson—Another former governor of Kentucky, and the namesake of the haunted building on E.K.U.'s campus (see "Ghosts" chapter).

- Walter Tevis—This is the final resting place for Kentucky's great pool hustler and writer.

- Fiddlin' Doc Roberts—Old-time country music star who baffled his fans by giving up his career at the peak of his success in 1935 and returning to a life of farming and anonymity.

- Earle Combs—New York Yankees Hall of Fame baseball star of the 1920s and '30s. (Is it just us, or is Combs's gravestone leaning drastically to one side?)

- T.C.—This is a delightful homemade stone, which is decorated with a primitive mosaic of broken Milk of Magnesia bottles, soda bottles, and marbles. You can find T.C.'s grave near the railroad tracks.

- French Tipton—Few people outside the area may have heard of him, but his grave is worth laying a flower on. Tipton was something of a Renaissance man during the nineteenth century. He was a newspaper editor for the *Richmond Register* and also published his own paper. He was an author, an attorney, and eventually a judge. He was, and is, considered the most important historian of Madison County. Unfortunately, he died before he could complete his masterwork history of the area. For reasons unclear, in September 1900, Tipton initiated a fistfight with Clarence Woods, the editor of a rival newspaper, while walking down North Second Street in downtown Richmond. Woods produced a pistol and shot Tipton point-blank. Tipton died from the wounds two days later in his home.

# Pets Rest Easy in Shepherdsville

***You can feel it coming*** from a long way off, as you drive down the winding country road toward Pet Haven. There's a very palpable vibe to this place. Even for those who don't believe in ghosts, bad karma, spooks, curses, or mojo, this cemetery just radiates sadness.

It doesn't help that the plot is largely treeless and wedged into a narrow strip of land adjacent to some sort of auto-work garage. Hardly feng shui for the final resting place of anyone, be it your great-grandmother or your Great Dane. But since pet cemeteries are difficult to come by in these parts, we suppose one has to accept it if they want to give their pet a superior final tribute other than a flush or a shoebox in the backyard.

Yet, paradoxically, the low-budget tackiness of Pet Haven is precisely what allows it to afford pets their superior final tribute. Most fancier pet cemeteries have the same restrictions on grave decor as a regular cemetery. But in Pet Haven, apparently anything goes! Many of the graves are piled high with elaborate decorations, offerings, and tributes that are sure to bring a tear to the eye of even the most hard-hearted. Like a public art installation on grief, these altars and shrines are profoundly moving and profoundly inspirational. It's nothing short of beautiful.

We asked a nearby resident if she'd ever encountered any sort of ghostly phenomena that might be attributed to the cemetery, and she said most emphatically that she has but refused to elaborate or to go on record.

Pet Haven is located near downtown Shepherdsville and is a must-see for any cemetery aficionado, but not for the faint of heart. It can be depressing for days afterward.

## Frankfort Cemetery

***Situated*** high on a hill with a breathtaking view looking down on the state capitol, Frankfort Cemetery is home to such notables as:

- Luke Blackburn—A former governor of Kentucky who pardoned the famous prostitute Belle Brezing (see "Local Heroes and Villains"), Blackburn is considered by some to be the "father of bioterrorism" because of rumors that he devised a plot during the Civil War to deliver clothing infected with yellow fever to northern states and even to Abraham Lincoln. Legend has it that Blackburn went to Bermuda during a yellow fever epidemic there in order to collect clothing from the sick and the dead for purposes of transporting it back to the United States. The plan was ultimately foiled, but it wouldn't have mattered anyway. What no one knew back then was that yellow fever was actually spread by mosquitoes, not by contact with people or infected articles of clothing. Somehow, instead of being lynched for attempted mass murder and attempted presidential assassination, Blackburn went on to become governor of Kentucky.

- William Goebel—Yet ANOTHER former governor of Kentucky, but one who held office for only a few days. He was assassinated on January 30, 1900, after a highly contested election fraught with irregularities. He lived for a few days afterward, but ultimately succumbed to his wounds while eating a dinner of oysters.

  Opposition to the generally disliked-by-all Goebel and his suspicious election (which was, in fact, rigged) threatened to tear Kentucky apart into a civil war of its own. Although Goebel's PR people released a statement that the governor's final words on his deathbed were, "Tell my friends to be brave, fearless, and loyal to the common people," it was later revealed by eyewitnesses that his actual last words were, "Doc, that was a damned bad oyster."

- Paul Sawyier—The well-known Impressionist painter led a happy and productive life until the 1914 death of his lover, Mary "Mayme" Bull, who is also interred here. Sawyier lost all will to live after her death and quickly dissolved into despair and alcoholism until his own demise in 1917.

- Daniel Boone—Well, there's a memorial with his name on it here, anyway, that much we can say for sure.

### *Daniel Boone's Grave—or Is It?*

By the end of his life, pioneer Daniel Boone, a beloved hero in Kentucky history, wasn't a big fan of the state he had helped create. He was hounded by creditors and lawsuits, wanted by the police for failure to appear at a court date, and ignored by the new governor, Isaac Shelby, when a high-paying contract to widen Boone's Wilderness Road was given to someone else.

Boone had seen this territory go from a wild, free, unoccupied forest to a growing hub of civilization, business, and government bureaucracy in just thirty years, and he'd had enough. Thumbing his nose at what Kentucky had become, he packed up his family in 1799 and left the United States for the territory of Missouri, which was owned by Spain at that time.

Boone died in Defiance, Missouri, in the year 1820, and was buried nearby in a small hamlet called Marthasville with his wife, Rebecca. In 1845, it was decided that he be reinterred in Kentucky, specifically in Frankfort. But according to Boone's relatives, the wrong body was dug up.

As the story goes, Boone had been buried at Rebecca's feet because the plot next to hers was already taken. At the time of the reinterment, Boone's family didn't correct the Frankfort officials, who made the assumption that Boone's body was the one buried next to Rebecca.

In 1983, forensic anthropologists who had studied the body in Frankfort's "Daniel Boone grave" announced the results of their analysis: It was most likely that of an African American. Frankfort disputes this, however, and naturally maintains that their Daniel Boone grave is the real one. The Old Bryan Farm Graveyard in Missouri, meanwhile, still insists that it has Boone's true remains.

# Maplewood's Grand Grave

***What may be*** the most elaborate grave marker in the entire commonwealth sits in this cemetery in Mayfield. Majestic and ostentatious at the same time, it marks the final resting place of Henry G. Woolridge.

Woolridge was a wealthy eccentric who lived with his niece in Mayfield. He seems to have come down with some sort of obsessive-compulsive disorder around the time he decided to pick out a grave marker for his burial plot. First there was a tall and majestic monument with various ornate touches such as a rifle, a horse, and the Masonic emblem. But that wasn't enough. At great expense, he had a statue of himself carved from marble by expert Italian sculptors. But it STILL wasn't enough. So he added another statue. And another. And another. It became a sort of addiction for Woolridge, and by the time of his funeral, there were no less than eighteen markers crowded together at his grave site.

Two of the statues depict Woolridge—one at a lectern and one astride a horse—and others portray various family members such as his mother, sisters, brothers, and nieces. (Pointedly, he chose not to include his father in the strange procession.) Also in the parade are a fox, a deer, and two dogs.

In another section of Maplewood, you'll find the grave of Henry Bascom Hicks, an accused spy who was executed by a firing squad in August 1864 (legend has it that he refused the traditional blindfold, stating, "I can look you in the eye"), and the grave for eleven people of the Drew and Lawrence families, who all died in 1921 in a mysterious house fire that some say was deliberately set to conceal the evidence that they were already dead, victims of a mass murder. The remains were so unrecognizable that all of the charred body fragments were stuffed into one coffin and buried in one grave with one stone.

# Eternal Embrace

***If you happen*** to pass through Maple Grove Cemetery in Bloomfield, you will find a historical marker describing the "Romantic 1825 Tragedy" that happened here. It's a classic bit of all-American trailer-trash drama that actually predates the trailer.

On November 7, 1825, Jereboam Beauchamp, a law student, stabbed former Kentucky attorney general Colonel Solomon Sharp to death in Sharp's home. Sharp had allegedly fathered a child with Beauchamp's wife, Anna, several years prior to her marriage to Jereboam. Reportedly, Anna married Jereboam only on the condition that he would murder Sharp, thus avenging her honor.

Jereboam, in a classic example of lawyer-think, assumed that no one would suspect him, precisely because he was in fact the most logical suspect. But suspect him they did, and he was sentenced to death for murder.

The part where this is supposed to be romantic is this: Anna stayed in the prison cell with Jereboam for the entire length of his incarceration. The couple made two suicide attempts together in that time. The first, by poisoning, failed. The second, by stabbing—attempted the day of Jereboam's hanging—succeeded, at least for Anna, who immediately died from her wounds.

Jereboam would have died from his wounds, but the police didn't want to be robbed of their right to kill him themselves. They rushed him to the gallows and quickly hanged him even as he was dying of blood loss. It was the first legal hanging in Kentucky, so the crowds really swelled up for it. There probably would have been a riot if they had been told the day's entertainment was cancelled because the one they had come to see die had already died.

As legend has it, Anna and Jereboam are buried together in an eternal embrace inside a shared coffin. How romantic is that? The Beauchamps rank high on the weird list of Kentuckians who did really stupid things for love.

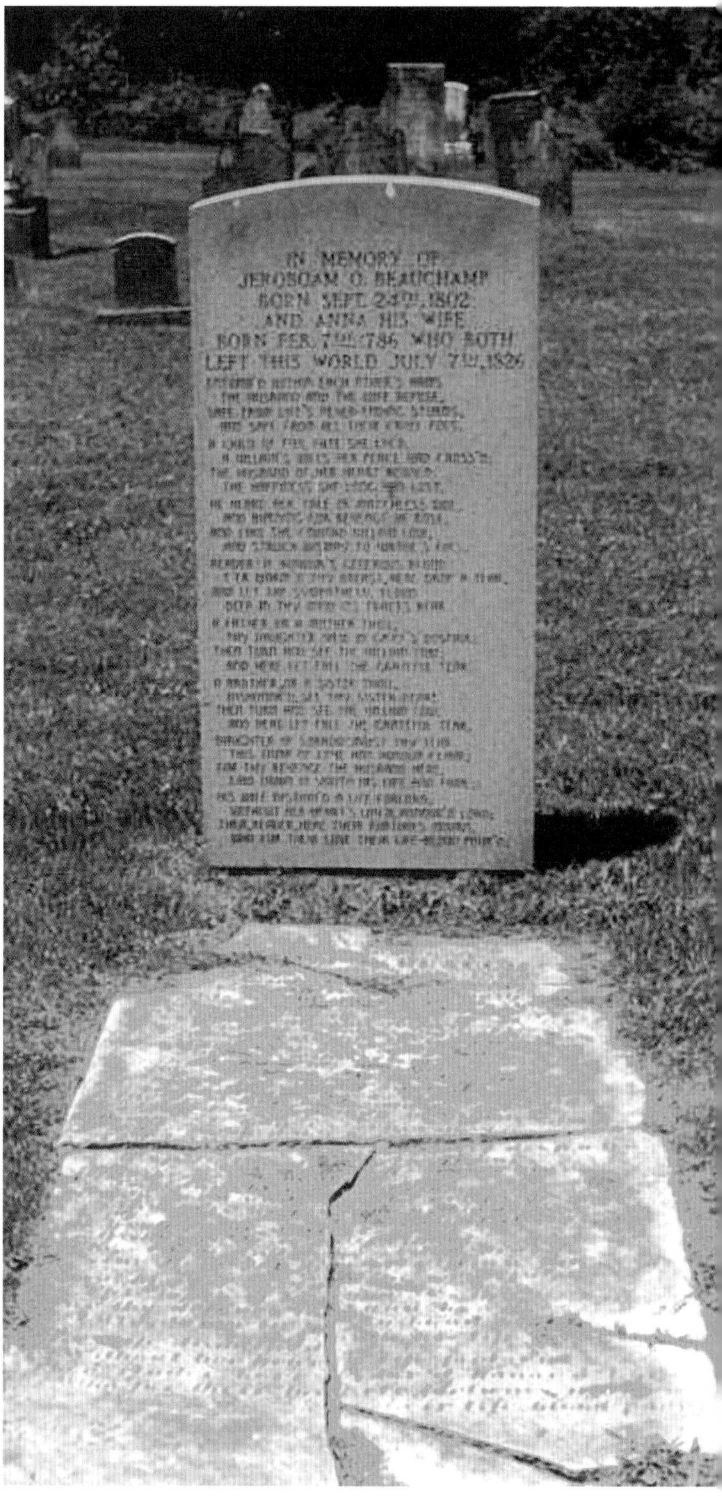

## How to Get into Heaven in Six Steps

***If you're looking*** for a surefire plan detailing how to pass through the Pearly Gates without stopping to explain yourself, look no farther than the grave site of Mr. Lesley Murdock. Conveniently, he provides this plan for you on a plaque at his mausoleum in Tri-City, where he and his wife are interred.

Forget the fact that this plan isn't really Murdock's own, entirely—he copped a lot of it from the Gospel of John. But still, he instructed that it be included on the mausoleum, and he even had a large sign installed on top of it that read STOP AND SEE A ROAD MAP TO HEAVEN. Somewhere along the line, the sign came down, but the plaque remains.

Murdock was a religious man who founded the Paradise Friendly Home, an orphanage that closed a few years before he died in 1979. What's left of the building (which mostly fell to a fire in the late 1980s) still stands, a few miles down the road from the mausoleum.

Since caring for defenseless orphans probably guarantees one a ticket into the big wonderland in the sky, Mr. Murdock likely didn't need to consult his own road map to find his way there.

## Baby Dolls in Jars

***Cowbell Cemetery*** is one of *Weird Kentucky*'s favorite graveyards, due to the odd custom of decorating graves with baby dolls in jars. Presumably the "canning" of the babies is to keep them safe from the elements, of course, but it's just a very peculiar sight to see these dolls staring out from jars and canisters on several different plots in the same graveyard.

Cowbell's located between Berea and Big Hill near the Jackson County border and is hidden off the main road. If you go, please don't mess with the bottled babies. Remember, the weird travelers' golden rule to "take only pictures and leave only footprints" applies to cemeteries too.

## For Whom the Bells Toll

***Thirty miles*** east of Bowling Green is the town of Glasgow, and here you'll find Ridge Cemetery, a small and simple graveyard worth visiting—not for its graves, but for its ghosts.

The story often told is that the spirits of two brothers have lurked here since the 1880s, after they killed each other in a duel held in the graveyard. Most of the evidence is not of a visual nature, but aural: The unexplained sound of tiny delicate bells can often be heard here, it is said, but why these ghostly bells are attributed to these brothers is a question with no apparent answer.

## Deadly Chain of Events

***In 1938,*** stories of a "killer ghost" began to be told around Pulaski County in southeastern Kentucky. Even though no one ever saw this malevolent apparition, it was said to have caused five very similar and unexplained deaths.

In June of that year, a man named Carl Pruitt came home from work one night and found his wife with another man. After her lover escaped by jumping out of a window, Pruitt strangled the woman with a small piece of chain. Immediately after, perhaps having just realized the depth of his madness, he committed suicide. He was buried in a separate cemetery from his wife.

Not long after Pruitt was buried, visitors to the cemetery started to notice that the pattern of a chain was slowly forming on the dead man's gravestone. Kentucky writer Michael Paul Henson first chronicled this strange phenomenon just a few weeks after Pruitt's death. The chain image was caused by an unusual discoloration in the stone, and it slowly gained links until it formed the shape of a cross. At that point, it stopped growing. A number of local residents suggested that perhaps the supernaturally marked tombstone should be removed from the graveyard and destroyed, but officials scoffed and nothing was done about it.

One afternoon a month or so after the chain stopped growing, a group of boys were riding their bicycles past the cemetery. One of them, James Collins, decided to throw a few stones at Pruitt's "cursed" gravestone, probably just to prove that he wasn't scared by its spooky stories. Whatever the reason for his actions, the hurled rocks managed to chip several spots from the stone. As the young men started home, Collins's bicycle suddenly began to pick up speed, to the point that he could no longer control it. It veered off the road and collided with a tree. In a gruesome turn of events, the sprocket chain somehow tore loose and strangled the boy. Rumors quickly spread about this horrible coincidence, especially after an examination of the Pruitt tombstone revealed that no marks or chips marred its surface. The other boys knew what they had seen, however, and their breathless accounts only fueled speculation about a vengeful ghost.

James Collins's mother was inconsolable over her son's death. Less than a month after his accident, she went out to the cemetery and destroyed the Pruitt gravestone with a small hand axe. She pounded and hacked at the stone until it lay in dozens of pieces. The following day, she was hanging the family wash on the line. The clothesline was made from small linked chain rather than the usual rope or wire. Somehow, she slipped and fell, and her neck became entangled in the chain. She tried to free herself, but it was no use, and she too was strangled to death. Legends say that after she died, the Pruitt tombstone once again showed no signs of destruction.

Needless to say, news of this most recent incident spread fast and furious. A short time later, a local farmer and his family were driving a wagon past the cemetery. The farmer announced that he had no fear of ghosts and fired several shots at the Pruitt stone with his revolver. Chunks flew off the marker, and immediately the horses pulling the wagon began to run faster and faster, until the wagon was out of control. The family all jumped to safety, but the farmer hung on, frantically pulling on the reins. Just as the wagon veered around a curve in the road, he was thrown from his seat and tumbled forward. His neck snagged on one of the trace chains, and the motion of the horses snapped his neck. For the third time, Pruitt's stone showed no signs of the damage that had been done to it.

The local residents were now convinced that the

grave marker was cursed. People were so frantic that two police officers were sent to the cemetery to investigate. When they arrived at the graveyard, one of the cops began to laugh about the stories and made fun of the idea of so-called ghosts and curses. Regardless, they took several photos of the stone and then left to go talk with the witnesses to the events surrounding it.

As they were leaving, the doubting officer happened to look into his car's rearview mirror. In it, he saw a bright light coming from the direction of the Pruitt tombstone. At first, he assumed that it was just a reflection from the car's taillights, but then it began to get closer to the car. Startled, he began to drive faster, but the light kept coming. He drove faster and faster, always watching his mirror. His partner pleaded with him to slow down, but it was no use. The light was still coming.

Just then the car swerved off the road and crashed between two posts. It rolled over and over several times. The officer on the passenger side was thrown clear of the wreck and was only slightly hurt. Shaken, he climbed to his feet and went to his partner's aid. He found that his friend was dead . . . but he had been killed before the car had wrecked. As the car passed between the two posts, a chain that was hanging between them had shattered the car's windshield and wrapped around the driver's neck. The force was so great that it had nearly severed his head.

After this death, residents began to avoid the cemetery altogether. Only one man, Arthur Lewis, dared to go there. He was determined to prove that the stories of a cursed tombstone were nothing but superstitious nonsense. One evening, after telling his wife what he intended to do, he went to the graveyard with a hammer and chisel and began to methodically destroy the grave marker. The sounds of the hammer and the shattering stone could be heard by all who lived near the cemetery . . . and they also heard the bloodcurdling scream that filled the night! Several men grabbed lanterns and went down to investigate. When they arrived, they found Lewis dead, with the long chain that had been used to close the cemetery gate wrapped about his neck. Apparently, something had frightened him and he had started running, forgetting about the chain that barred the entrance gate. Oddly, even though ten or fifteen people had heard the sound of the man breaking Pruitt's gravestone, there were no marks or broken places on it.

After this last death, other bodies in the cemetery were removed and buried again in other locations. People gradually moved away, and the small burial plot was forgotten. Since Pruitt had no family left to care for his grave, the site became overgrown and tangled with weeds. In 1958, it was destroyed for good by a strip-mining operation. The five strange deaths, all linked by chains, were never explained.—*Troy Taylor*

## Bert & Bud's Vintage Coffins

*"Don't Be Caught Dead Without One"*

***Bud Davis*** is an artist, but some of his masterpieces can be hard to find. As he'll gladly tell you himself, most of the art he's made is buried!

Davis, sixty-eight, a Kentucky native and former museum curator, makes coffins. And not the big, generic kind you might get offered at your run-of-the-mill funeral home, either. No, Davis's coffins are lovingly designed for each unique individual who commissions one, because as he points out on the Web site for his business, Bert & Bud's Vintage Coffins, in Murray, your coffin is your last chance to make a first impression.

What type of coffin can you order from Davis? Well, any kind you like! While he specializes in an old-fashioned "toe pincher" design, he is happy to work to create a final resting place that is as original as its owner. For an average price of between $1,200 and $1,800 (Davis notes: cheaper than most!), you can order a coffin that speaks to who you are, or were, with a customized shape, fabric color, type of wood, decorative design, and so on. Or, if you are looking for an unusual weekend project, Davis will send you a "coffin kit." Your coffin will arrive flat in a box, complete with the tools and glue needed to put it together, so you can assemble it yourself.

Davis's coffin-making business started out as an art project and a labor of love. In an effort to commemorate some long-gone family members, he built half-coffins to serve as memorials to them. He thought about making his own coffin, and then it hit him that everyone's coffin deserves to be a work of art. He launched Bert & Bud's Vintage Coffins with his friend Bert Sperath—another artist who offered studio space and accounting abilities—and got to work. Thirteen years later, the business is still going strong. Guess there's always a need for coffins!

Bud now runs the business on his own, as Bert moved to Mississippi to curate a museum. Among his more attention-grabbing coffins are one he designed for *Maxim* magazine in the shape of a beer bottle, a steamboat coffin owned by—as Davis puts it—"a real live Mississippi riverboat captain," and a coffin for Kentucky local legend Leonard Hobbs. Hobbs is a Santa Claus impersonator who uses the casket as a coffee table. It's also a great place to hide his wife's Christmas presents, as she finds it too creepy to open.

While Davis does a good deal of business with people who are planning in advance for their day of reckoning, there are many others who don't actually want to be buried in their coffins. These folks use them as blanket chests or tables. For instance, as Davis laughingly tells the tale, he has one customer who "keeps hers in her living room and calls it her 'end' table!" Another customer had her coffin built with a padded top and uses it as a window seat. She stashes her sewing supplies inside.

Davis can't put a finger on his typical customer, but he finds that most are "practical people over the age of fifty who have a sense of humor about them." At first Bud and Bert thought that Civil War reenactors would be their target market, because reenactors seemed willing to "spend a lot of money on authenticity." But Davis says, "Most were only interested to see if we would line a coffin with Styrofoam so they could carry their beer in it!" (They wouldn't.)

If you're interested in designing a coffin for short-term (coffee table, sewing caddy) or long-term (ahem, burial) use, visit www.vintagecoffins.com.

*—Abby Stillman Grayson*

Bert & Bud's
Vintage Coffins

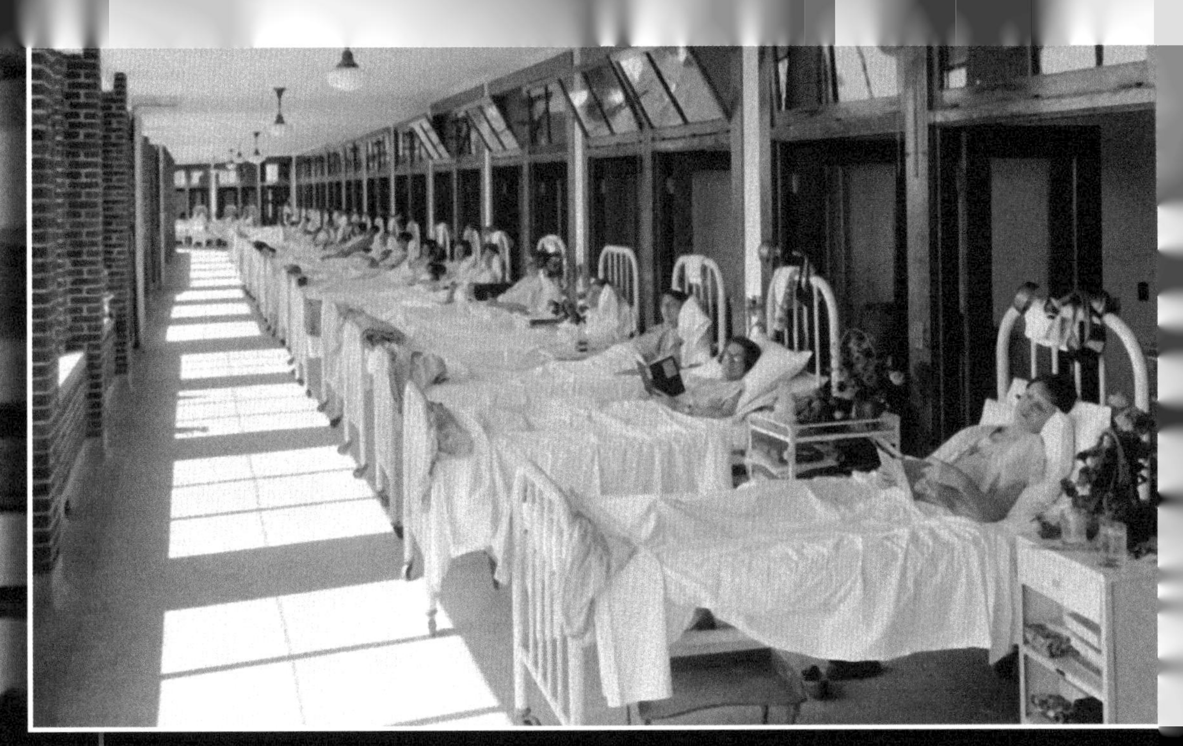

# Abandoned in Kentucky

**Abandoned places are a constant source of intrigue and fascination. They seem to carry with them the imprint of their pasts, the days before they were gutted and rotting husks. Items littered on the ground—from papers to machinery to the personal belongings of those who walked their hallways long ago—serve as reminders that living, breathing humans once lived or worked in these now empty spaces. These places allow u the voyeuristic pleasure of seeing how life once was, up close, personal, and in way that no museum could ever match.**

**Besides all that, and more simply, there's just nothing creepier than an old creaky building on a foggy night.**

# Waverly Hills Sanatorium

***To those interested*** in the paranormal, Waverly Hills Sanatorium is a national landmark. Ghost hunters travel to Waverly in the same way religious folks head to Mecca and Jerusalem. It is a revered, respected spot for some serious weirdness. Waverly sits upon a hill in southern Jefferson County, abandoned and slowly succumbing to the ravages of time. Vandals have long ago broken every window in the building, and graffiti covers the walls like ugly tattoos. All the doors on the lower levels have been boarded shut in an attempt to keep out trespassers, and piles of dirt and rubble are strewn about the building. It is an inhospitable place, plain and simple. But despite all its shortcomings, some say there are those who still live within its walls. Not vagrants looking for shelter or teenagers holding clandestine meetings, but the spirits of those who came to the hospital for treatment of what was known as the white plague.

At the turn of the century, Jefferson County had one of the highest tuberculosis rates in the nation. With no cure for the disease, the only alternative was convalescence away from the general public. The hope was that the disease would not be spread farther and that the patients would enjoy the benefit of clean country air. The original hospital opened in 1911 with facilities for forty patients. Soon it became painfully apparent that more beds were needed, so in 1924, construction began on the building that currently stands. It was five stories tall and large enough to house four hundred patients.

Many patients who came to Waverly were actually cured enough to once again enter society. For those not so fortunate, Waverly was the last place they ever saw. Records have been lost, but it is estimated that tens of thousands died here. It is reported that at the height of the tuberculosis epidemic, one patient an hour died. Corpses were taken from the hospital and transported down a steam tunnel, now known as the Body Chute, to hearses waiting at the bottom of the hill. This was done so as to avoid lowering the morale of the patients still alive.

With the discovery of streptomycin, the tide of tuberculosis was turned and the need for the hospital was no more. Waverly Hills closed its doors as a TB hospital in 1961, but reopened two years later as a geriatric center. The state closed it for good in 1980, citing mistreatment of patients. Details of the mistreatment were never released, so we are left to assume the worst.

Since 1980, Waverly Hills has stood vacant, a destination for the homeless and teenagers looking for a place to hang out. As time passed, legends started to grow about paranormal activity. Three stories in particular have cemented themselves as sort of emblematic of the decrepit building. One involves a young woman named Mary who can be seen staring out of a third-floor window. Another tells of an elderly woman who runs out of the main entrance, her wrists slit and bleeding, pleading for help. A third concerns a nurse who hanged herself in room 502, depressed over the pain and suffering that surrounded her. To many these are just legends, but to some they are as real as the building itself.

A former security guard reported an encounter at Waverly that caused him to walk off his job in the middle of his shift and never return. The other guards had gone out for something to eat, so he was left alone at the old and now abandoned building. He was sitting at the far end of the dirt parking lot, away from the building, when he spotted a hearse driving up the road and through the open gates. He watched as it went up to the side of the building and stopped in front of the old loading dock. Before he could call out or move toward it, two men wearing white orderlies' uniforms exited the vehicle and went directly into the building, using the door adjacent to what was once the morgue. The security guard stood amazed for a moment. Unable to decide his next course of action, he continued to stare at the hearse, not letting it leave his sight. He then saw the door next to the morgue reopen and the two men reappear, carrying what seemed to be a large box. The men carried the object around to the rear of the hearse, and one of them opened the swing-out door. As the door opened, the overhead dome light came on, giving the guard just enough light to see what it was the men were loading into the hearse. It was a casket. They lifted it up and placed it in the back of the hearse. The men then got back into the hearse and drove down the drive the same way they had come in.

After he was sure that they were gone, the guard ran to his own car and drove away. When the rest of the security team returned, they found the grounds deserted. The next day the head of security called the guard who had abandoned his post to ask why he had left. He told his supervisor what had transpired the night before and told him that no amount of money could get him to return to Waverly. He never returned to his job.

Over the years, Waverly has passed through many hands. Most of the owners had visions of developing the site in one way or another, and turning a tidy profit. No matter what the plans were, things never seemed to work out. The current owner, who bought the property in 2000, is different from those who came before him. His main motivation for the purchase was not profit, but love for the building and the history behind it. His goal is to restore Waverly to its former grandeur, not to tear it down and build something else. He is also aware of the building's paranormal past and has allowed the Louisville Ghost Hunters Society access to Waverly to conduct a full investigation. The official investigation has not yet begun, but there have been many preliminary studies.

## Strange Lights and Flying Bricks

During these preinvestigations, the LGHS has observed things that cannot be explained by reasonable means. One

of the main pieces of equipment used in ghost detection is an electromagnetic field, or EMF, meter. It is believed that ghosts are a form of energy and that when they are present, they disrupt the natural electromagnetic fields in their vicinity. EMF meters detect these disturbances, and while it is not solid proof of the presence of a ghost, it is a good indicator.

Of all the rooms in Waverly, room 502 has produced more EMF readings than any other. On one occasion, Keith picked up a disturbance so strong and long in duration that it fried the EMF meter. The solder on the circuit board actually melted and started to drip out of the meter. Cameras have also been a victim of room 502. On one investigation, Steve was taking pictures with an Advantix point-and-shoot camera. After finishing the first roll of film, he unloaded it and loaded in a second. As he waited for the film to advance, there was only silence. The camera had gone completely dead. He tried a second and a third roll of film only to get the same result. The ready light and the small LCD screen were also dark. Steve concluded that the batteries must have died, even though it was strange to have them die right between rolls of film. But when the group got down to the third floor, he found that the camera was working perfectly. Maybe someone or something in room 502 was a little camera-shy.

Strange lights and shapes have also been seen in the abandoned hospital. On consecutive nights during a weekend in October, LGHS members were able to see what looked like shadows moving up and down the fourth-floor hallway. One shadow in particular actually peeked around corners and crossed in front of open doorways. A faint red light, about the size of a lit cigarette, was also seen moving at the other end of the hallway. Immediate investigation found no one in the vicinity of the light, and no natural explanation could be given. During the second night of watching the shadows in the hallway, a room on the right-hand side of the hallway lit up with a brilliant white light. The light jumped across the hallway to the room directly opposite, only to extinguish as quickly as it had appeared. Again a closer investigation gave no clue to a natural cause for the light.

Perhaps the most frightening experience was one that Keith had in one of the rooms. He was walking the fourth floor with an EMF detector while two other members trailed him with a video camera. He started to pick up readings that led him to a room that was once a treatment room. The intensity of the readings increased and seemed to move around the room; the strongest reaction seemed to be coming from its southeast corner. Keith was standing there watching the meter when suddenly an empty plastic soda bottle seemingly came out of nowhere and hit him in the back. As he turned around to see what had struck him, an overhead fluorescent light fixture fell. With one end still anchored to the ceiling, the other end swung down to hit Keith in the side of the head. Amazingly, there was a fluorescent tube still in the fixture, and when it struck Keith, it smashed into a thousand pieces, showering him with glass. Before he could get his bearings, he heard the sound of a brick being scraped across the concrete floor. He looked to the opposite corner of the room and saw a brick moving along the floor toward him. All at once, it took off like a shot and flew directly at him. Without time to move out of the way, Keith quickly turned, and felt the oncoming brick strike him in the small of the back. He had seen and felt more than enough. He quickly retreated from the room, barely giving the two LGHS members in the doorway time to move. Shook up but not frightened, he asked if they had gotten a video of any of what had just transpired. They reported that they had the video camera trained on Keith while he was taking the readings, so they had gotten the bottle and the light fixture hitting him, but they could not tell from exactly where the bottle had come. They were also able to capture the brick as it moved across the floor.

From time to time, psychics have been to Waverly. Most have reported feeling or seeing spirits there, but none were able to offer proof. That all changed in the summer of 2000. Earlier in the year a major television network had been to the facility to shoot an episode for one of its shows. In July, about two months after the taping, a woman showed up at the gate, claiming to be doing some postproduction work for the network. As it turned out, the woman had fabricated that story. She was a psychic who had been drawn to the building, and claiming to be with the network was the only way she could get in. Waverly's owner happened to be there that day, and when he learned that an unknown woman was in the building, he called his contact at the network to ask why they hadn't called ahead. That's when he learned that the network had sent no woman. He immediately radioed the rest of the security team and then headed into the building to find the intruder.

They found her walking down the third-floor hallway. The owner confronted her with the information he had, and she admitted that she had lied to gain access to the building. She gave a different name—whether or not it was her real name may never be known—and said she was a psychic. She told them that the spirit of a young girl named Mary had drawn her to Waverly, in particular to the third floor. The owner was not impressed: Almost everyone knew the legend of Mary, the girl who peered out of the third-floor window. He was ready to usher the woman out, when she turned and entered one of the rooms. When he followed her in, meaning to stop the charade, the woman spoke up. She said that this had been Mary's room and that if he would look in the closet, he would find items that belonged to the girl.

The owner decided to pacify her and look in the closet. He found nothing but plaster and dirt. But before he could say anything, the woman told him he was not looking in the right place. He needed to reach into the back of the closet, behind a part of the rear wall that had been broken away. With a sigh of resignation, he knelt down and felt behind the wall. To his surprise he felt a large, thin metal object. Pulling it from behind the wall, he discovered that it was a large metal serving fork. "There's more," she said. He reached back in to pull out a lady's house slipper and three pictures. One was of a wooded road, the second was of four men sitting on a brick wall, and the third was of a young woman, possibly in her early twenties. On the back of the picture a name was written. The name was Mary Lee.

The owner was dumbfounded. He turned to the woman, only to see her leaving the room with a slight smile on her face. She continued on down the stairs and through the gate. She never spoke another word, and she has not been heard from since.

Waverly has many more secrets and many more questions to be answered. Even though a full investigation is scheduled, those questions may remain unresolved. Most of the records have been lost, and a lot of time has passed since Waverly's unfortunate patients walked its halls. Despite these problems, the search for answers will continue. Who knows what might be revealed by hard investigative work or by paranormal means? Only time and patience will tell.—*Thanks to Steven Conley and Keith Age, American Ghost Society, Louisville*

## *Spook Hunter Sees His First Spirit at Waverly*

One of the first questions that people ask me when they learn what I write about for a living is whether or not searching for real ghosts ever scares me. For a very long time, I assured them that I was never frightened during these outings to haunted places, and for the most part, this was true. My reply would have to change, though, after I experienced Waverly Hills.

The first time that I visited the hospital was in September 2002. I was in town for the first Mid-South Paranormal Convention, and one of the places that I asked Keith Age to show me in Louisville was Waverly Hills. I had heard about the investigations that had been conducted there and was eager to see things for myself. It was literally a dark and stormy night when we arrived at the hospital, and it had been raining all day. By this time, I had traveled all over the country and had been to hundreds of places that were alleged to be haunted, so a visit to a place like Waverly Hills was not a new experience for me. It was just an old, spooky building with a fascinating history, and I wanted to see it. I had long since abandoned the idea of going in expecting too much. This is likely why I was so surprised by what actually happened that night.

After meeting with the owners, Keith and I went inside and started our exploration. Once we were away from the activity going on downstairs, the surroundings fell silent. The only sounds that I heard in the dark building were of our footsteps, our hushed voices, and the drip of rain as it slipped through the cracks in the roof and splashed down onto the floor. Keith led me through the place and pointed out the various rooms, the treatment areas, the kitchen, the morgue, and on and on. We climbed the stairs to the top floor, and I saw the legendary room 502, as well as the lights of Louisville as they reflected off the low and ominous-looking clouds that gathered above the city.

During our excursion, I mentioned to Keith that there was one floor that we had missed—the fourth. He explained that this was the only floor in the building whose entrance was kept locked, and he had saved it for last. Many regarded it as the most active—and the most frightening—area of the former hospital. This is where, I knew, a brick had leaped from the floor and hit Keith in the small of the back! The other investigators had clearly seen it strike him. This is still regarded as one of the most chilling events to occur in the building.

When I entered the fourth floor for the first time, I got the distinct feeling that something strange was in the air. I make absolutely no claims of any psychic ability whatsoever, but there was just something about this floor that felt different from any of the others. I can't really put into words what felt so strange about it, but there seemed to be an almost tangible "presence" that I had not encountered anywhere else in the place. And right away eerie things started to happen.

We had arrived on the floor at what I believed was the center of the building. Behind us was a wing that I was told was not safe to enter. Sections of the floor had fallen in, and this area was off-limits to visitors. The strange thing about it was that both Keith and I clearly heard the sounds of doors slamming from this part of the building. I can assure the reader that it was not the wind; it was not strong enough that night to have moved those heavy doors, and this clearly sounded as though someone was closing them very hard. When I questioned Keith about who else could be up there with us, he explained about the floor's being closed to visitors. I investigated on my own and determined that he was correct; there was no one walking around on that part of the fourth floor.

I switched off my flashlight, and we walked down the corridor using only the dim ambient light from outside. The hallway runs through the center of the building, and on either side of it are former patient rooms. Beyond the rooms is the porch area, which opens to the outside. It was here that the patients were placed to take in the fresh air. There was no glass in the huge outer windows; therefore the interior of the floor was open to the elements. On this night, the windows also illuminated the corridor, thanks to the low-hanging clouds that glowed with the lights of Louisville.

We walked down through the dark and murky corridor, and I began to see shadows that flickered back and forth. I was sure that this was a trick of the eye, likely caused by the lights or the wind moving something outside, and so I urged Keith on for a closer look. It was where the corridor angled to the right that I got a look at something that was definitely not a trick of the eye!

So that the reader can understand what I saw, I have to explain that the hallway ahead of us continued straight for a short distance and then turned sharply to the right. In the early 1900s, most institutions of this type were designed in this "bat-wing" manner. There was a main center in each building; then the wings extended right and left, then angled again, so that they ran slightly backward like a bird's or bat's wings. Directly at the angle ahead of us was a doorway that led into a treatment room. I noticed the doorway in the darkness only because the dim light from the windows beyond it had caused it to glow slightly, making it impossible to miss since it was straight ahead of us.

Without warning, the clear and distinct silhouette of a man crossed the lighted doorway, passed into the hall, and then vanished into a room on the other side of the corridor! The sighting lasted only a few seconds, but I knew what I had seen. It shocked me so badly that I let out a yell and grabbed hold of Keith's jacket. I am not sure why it affected me in that way—the setting, the man's sudden appearance, my own anxiety, or perhaps all these things. Regardless, after my yell, I demanded that Keith turn on his flashlight and help me to examine the room into which the man had vanished. I was convinced that someone else was on the floor with us. Keith assured me we were the only ones there, but he did help me search for the intruder. He was right; there was no one there. Whoever or whatever the figure had been, it had utterly and completely vanished.

I was not the first person to have seen this mysterious figure on the fourth floor, and it's unlikely that I will be the last. However, for me, this put Waverly Hills into a unique category, for there are not many places that I will firmly state are genuinely haunted. Before I can do that, I have to have my own unexplainable experience, something that goes beyond a mere "bump in the night" or spooky photograph. In this case, it was much more than that, because I actually saw a ghost. In all my years of paranormal research, I can count the times that I have seen ghosts on just two fingers, and one of them was at Waverly Hills. In this case, seeing really was believing.—*Troy Taylor*

### *Shadow People Roam Waverly Hills*

A group of us toured the haunted Waverly Hills Sanatorium in Louisville during a torrential downpour. The place is immense and leaked with water.

We made it to the floor they call the Hall of Shadows. I looked to a room on my left and saw a shadow about four feet tall pass in front of me. It moved across the room and through the wall. When I saw this I became spellbound, not even hearing the others in the group.

After the tour I went back to the hotel room. I was soaked to the bone, so I took off my shirt. I noticed in the mirror these marks on my left side. They were like welts or scratches. I did not feel anything that could have caused them. From what I could read, it spelled out the word Dad,

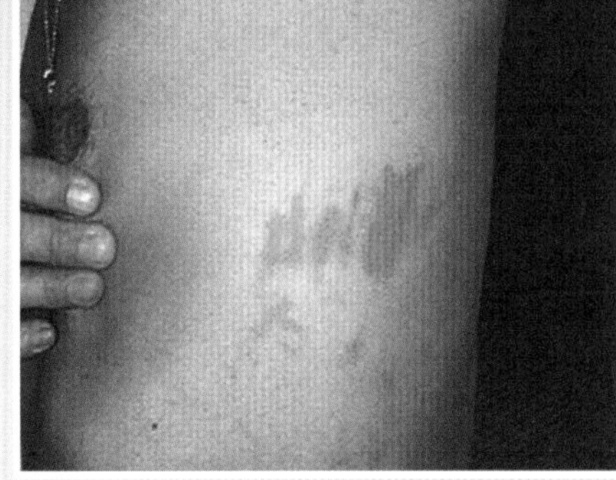

with an X and an O appearing to be underlined. When I touched these marks I received a sensation like a burn.

The next morning the marks were gone. My only conclusion is that when I walked through the Hall of Shadows, the image I saw must have made some kind of contact with me. Waverly Hills is haunted, and from my experience, souls still roam the halls.—*Brian K. Wilson Sr., President, Wilson's Paranormal Research*

### *Death Tunnel at Waverly*

I've heard plenty of stories about the Waverly Hills Sanatorium. They used to send people with TB there because they thought they were contagious and would lock them up and never let anyone leave.

They say these people went crazy and killed everyone in the place. They have a tunnel that is called the death tunnel where they used to put dead bodies and they were taken away and burned. They say people were trapped in the tunnel trying to get out and died in there. They also say that afterwards there were no bodies left because they had all been burned.

Kids have been going there for years and swear it is haunted. The new owners run a haunted house there every year, but I've heard there are parts of the building that are off limits supposedly because they are dangerous—but I think it's because of the ghosts.—*Jessica*

## Waverly Ain't the Only Abandoned Hospital!

**Waverly is a big fish in the pond of abandoned hospitals, but Kentucky is literally littered with them. Here are some other hospitals in the Bluegrass State that urban explorers have found up their (abandoned) alley.**

### John Ford Graves Hospital

***On West Main Street*** in Georgetown stands a crumbling reminder of the past. Built in 1917, the John Ford Graves Hospital was discontinued for use as a hospital in 1984. Parts of it were used intermittently as office space until 1990, when the entire facility was abandoned. In 1999, it was condemned, and it has recently been totally demolished. This is a shame, as hundreds of urban explorers found the place to be a terrifying glimpse into the past.

Inside the hospital, rooms with peeling paint and cracked ceiling tiles housed dozens of creepy reminders of the building's medical history. Steel gurneys littered the silent hallways. Ancient machinery that looked more reminiscent of Buck Rogers than reality could be found tucked away in corners. Large portions of the grounds had been trashed by visitors—and the large amount of Nazi and K.K.K. graffiti spray-painted on the grounds must have made even the most stoic explorer wonder exactly who visited.

## Paris Tuberculosis Sanitarium

***Paris is a small town*** of less than ten thousand people on the Stoner Fork of the Licking River. It's known for its arboretum, rich history (the town has existed since 1775), and the grave of Triple Crown–winning horse Secretariat. To say the town has embraced its quaint side would be a vast understatement.

And yet, even a place as idyllic as Paris has its darker aspect. Standing abandoned in town is a visually haunting series of brick buildings known as the Paris Tuberculosis Sanitarium. Abandoned for many years, the buildings are a reminder of the immense amount of pain and suffering that once took place at this spot. While a lucky few of the tuberculosis victims managed to fight off the disease and walk away from the sanitarium, most died after being committed.

Today the red brick buildings stand silent, their windows broken, their secrets, whatever they are, lost to time. These days, the Paris Sanitarium is visited only by those who come to explore its empty husk.

# Hayswood Hospital

***On the West McDonald Parkway*** in the town of Maysville is an abandoned red brick hospital. Legends of ghosts have surrounded this place since its closing in 1983. Most often visitors report strange lights in the windows. Perhaps more terrifying are the accounts of screams coming from the upper levels of the building. Many who have heard these sounds claim vehemently that they are the cries of children.

While these hauntings happen at a distance, there are some who claim to have seen evidence of ghosts close up while visiting Hayswood. Some reports say that people who attempt to enter the hospital are often met with a sense of foreboding coming from the upper floors. Those who happen to glance at the third floor often see a shadowy figure staring down at them from the window at the end of the hall. This has been more than enough to scare away many a midnight visitor.

People who have made it inside report a terrifying phenomenon. A gurney on wheels stands in one of the abandoned hallways of the building. Explorers have noted that in their travels around the hospital, this gurney appears in many spots throughout the building—even though no human hand has moved it.

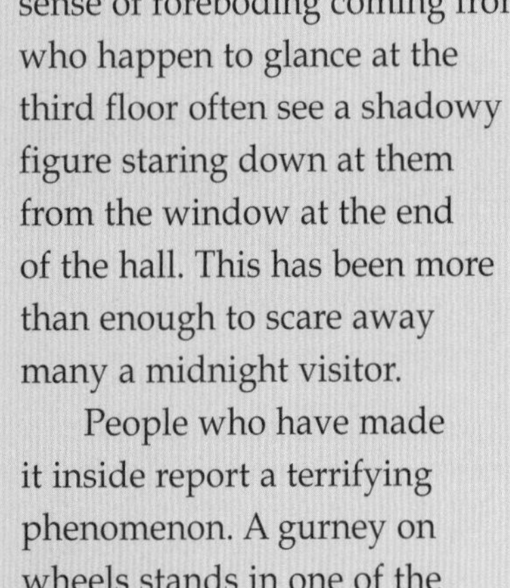

# The Phoenix Hotel

***The hotel*** once towered over the corner of Main and Limestone in Lexington, a proud and unrepentant throwback to the good old days of elegant-but-creepy commercial lodging facilities. It was a swingin' spot for nightlife even into its declining years, and the city's older degenerates have fond memories of warped good times within its dusty confines. Sadly, the greatest and sleaziest of all Lexington hotels is no longer with us. The controversial Wallace G. Wilkinson decided in 1981 that he wanted to build a forty-one-story skyscraper housing something called the World Coal Center in Lexington, and he tore down the Phoenix so the center could be built on that site. Many were very unhappy about this longtime historic landmark's being reduced to rubble and were doubly dubious about its being done in the name of this coal center.

But things didn't go so well for Wilkinson's dreams of glory. Allegedly beset by funding problems, the project was scaled down to a smaller plan, and much fund-raising was done. Years passed, and still the lot remained nothing but a pile of debris. Finally the World Coal Center idea was abandoned, and now the site is a very unpleasant public park that stretches the definition of "park" by being made primarily of concrete. Even more insulting, they named it Phoenix Park in honor of the magnificent old hotel that became just another casualty of just another failed construction-project scheme.

Reportedly, the basement and subbasement floors of the Phoenix Hotel remain intact but permanently encased underground. The floors below street level were never excavated when the building was razed, and were then hastily paved over when Wilkinson's plan flopped. These abandoned subterranean rooms would be the Holy Grail for urban exploration enthusiasts, and perhaps one day they'll be reopened like a time capsule. As of now, there is no known way to gain access to them, short of employing a pneumatic drill and an hydraulic excavator.

# INDEX

Page numbers in **bold** refer to photos and illustrations.

## D–E



## F



## G

# PICTURE CREDITS

All photos by the author or public domain except as listed below:

**Page 1** © Rob Southard; **2** background © Ryan Doan/ryandoan.com; **3** top © Kelly Hosford; **4–5** © Amy Gleske; **7** © Dan Walworth; **9** © Rob Southard; **11** top center © Raymond Gehman/CORBIS, top right © David Ward; **12** © Sanford/Agliolo/CORBIS; **13** Chris Jung, ES 771 Remote Sensing, Emporia State University; **16** bottom left © David Ward; **20** © Rich Griffith; **21** © Raymond Gehman/CORBIS; **24** © Daniel Dempster Photography/Alamy; **27** Jim Leslie/midwesternepigraphic.org; **31** top left © John Pike/globalsecurity.org, bottom left © Bettmann/CORBIS, bottom center Library of Congress, Prints and Photographs Division; **38** top © Joe Oesterle, bottom © Mark Moran; **39** top Library of Congress, Prints and Photographs Division, bottom © Eileen Hart; **40** right © Bettmann/CORBIS; **43** bottom © POPPERFOTO/Alamy; **46** top © Joe Oesterle; **47** bottom © iStockphoto.com/Eduard Härkönen; **49** © courtesy John Pike/globalsecurity.org; **50–54** © Ryan Doan; **56** background © iStockphoto.com/DIGIcal; **57–62** © Ryan Doan; **63** © iStockphoto.com/birdseye; **64–67** © Ryan Doan; **68** © iStockphoto.com/Kristen Johansen; **70–73** © Ryan Doan; **76** top © Ryan Doan, bottom © Barton Nunnelly; **77** © Ryan Doan; **78–79** © Charles O'Rear/CORBIS; **81–87** © Ryan Doan; **88** © Cathy Wilkins; **89** © Barton Nunnelly; **91–93** © Ryan Doan; **94** top © Ryan Doan; **95** top © Bettmann/CORBIS, bottom © Louis Psihoyos/CORBIS; **98** left © Owen Franken/CORBIS, right © Bob Rowan, Progressive Image/CORBIS; **100** right © Ryan Doan; **102** © John Springer Collection/CORBIS; **103** © Bettmann/CORBIS; **106** © Louis Psihoyos/CORBIS; **107** © Ryan Doan; **108** © Underwood & Underwood/CORBIS; **113** © Bettmann/CORBIS; **115** top left Wildwood Inn; **115** top right, **116, 117** © Kelly Hosford; **118–119** bottom © C. M. Laster; **120** inset, **122** © abandonedbutnotforgotten.com; **123, 124** Wildwood Inn; **125** © Wm. Baker/GhostWorx Images/Alamy; **126, 126–127** top © Steve Minor; **127** bottom © Debra Jane Seltzer; **130** left © J. T. Dockery, top © Kathleen Lolley, bottom © Adrian Wright; **134, 135** © Larry Harris; **138** top © Tiffany Vincent, bottom © Amy Gleske; **139** top © Rob Southard; **140** Vent Haven Ventriloquism Museum; **141** © Tiffany Vincent; **142, 143** © Woody Myers; **146** bottom left © Debra Jane Seltzer, top and bottom right © Kelly Hosford; **148** © Debra Jane Seltzer; **149, 150** center, **151** © Amy Gleske; **152–153** © Rob Southard; **154** top © Amelinda Burich; **154–155** bottom © Chuck Bowden; **157** © Cindy Seigle; **159** right © Wm. Baker/GhostWorx Images/Alamy; **160** © Thomas J. Hodge; **162** © MuseumPlaza.net; **163** © Debra Jane Seltzer; **164–165, 167** © Ryan Doan; **169** © iStockphoto.com/Jed Brown; **170, 171, 172, 175, 176, 178** © Ryan Doan; **180** left © Russell Chowning; **184–185** © Ryan Doan; **189** bottom Library of Congress, Prints and Photographs Division; **190, 197** © Ryan Doan; **200** background © Hulton-Deutsch Collection/CORBIS; **205** © Ryan Doan; **206** © Bettmann/CORBIS; **208–209** © Tim Connor; **218** top © iStockphoto.com/Jeff Salvant; **220** © Ryan Doan, Mark Moran; **222** top left © Richard Wong/Alamy; 224 right © Bettmann/CORBIS; **226** © Kentucky Historical Society; **227** top © Donnali Peters; **228-229** © Rob Southard; **235** courtesy Roy "Bud" Davis/www.vintagecoffins.com; **236** © Christina Gnadinger; **238** right © Ron Donald/abandonedbutnotforgotten.com; **240** © Christina Gnadinger; **244, 245** © Ron Donald/abandonedbutnotforgotten.com; **246** bottom right © Ryan Doan; **247** top Library of Congress, Prints and Photographs Division.

HILLERICH & BRADSBY C°
MADE IN U.S.A.
LOUISVILLE, KY.

By

**JEFFREY SCOTT HOLLAND**

**Executive Editors**
**Mark Sceurman and Mark Moran**

## ACKNOWLEDGMENTS

In some way or another, the following wonderful friends and associates have contributed to this book, and/or the maintenance of my sanity during the process. You're all on my "free drinks" list in the foreseeable future. And if you don't drink, cigars are on me. And if you don't smoke, well, I'm sure we can negotiate something.

Sherry Deatrick, Carla Watson, David Deborde, Amy Deborde, Cary Q. Lyle, Bob Morgan, Rebecca Quartieri, Fu Wu, Andrea Markston, Leah Baker, Gene Simmons and KISS, Brian Galvin, Debbie O'Connell, JLK, Rob Southard, Bryan Renfro, Eddy Riou, Cynthia "Ninnie" Norton, Cindy Seigle, Marie Metcalf, Lila Afiouni, Elizabeth Kramer, Paula Kounse, Ann Sturdevant, Marcia Goss, Erica Cefalo, Amy Barnes, Terry Wunderlich, Tim Stamps, Jon Shelton, MagicTom, Rocky Karlage, Sherry Rine, Mark Givens, Alicia K, Spinelli's Pizza, Telecrylic International, Ron and Sarah Whitehead, the crew at the Middletown Starbucks.–*Jeffrey Scott Holland*

As with all of the books in our Weird series, the creation of *Weird Kentucky* was very much a team effort and would not have been possible without contributions by, and the collective talents of, Joanne Austin, Ryan Doan, Abby Stillman-Grayson, Chris Gethard, Emily Seese, Gina Graham, Richard Berenson, Marjorie Palmer, Alexandra Koppen, Dave Hall, and all those folks who have sent us letters over the years offering stories, photos, or simply cryptic tips leading us off into parts unknown. We thank you all!–*Mark and Mark*

## SHOW US YOUR WEIRD!

Do you know of a weird site found somewhere in the United States, or can you tell us about a strange experience you've had? If so, we'd like to hear about it! We believe that every town has at least one great tale to tell, and we're listening. It could be a cursed road, haunted abandoned site, odd local character, or bizarre historic event. In most cases these tales are told only in the towns in which they originated. But why keep them to yourself when you could share them with all of America? So come on and fill us in on all the weirdness that's lurking in your backyard!

You can e-mail us at: Editor@WeirdUS.com,
or write to us at:
Weird U.S., P.O. Box 1346, Bloomfield, NJ 07003.

www.weirdus.com